CORVETTE RACERS

Race History of America's Sports Car and the Drivers Who Pushed It to the Limit on Tracks from Sebring to Le Mans

Gregory Von Dare
Photography by Dave Friedman

Motorbooks International
Publishers & Wholesalers ®

To my dear wife, Mary, for her stamina, and to
all those great Corvette racers out there who
helped make this book possible.

First published in 1992 by Motorbooks International
Publishers & Wholesalers, PO Box 2, 729 Prospect
Avenue, Osceola, WI 54020 USA

Library of Congress Cataloging-in-Publication Data
Von Dare, Gregory.
    Corvette racers / Gregory Von Dare.
        p.   cm.
    Includes index.
    ISBN 0-87938-574-X
    1. Automobile racing—United States.
2. Corvette automobile.   3. Automobile racing
drivers—United States.   I. Title.
GV1033.V66   1992
796.7'2'0973—dc20   91-32108

On the front cover: *One of four factory entries in the 12
Hours of Sebring race in 1956, this car finished first in
Class B with team captain John Fitch at the wheel. It was
the first factory race effort with the Corvette. Rich Chenet*

On the frontispiece: *Al Daniels hurls his solid-axle
Corvette up the mountain at Pikes Peak in July of 1960.
The Peak is one of the most challenging and dangerous
tests in the world for racer and machine alike. Dave
Friedman*

On the back cover: *An Owens-Corning Sting Ray (2) at
Sebring in March 1969. The GTP Corvette (52) races at
Palm Beach in 1986. Don Yenko's Sting Ray (6) races at
Sebring in 1965. A Corvette Challenge car (22) swings
through a turn. Dave Friedman, Ron Howard, Dave
Friedman, Chevrolet*

Printed and bound in the United States of America

Contents

Acknowledgments

So many people who cherish Corvettes and racing gave their time and advice to make this book better, more complete and more exciting. To them and to the many Corvette racers themselves who spent hours talking to me while the tape recorder ground away, my utter thanks. Those who were of special aid and comfort are:

Ralph Kramer and Tom Hoxie of Chevrolet Public Relations
Kari St. Antoine, Chevrolet Public Relations
Andria Williams of Southern California Timing Association
Dan Luginbuhl of Penske Racing
Kipp Kington of *Turbo* magazine

Cindy Finster of Autostar Productions
Billy Cunningham of IHRA
Lew Spencer of Carroll Shelby Enterprises
Otis Meyer, Librarian for *Road & Track*
Orwin Middleton, Corvette restorer extraordinaire
Judy Cunard of SCCA Public Relations
Harry Handley, SCCA's archivist
Judy Stropus
Don Prieto
Ron Centra of *Keeping Track of Corvettes* magazine
Robin Herring
Michelle Preddy, Dick Smothers' PR agent
Bill King of Goodyear
Racing Information Systems on Compuserve

Introduction

A Corvette on a racetrack: its exhaust blaring, tires screaming, the car cocked sidewise in a powerslide. What could be more natural? As it thunders past, it blankets you with the acid smell of racing gas and the bitter stink of scorched rubber, yet to the buff, these smells are ambrosia. Not only is the Corvette America's sports car, as it has often been called, it's America's race car as well.

No other American production car has taken to racing as has the Corvette. In fact, no other production car in the world has raced in so many forms and at so many different venues and in such overwhelming numbers.

You would find Ferraris at Le Mans, but not cutting a light at the local drag strip. You could glimpse a Jaguar on a road-racing course, but there

Jerry McGee attends the Church of Oversteer at Palm Springs in November of 1957. Dave Friedman

7

would be ten Corvettes in front of it and twenty behind. And you certainly would not find a Lotus dominating its class at Bonneville.

Only the Shelby Cobra ever challenged the Corvette for dominance of SCCA (Sports Car Club of America) racing, and Cobras number in the hundreds, not in hundreds of thousands like the 'Vette. The unique persona of the Corvette is as American as the World Series and, ultimately, as fiercely competitive.

The Corvette has been America's race car for four decades, but the beginning of the Corvette racing story goes back further than Motorama of 1953 when the Corvette was formally introduced. It goes back to the turn of the century.

Speed, American Style

Americans love fast cars, unless they belong to somebody else. Our history is crammed with Stutz Bearcats, Marmon Wasps, Mercer Runabouts, Cord Sportsmen, supercharged Dusenberg SJs and so on. In 1901, an endurance race organized by the Automobile Club of America was reluctantly stopped at half distance when it was learned that President McKinley had been assassinated!

In 1904, millionaire W. K. Vanderbilt, Jr., brought international derring-do to the United States. The first Vanderbilt Cup race took place on October 4 and covered 284 miles on a thirty-mile-long track on Long Island, New York. It was won by a French driver in a Panhard.

Racing grew quite popular through the roaring 1920s with dirt ovals and wooden-board tracks dotting the country. Automobile races became a regular item of every county and state fair. American motor sports overall took a big dive with the stock market in 1929.

Sadly, by the late 1930s, the average American car was a truck with a passenger body on it. Fast cars were for the rich or the demented. Everyday people puttered along in their Model As and cheered for their favorites on Memorial Day at the Indy 500.

In Europe, wealthy aristocrats with an obsession for danger had made road racing a continental passion. Automobiles rapidly advanced to meet the demand for greater speed. In the years before World War II, Dr. Ferdinand Porsche in Germany, Ettore Bugatti in France and Enzo Ferrari (working for Alfa-Romeo) in Italy led the way to remarkable technological advances in race machinery. In the United States, we still cheered our favorites on Memorial Day.

When American servicemen returned from World War II, they brought back a desire for speed and adventure. It's hard to step from the cockpit of a P-51 Mustang or a P-38 Lightning into an old Dodge, just as it's difficult to turn from commanding a submarine or PT boat to steering a bus.

When those GIs and officers returned home to leftover prewar cars from Detroit, a collective sigh went up all across the country. Some wild and crazy types in Southern California created the hot-rod scene, a protest movement which was the mechanical equivalent of the Beatniks in Greenwich Village, New York.

The West Coasters put their wartime experience to work in making engines sing at the dry lakes and drag strips. They swapped big sixes and flathead Ford V-8s into smaller chassis. Model T roadsters and '32 coupes were popular choices for this crowd. They soon discovered that the cars they made were very fast in a straight line but couldn't stop or turn well. Thus drag racing was invented.

The Awful Yet Wonderful MG-TC

At the same time, many returning officers and GIs on the East Coast abandoned their Fords, Chevys and Buicks for the kind of small, light and relatively agile roadsters they had driven in England and on the Continent. Most popular at first with this blossoming "sports car" crowd was the primitive but delightful MG-TC.

When this writer recently drove a perfectly restored, right-hand-drive MG-TC, it was easy to understand the attraction. The TC begged to be driven with spirit. Even though it was a senior citizen in automotive terms, its little motor revved freely, with a bravura and buzzing exhaust note.

The gearshift felt odd in my left hand, but the mental gymnastics required to keep the reversed shift pattern correct added to the heightened sensations of driving the car. Yes, its steering was slow and inaccurate, yes the suspension was crude, and yes the tiny, cramped car was a nightmare in rain and heavy city traffic. No matter.

What I truly remember about the car was its feeling of fun, and for-real readiness to go fast, to attack the road, to dive into a corner and power out of it. And for the driver, it was a case of hang on for dear life. What fun that was!

While technology has brought us a long way from the TC, it hasn't dimmed the fun-to-drive factor of that car. English sports roadsters were a secret code for a new, free kind of lifestyle. Then, in 1948, when Jaguar introduced its seductive, haunting, powerful XK-120 at the Earl's Court Motor Show in London, the dam broke. Even Clark Gable rushed to buy one.

Detroit Yawns

Detroit's response to this growing crowd of sports car enthusiasts was a loud yawn. Wrapped up in the hustle of the yearly model change, Ford, GM, Chrysler and the scattering of smaller makers had little or no time to experiment with something new. Some exceptions to this rule were the Kaiser-Darrin, the Kurtis or Muntz Jet, the Cunningham and the Crosley Hotshot. If it wasn't big, heavy and family oriented, Detroit was not interested.

T. C. Browne has been called "one of the graybeards of automotive journalism," and so he is. After his wartime hitch in the Navy, Browne was part of what he called "the sports car movement" from its golden days in the early 1950s. He has been an editor and publisher of automotive enthusiast magazines and has owned and driven many of the world's great cars.

"In 1952 Alan Selby and I drove to Palm Springs and went to the road races," Browne narrated. "I had never been to a road race before, and I never saw such a thing in my life.

"The next year, I bought an MG-TC of my own. Selby had one and I had one. And we built a race car out of his. I drove my first race at Stockton in '53 I guess. Doug Trotter had an Aston Martin DB-2, it was a marvelous car and our eyeballs were sucked out of their sockets. At that time, the Kingston Trio and sports cars was what it was all about!"

David E. Davis, Jr., today the distinguished publisher of *Automobile* magazine, was then a young man with a love for fast cars. He told me, "I think it was the XK-120 as much as anything that got Harley Earl's attention. There were Allards around the city of Detroit that also got a lot of attention.

"Fred Warner who worked for General Motors raced an Allard, and he was Charlie Wilson's personal pilot so his Allard got a lot of visibility around General Motors. And it was, of course, powered by a Cadillac engine."

European sports cars that came into the United States after World War II had an explosive effect on the driving tastes of the maturing postwar generation. The Austin A40, MG-TC, Triumph TR-2, Jaguar XK-120 and Porsche Speedster altered the perceptions of many Americans as to what a car should be and how it should handle. This new definition was finally acknowledged by Detroit in the Corvette.

Harley Earl to the Rescue

History is pretty clear on one thing: General Motors didn't want to make the Corvette in the first place. They had to be sold on the idea. From our perspective, forty years later, this seems incredible, absurd. But, at the time, those top GM executives were riding high. They saw no need for an American sports car, partly because they had no interest in sports cars themselves.

One certainty was that postwar America was a boom town. The economy was running like a thoroughbred in the Derby, and Americans were looking for newness everywhere: in their homes, their clothes, in their relationships and very much in their automobiles.

Fortunately, we had a man on the inside. His name was Harley Earl. As head of the Styling Section of GM and a vice-president of the corporation, Earl had clout. He also had charm and a habit of wrapping top management types around his cuff links.

When Earl saw the Jaguar XK-120 with its sensuous envelope body and glorious flowing fender lines, something snapped. He wanted GM to make a similar car and tap into the excitement this import vehicle was creating. Little did he know that he'd be fathering a legend in the Corvette, not just a low-cost, two-seater runabout!

Chapter 1

Design and Development
of the Corvette—The Early Fifties

On June 2, 1952 Chevrolet engineers were shown a plaster model of a proposed car of 102 in. wheelbase, for which a chassis was required. The chassis sketches were started right away. The body, which is in one piece with the fenders, is mounted at eleven points to the boxed X-braced chassis.
— Maurice Olley, Chevrolet engineer,
writing in an SAE paper of 1953

One day in 1952, all the chips would be bet on a single roll of the dice. Harley Earl was about to show a two-seat roadster styling exercise to Chevrolet's chief engineer, Ed Cole. If Cole liked the car, he might get behind it and help Earl sell it to upper management. If he didn't like it, the Corvette was a dead issue, destined to be a brief footnote in a history of GM's design department.

Styling for the Corvette was a mix of elements, many of them from other Harley Earl designs. Seen here with soft light from above, the fine lines and excellent proportions *of the original Corvette are clear. But if you walked closer, you'd start to see the gaps between fiberglass panels.* Chevrolet

Earl had the car up on a platform. At a signal from him, spotlights shone down on it and the cloth cover was whisked off by an assistant in the wings. Cole caught his breath. What he beheld was a compact two-seater with racy but restrained looks.

When Cole saw the sporty roadster, he was so delighted he jumped right up off the floor. Cole would become one of the Corvette's most aggressive boosters, and its first engineering mentor. Within a year, the first Corvettes would be on the street. The dice had come up seven, the easy way!

Corvette Styling Influences

Styling for the original Corvette was not radical in its day but it was forward looking. The first roadster body blended the sweeping curves of the Jaguar XK-120 with several other ideas that were rumbling around in Harley Earl's mind at the time.

One contributor was Earl's own low-slung and streamlined two-seater LeSabre show car of 1951, which contained a number of signature items, such as the recessed side coves that showed up on the '56 Corvette, and a "panoramic," wraparound windshield that the Corvette inherited directly. The small tail fins on the LeSabre were similar to the Corvette's in idea but not in shape.

The famous Corvette grille was related to the wide "mouth" seen on Earl's Buick show car the Y-Job, one of the first modern cars envisioned by General Motors after World War II, but never put into production.

Another prototype car called the Alembic also had an influence on the original Corvette, in several ways. The Alembic was a GRP-bodied car (glass-reinforced plastic), which was touring the country to show the potential of fiberglass, at that time a new miracle product. The Alembic spent some time in the large, ground-floor display area in the GM Styling Center, where Earl and others saw it every day.

At that time, Earl began referring to his sporty roadster as Project Opel. This clever ruse made use of the German Opel nameplate which was part of General Motors, and which had a genuine styling project in progress. It also made an ideal cover story for the Corvette's development, to confuse the curious.

For chassis layout, Ed Cole and Harley Earl went to a young GM designer, Robert McLean. A graduate of Cal Tech, McLean was a sports car fan himself. He got the idea that if he moved the engine and transmission as far back as he could, the resulting car would have a favorable weight balance and consequently, good handling. Corvette's early success as a competition car is directly traceable to McLean's decision.

Unorthodox Chassis

While laying out the Corvette chassis, Bob McLean did the unusual, and it was a crucial moment in the Corvette's development. If someone with less understanding of sporty handling had drafted the car, who knows what cruel fate might have awaited it on the racetrack, rather than decades of glory?

That clever McLean touch was to engineer the chassis from the rear axle location point, forward. He placed the driver and passenger seats almost in the middle of the car's 102 in. wheelbase, a specification exactly the same as the XK-120.

Where the Corvette differed most from the Jaguar was in track, the distance between the left and right wheels. Project Opel had a 57 in. front track, and a 59 in. rear, compared to the Jaguar's 51 in. front and 50 in. rear. This meant that the Corvette would corner better and flatter than the Jaguar and would show better transient response, such as in a slalom test, or sudden lane change, or negotiating a chicane on a racetrack.

At this point the "Opel" would have an overhead valve, six-cylinder motor and two-speed automatic transmission, both off-the-shelf parts. Front suspension would be twin A-arm and rear suspension and drive would be a live axle sprung by half-elliptical leaf springs. Tube shock would be all around. The car's frame was completely in the mode of the era, twin steel frame rails comprised of boxed beams with a heavy X-brace in the center, forming a ladder that kicked up over the rear axle.

While this frame was heavy, in racing terms, it was also strong and fairly stiff. With a fiberglass body, good weight distribution and comparatively solid frame, the Corvette-to-be had some virtues that go a long way on the racetrack. As the Corvette began to emerge, all it really lacked was horsepower.

Olley's Corvette Notes

The Chevrolet Research and Development department, under Maurice Olley, had the official job of developing the Corvette chassis. In a 1953 paper to the Society of Automotive Engineers, or SAE, Olley wrote: "On June 2, 1952 Chevrolet engineers were shown a plaster model of a proposed car of 102 in. wheelbase, for which a chassis was required. The chassis sketches were started right away.

"The body, which is in one piece with the fenders, is mounted at eleven points to the boxed X-braced chassis. The complete chassis frame weighs 213 lb. Front suspension consists of standard double 'A' arms and coil springs, but is rather stiffer than normal, and is fitted with a fairly stiff front stabilizer."

Olley mentioned that fiberglass is a desirable material for building limited-production bodies

Harley Earl—Dictator and Dreamer

There are few men in the history of the automobile who have been as powerful and influential as Harley Earl. Had a lesser man in the GM hierarchy been the booster of the plastic two-seater, it might never have seen the light of day.

As founder and then head of GM Styling Section, originally called Art and Colour, Earl put a personal stamp on every car to come from General Motors from the late 1920s to the late 1950s, even though he did little of the actual designing.

While he was called a dictator by some of the designers who worked for him, Earl was also a charming man, a superb salesman and one of the few designers to ever feel and act the equal of GM's top management.

His father designed carriages for the wealthy of Hollywood in the years before World War I. Earl imitated his father's drawings and improved on many of them. He attended Stanford University, in California, where he spent most of his time drawing chassis for the increasingly popular horseless carriages.

When Earl returned to Los Angeles after college, he went to work for Don Lee coachbuilders, designing special bodies for limousines and other exclusive, one-off cars.

On a trip out West, Lawrence Fisher, one of the brothers who owned the Fisher Body Works, met Earl and was very impressed by his sketches. At Fisher's insistence, Earl went to Detroit first as a consultant, then a designer for the company. One of the first projects Earl turned his hand to was the debut of the LaSalle in 1927. Seen as a smaller companion make for Cadillac, the LaSalle had to look substantial, graceful and rich, while not dethroning the big Caddys.

Earl came up with a striking design, somewhat similar to the ultra-luxurious Hispano-Suiza town cars of Europe. The '27 LaSalle was a great success. Earl was on his way.

Based on the success of the LaSalle, Earl was recruited by General Motors master planner, Alfred P. Sloan. His assignment was to create a complete styling department that would oversee the look of every GM car produced from that time forward. History shows that Sloan picked the perfect man for the job.

Earl hired designers by the dozens and split them into competitive groups, some working on one model line, others on advanced ideas while others built full-size models in clay, another new technique Earl brought to Detroit.

This new division was called the Art and Colour section. Earl liked the Europeanized spelling of colour; he thought it gave his struggling enterprise a dash of class.

Another innovation Earl brought to GM was the use of show cars or dream cards as a way to project styling ideas into the future. These exotic show

Harley Earl, the dean of General Motors design, founder of the Styling Section and the man who had a vision which became the Corvette. Earl loved to make cars longer, lower and wider, which became a worldwide trend. Chevrolet

cars also acted as a barometer of public taste, with the popular cars inching toward production and the ones nobody liked quickly consigned to history's scrap heap.

His image was as carefully conceived as a side rendering of a show car. Earl was an excellent dresser, and he looked like an original in the hallways of General Motors where everyone wore a black or dark blue suit. He once said that when his designers were stuck on some detail of a car, he would come into the studio and say or suggest something wacky, just for effect. He thought that his odd behavior would jolt the stylists' imagination. Often it did.

While Earl may have been a dictator, he was a benevolent one. As a manager of design, he is unsurpassed, even by his brilliant successor, Bill Mitchell. As a designer himself, Earl's portfolio is unmatched. It includes the 1927 LaSalle, the classic 1955-1957 Chevy, the Buick Y-Job show car, the Olds F-88 and Cutlass, the Cadillac Cyclone and, of course, a car that changed history, the Motorama Corvette.

because it is easy to work and because, if the resin and glass mat are in the right proportion to each other, "a fiberglass panel of body quality will be three times as thick as steel, will weigh half as much and will have approximate equal stiffness." The only trouble was that fiberglass was more flexible than steel, so a steel chassis was still needed.

Brakes were also from the Chevrolet parts bin. They were the standard-production iron brake drums with composite pads on two internal, expanding shoes. The front drums were 2 in. wide and the rears 1¾ in. However, the Corvette's master cylinder was bigger than those used on sedan models. It's a shame that no more effort was put into giving the Corvette outstanding brakes at this point as the lack of a good braking system was to plague the car in its first two decades as a racer.

Steering for the Corvette was the usual Saginaw worm and sector box, with a higher ratio than stock. A single-piece steering column ran from the steering box on the frame rail to a thin, plastic-rimmed wheel in the cockpit. This steering wheel was positioned so far out from the dashboard, many early racers cut several inches off the steering column for better leverage.

Inside, the Corvette had two bucket seats, a dashboard which put many of the instruments in the center console, where the driver couldn't see them, and a carpeted floor, with the shift lever for the two-speed Powerglide transmission rising from the center hump. There was a grab bar for the passenger and both doors were hollow, with bolt-on side curtains serving for windows.

The first Corvettes had a perimeter-type frame of boxed steel beams, heavily X-braced in the center. This type of structure was relatively heavy, but it was solid as well. Chevrolet

Early Corvette rear suspension reflects Detroit thinking of the era. There's a live axle, semi-eliptic leaf spring and a tube shock at the front side of the axle to defeat squat under acceleration. The canvas strap under the axle was the subject of many demon tweaks during the solid axle years. Some cut it off, some shortened it to reduce suspension travel, some just ignored it. Bob D'Olivo

Corvette front suspension (shown at the right front, from below) has twin, unequal length A-arms, coil spring and tubular shock absorber. This arrangement continued through the Sting Ray years, indeed up till the eighties. Bob D'Olivo

Roll-up windows were several years away for the Corvette. The ragtop stored under a hinged fascia on the rear deck, setting the pattern for all Corvette roadsters, the cleanest looking production convertibles in the world.

Blue Flame Six—The Stovebolt

Next Olley discussed Corvette's first powerplant, the infamous Blue Flame straight-six of 235 ci. The former truck block had been introduced in 1941 and was updated in 1953. This update gave the workhorse motor aluminum pistons, to reduce reciprocating mass, reinforced rod bearings and a pressurized lubrication system for the crankshaft. The stovebolt six had a bore of $3\frac{9}{16}$ in. and a stroke of $3\frac{15}{16}$ in.

The 115 hp engine was modified by Ed Cole and his powertrain team for mildly increased performance and to take premium fuel. Compression was raised from 7.5:1 to 8.0:1, and the six was fitted with a relatively high-lift camshaft and metal timing gears. Solid lifters were specified, as were dual, concentric valve springs, because, Lord have mercy, the engine might rev over 5000 rpm.

Because of the low hoodline of the Corvette several other changes to the standard versions of the six were necessary, all of which became part of Corvette lore in the early days. The rocker arm cover with its front end flattened, the three, side-draft Carter carburetors and a water pump moved to the bottom front of the engine were all part of the changes.

According to Maurice Olley: "The exhaust manifold is dual and of a special type to keep the exhaust gasses in the throat of each of the two downpipes always whirling in one direction. This was found essential and picked up some 8 or 10 lb-ft. of torque in the mid-range." The twin downpipes extended under the car, each with its own muffler for a complete dual-exhaust system, one element of Corvette technology which has remained to the present day.

These improvements were good enough to produce 150 hp at 4200 rpm. Torque was raised from the previous stovebolt standard 204 lb-ft at 2000 rpm to a heftier 223 lb-ft at 2400 rpm. Even

At the front of the first Corvette chassis sat the infamous Blue Flame six engine and two-speed Powerglide transmission. This crude, truck engine was refined with a better cam and three Stromberg sidedraft carburetors, but no one was fooled by the lightning bolt on the valve cover. This print was taken from a damaged original Chevrolet negative. Chevrolet

Viewed in profile, the balance of the original Corvette is obvious. Bob McLean worked hard to place the driver in the middle of the car, both for comfort and handling. Note the steeply angled driveshaft and long steering column. Chevrolet

Yesiree, Bob! A Chevrolet executive gets enthusiastic about a 1953 Corvette at the Waldorf Astoria Motorama show in New York City. The car's interior was nicely turned out with simulated tuck-and-roll upholstery, but instruments were grouped in the center of the dash, not near the driver. Chevrolet

While a large crowd looks on, Dinah Shore takes her turn playing with a Motorama Corvette. Her hat and gloves tell you it's the fifties. Chevrolet

with the triple carb setup, specific fuel consumption was about the same as if the engine were in a sedan. Olley figured that the car would have a top speed of 108 mph, running at 4800 rpm with a 3.55 final drive, but they suspected a higher speed was possible. They were right.

Grounding the Plastic Body

The car's 6 volt electrical system didn't work the first time it was tried, until engineers shockingly realized that they had no ground channel through the fiberglass body! The ignition system including coil, plugs, distributor and plug wires had to be shielded by a shaped metal plate, again because of the plastic body, to reduce RF (radio frequency) radiation, so that the radio could be played without the whining crackle of engine acceleration. Chevrolet equipped the stock Corvette with AC 44 spark plugs but recommended to owners that they replace the stock plug with one range colder—AC 43s—for high-speed driving.

Going to bat for the use of the two-speed Powerglide in a sports car chassis, Olley defended the move by saying that the typical sports car buff is like the square root of minus one, an imaginary thing, and that any car with an automatic will be received by a wider section of the public. Olley concluded his paper with what sounds like a quote from today's newspapers comparing American and Japanese industry:

"Outside the United States it is generally considered that American manufacturing methods are too inflexible to meet modern conditions. This

Shown here with a proposed hardtop, the 1953 Corvette wowed crowds across the country. It was the enthusiastic reaction of these folks that convinced Chevrolet to build the two-seat roadster. The bolt-on side curtains and other drawbacks weren't apparent to the public until the Corvette went on sale in late 1953, and then the results were discouraging. Chevrolet

Ed Cole, Chevrolet Chief Engineer

It would be wrong to give the impression that the Corvette was solely inspired and nurtured by Harley Earl. Yes, Earl was the point man for the project and yes, he was responsible for the original shape. But there was more to getting a car into production than having Harley Earl give it his blessing. First of all, Earl needed allies within the corporation. For support, he went to another racing fan, a man with substantial power in the GM corporate world, Edward N. Cole, chief engineer at Chevrolet.

Cole had been an engineer at Cadillac and was involved with the creation and development of Caddy's groundbreaking overhead valve V-8, the engine upon which all of GM's later V-8s were based. In May of 1952, Cole was promoted to the post of chief engineer at Chevrolet, at least in part to bring V-8 technology to the lower priced range of GM cars. Cole had helped Briggs Cunningham's Cadillac racing efforts and had kept up with the latest speed and power developments of the hot-rod world in California. Cole was also responsible for bringing British engineer Maurice Olley to GM for advanced chassis work. Olley himself supervised several Corvette engineering projects.

Cole had a substantial impact on the Corvette, overall, especially its history as a competition car. He was personally responsible for seeing that it got the division V-8 as soon as practical, and for lending support and encouragement to a web of private owner-racers as they campaigned their cars across the country.

The Corvette's first engineering guru, Ed Cole, then chief engineer at Chevrolet. Cole did the best he could with the Blue Flame six and the uneven handling of the Corvette. Chevrolet

was well disproved by the wartime performances of the automobile industry [World War II]. It is proved to the whole world by such a specialized vehicle as the Corvette."

Corvette Gets a Name and Logo

At this point GM had a fiberglass/two-seat sports car body, custom chassis and straight-six motor, but the car we know as the Corvette was still called Project Opel. Time was running out before the car's public debut, and the General's executives still hadn't come up with a name or logo for it. Both seemed to happen overnight.

According to *Webster's Unabridged Dictionary,* the word corvette is derived from the Spanish word *corbeta,* for an armed cargo ship, but the most recent definition says, ". . . a small warship of about 1,000 tons, used for antisubmarine and convoy duty."

The corvettes used by the British and Royal Canadian navies in World War II won their measure of fame in the forbidding "submarine alley" of the mid-Atlantic. They were in some part responsible for the successful entry of the United States into the European theatre because they checkmated the precision attack patterns the German U-boat skippers had been trained to run.

Chevrolet burned the midnight oil trying to find a name for their upcoming sports car. They wanted something with a C for Chevrolet, but it had to fit the car and satisfy a host of other corporate demands. More than 1,500 names were submitted by outside advertising and marketing agencies as well as by internal engineers, marketing executives and design studios. None was accepted. Four months prior to the Corvette's debut at the January Motorama in the Waldorf Astoria in New York, no one had turned up a name that Ed Cole and Harley Earl liked.

Myron Scott saved the day. Scott was an assistant advertising manager at the time. He retired from GM in 1977 as assistant director of public relations. In 1952, he mentioned the name Corvette to Ed Cole, who immediately seized on it as a winner. The definition of "corvette" was sure to appeal to all red-blooded Americans. Legend has it

To increase public awareness of the Corvette, Chevrolet pulled stunts like this parade of 1953s on Chicago's Lake Shore Drive and the Harbor Freeway in Los Angeles. While the average guy might have liked a Corvette, the *wealthy and elite didn't take to the car as Chevrolet had hoped. Without strong sales, the Corvette was in trouble with GM management.* Chevrolet

that Myron Scott went through every C word in the dictionary until he found one that sounded right and had an acceptable meaning.

Furthermore, the Corvette was supposed to have an emblem which consisted of two crossed flags, a checkered flag for racing on the left, and an American flag for its country of origin on the right. But some legal genius at GM got cold feet about using the Stars and Stripes on a commercial logo and nixed the idea.

Bob Bartholomew was then a GM designer working in the Chevrolet design studios. He had experience designing emblems for Chevrolet passenger cars and was given the assignment of drafting a revised emblem for the motorama Corvette immediately.

Working around the clock with a local plastics firm, Bartholomew created a heraldic flag to re-

place Old Glory and had new emblems custom-made by the vendor. The finished products were put on a plane, delivered to New York and installed on the prototype just before Motorama's doors opened.

While many other aspects of the Corvette's design and development were the product of considerable thought, the name and logo of the car were both the result of last-minute necessity.

Slow Sales—Corvette Is in Trouble

The newly dubbed Corvette made its public debut in January of 1953 at the New York Motorama, held in the Waldorf Astoria Hotel. The Corvette sat on a turntable and was attended to by a pretty model. For those who may not know, Motoramas were national touring shows that

18

showcased General Motors products, American industry and the button-down values of the Eisenhower era. They were hugely successful in stimulating public interest in new and exciting cars, foremost of which was the Corvette itself.

The public was wowed by the Corvette, by its sporty lines and modern look. The enthusiasm it generated in New York held through the Midwest and the West. The whole country was crazy about the Corvette.

So, if GM brass needed a confirmation that they had something special on their hands, they got it. But back in Detroit, once the cheering stopped, they still had to manufacture the car, and that would not be so easy.

The first 300 Corvettes were more or less handmade in Flint, Michigan, in mid 1953, although regular production would take place in St. Louis. The first production run of cars were all white, Polo White, with Sportsman Red interiors.

They looked good, but the fiberglass bodies, contracted out to a vendor, had a number of fit and finish problems, as everyone learned from scratch how to mass-produce a plastic-bodied car.

Chevrolet had an odd marketing plan. They wanted to sell Corvettes only to the elite. The idea was simple: get influential people, the ones everybody wants to copy, driving Corvettes, and the demand will take off like a rocket. But community leaders and other influential persons are not necessarily the same group that will be interested in sports cars, especially if they don't have crank-up windows, and their cloth tops are balky and confusing to former sedan drivers.

In the 1954 model year some other colors were introduced, but the clamp-on side curtains continued, as did the Powerglide and straight-six engine. It was becoming clear that the Corvette was far too much sports car for some, and not nearly enough for others.

Chapter 2

The Corvette Comes Alive on the Racetrack

What had seemed a dream a few weeks ago, and what had seemed impossible in the first hours of the race was now a reality! Two dirty, crippled Corvettes streaked and battered from their ordeal, roared into the pits from the darkness and were treated as if they had won the race itself.

Later we got the official verdict: winner in Class B, Corvette; winner of the production sports car prize, Corvette; winner of the team prize, Corvette . . .

—John Fitch, writing in *Adventures on Wheels*

For the second model year, in 1954, a new cam brought more muscle to the humiliated Blue Flame Six, a big 5 hp. Corvette's price was lowered, but still the cars were not selling very well. Strangely enough, this year may have marked the competition debut of the Corvette.

As David E. Davis relates: "I remember seeing the first one. Seeing somebody actually doing something with one, when one turned up at the Press On Regardless Rally in Michigan driven by a couple of General Motors guys in 1954—but I don't

John Fitch at speed on Daytona Beach in 1956. Note how carefully prepared this car is. The headlights have turned aluminum cones for streamlining, the grille is half taped over, there is the racing windscreen and

tonneau, and an abbreviated side pipe exhaust. The Corvette ran about 150 mph at these trials, and the checkered flags began waving in earnest. Daytona Speedway

remember how they placed. We still had high hopes that something would come of it. But there was absolutely no question in anybody's mind that in the form in which it was introduced it was hopeless."

The truth was that the car was not an outstanding performer. It was plain that acceleration times from 0–60 mph of eleven and twelve seconds just wouldn't do. Other GM cars with V-8 engines were capable of performance equaling the Corvette. The pain of driving a sports car and having your date watch a big sedan pass you never quite goes away.

If it wasn't for a challenge from the competition, the Corvette might have been dumped after 1954 and been forgotten. But in September of 1954, the Ford Motor Company unveiled its own personal sporty car, the Thunderbird. Sharp looking and powered by a V-8, the Thunderbird crackled with personality. The little Ford roadster seemed to catch on with buyers in a way the Corvette did not.

A few minor changes were made in the Corvette for 1954, but not nearly enough. The car was still underpowered and struggling to find its identity. Fortunately, Zora Arkus-Duntov was just around the corner. Campbell-Ewald

THE REAL McCOY

CORVETTE

The 1956 restyle also brought with it the Corvette's saving grace, the Chevy small-block V-8. One reason for racing was that a victory of any kind would make terrific advertising ink. The Campbell-Ewald ad agency became Chevy's Skunk Works for its motor sports program. Campbell-Ewald

The hot setup before fuel injection appeared in 1957 was this twin four-barrel system. The hand holding the pencil belongs to Hot Rod magazine's Racer Brown. Bob D'Olivo

Ed Cole was darned if his favorite Chevrolet was going into the dumpster. He made a powerful case to upper GM management, especially Harlow Curtice, Chairman of General Motors, that the Corvette needed a V-8 like Thunderbird had, to fire the American imagination.

Chevrolet engineer Russ Sanders once remarked that it was a natural thing to place Chevy's brand-new V-8 in a Corvette, "to see how this engine would perform." The neck-jerking acceleration and effortless cruising speed of the car with the V-8 couldn't be denied. Chevrolet Division decided to make the 265 ci, 195 hp motor an easy access option on the 1955 Corvette, and to make a three-speed manual transmission available with it.

The Classic Small-Block

Developed by Ed Cole, Harry Barr, Al Kolbe and Donald McPherson among others, the Chevy small-block or mouse motor has been one of the most popular automotive powerplants of all time. Today displacing 350 ci, it still powers the stock Corvette.

The one, the only, Zora Arkus-Duntov, a gifted engineer and highly competitive sports car racer. The Corvette owes its racing victories to Arkus-Duntov, who changed the car from a limp boulevard cruiser to a road rocket that dominated American amateur racing in the 1950s, and again in the 1970s and 1980s. Chevrolet

The engine's short stroke was valuable in racing because it reduced piston speed and friction, and it cut down on vibration as well. The engine could be spun for hours at the limits of the valvetrain, 5600 rpm.

The small-block had three major virtues. It was light in weight, 41 lb. less than the Blue Flame six it replaced. It was strong, with iron webbing stretching between cylinder banks, a massive girdle of metal surrounding the central camshaft and five heavy, arched main bearing caps on the bottom end. And, most temptingly, it had the ability to be bored and stroked to much higher displacements than 265 ci.

For 1956, compression was raised from 8.0:1 to 9.25:1, and tougher exhaust valves were used. Both intake and exhaust manifolds had larger cross sections for greater flow. With one Carter carburetor sitting atop a power pack manifold, the motor produced 210 hp. With two four-barrels and progressive linkage, 225 bhp was advertised at 5200 rpm, and 270 lb-ft of torque at 3000 rpm.

As a racing machine, the Corvette always owed its tremendous speed to its beating heart, the Chevrolet V-8. Both small- and later big-blocks, gave Corvettes the swiftness and endurance to shoot past the competition.

Zora Arkus–Duntov to the Rescue

At this same time, destiny entered its own radical element into the Corvette equation. A European-born engineer with a racing background and a profound love of performance was a new employee at General Motors. He was assigned to discover why exhaust smoke was darkening the rear quarter panels of early Corvettes.

His name was Zora Arkus-Duntov. As time would prove, this man was one of the great rebels of the 1960s and one of the finest automotive performance engineers in history, as well as an experienced racing and test driver.

It is with great justice that Arkus-Duntov is often called the "father" of the Corvette, because it was he who moved the car from an ineffective boulevard cruiser to a muscular street racer, with the potential for world-class response from chassis and engine alike.

In late 1952, Arkus-Duntov wrote Ed Cole a letter mentioning that he would like to work for General Motors, in their Research and Development department. Cole responded that Arkus-Duntov should drop in to see him the next time he was in Detroit. Instead, Arkus-Duntov took a job with Fairchild Aviation, where he continued the work he had done between the wars on supercharged, high-performance engines for aircraft. Based on this work, he wrote an engineering paper exploring supercharging and fuel injection in high-performance engine design. After sending a copy of this study to Ed Cole, Arkus-Duntov received an offer from Maurice Olley to come to Detroit and discuss employment terms.

Arkus-Duntov was hired and assigned several engineering projects, none of them to his complete liking. It wasn't long before he decided on his own initiative to improve the Corvette's handling.

"The front end was oversteering," he was quoted as saying. "The rear end was understeering, an atrocious amount of understeer. I relocated the bushing in front of the rear spring, then I put a two-degree positive caster in front. Then the car was fine. Put the Corvette in a drift at maximum speed and nobody could outdrive you."

Both Maurice Olley and Ed Cole couldn't believe it when Arkus-Duntov told them that he was taking ten days off to drive a Porsche at Le Mans in June of 1953. He had been working at GM for only a few weeks at this point and his superiors were not used to their engineers flying off to Europe to slip into the cockpits of race cars.

Arkus-Duntov shrugged, saying, "The importance I attached to racing was not yet shared nor understood by others at General Motors. I felt rather than encourage me, the whole matter did not sit very well with them. I purchased a one-way ticket to France, never intending to return. In Paris after the race, I tried to make contact with some people. Then I ran into an old friend who listened to my story and insisted that I go back. He rushed to an airline office and came back with a ticket. So I went back."

In 1953, Arkus-Duntov drove a Porsche Type 550 Spyder at the 24 Hours of Le Mans, but he DNFed. Fast lap in le Sarthe that year was set by Alberto Ascari in a Works Ferrari 250 Sport prototype, and the overall race was won by a factory Jaguar D-Type, a car Arkus-Duntov would try to recreate in the Corvette Sebring SS—in a few years.

The Classic 1956 Restyle

Still, the V-8 in the 1955 Corvette was only an interim fix. The entire Chevrolet staff knew that it would take more than horsepower to match the classy looks and solid performance of the Ford Thunderbird. For 1956, Chevrolet designers, led by Harley Earl, sculpted an all-new body—one of the most graceful and memorable ever formed.

The new roadster was only slightly changed from the year before, but now it was a mature design, handsome and complete. Headlights now popped forward from the fenders in a manner similar to the Mercedes 300 SL, although the car's face was unmistakably Corvette. In the rear, the little rockets on the rear wings were gone and the trunk shape had been refined. Interestingly, the taillights were now frenched into the bodywork, much as the headlights had been on the first bodystyle. Also, brake cooling ducts appeared on the car's face. This distinctive bodystyle would continue through the introduction of the Sting Ray in 1963, with several minor cosmetic updates.

In the garages at Daytona Beach in 1956. This was where the legend began. Now powered by a 283 ci V-8, the Corvette was ready to trounce its arch rival of the day, the Ford Thunderbird, one of which is pitted right next to the 'Vette. The twin-carb manifold in front of the white Corvette begins to look like familiar hardware, doesn't it? Daytona Speedway

On the sands of Daytona Beach, the Corvette is poised for its moment of glory. Here a NASCAR technician supervises a change of plugs between speed runs. Note the small racing windscreen, soon copied by other Corvette racers, and the nifty tonneau cover with its racing stripes. Daytona Speedway

Racer John Fitch, one of America's finest drivers of his time. Fitch was the man who sweated the details in converting the Corvette from a nice sports car to a hard-charging racing machine. Fitch brought superb organizational skills and a brilliant driving technique to his job as team manager of the Corvette racing effort at Sebring in 1956. Chevrolet

To match the new body and improved V-8 engine, some refinements were called for in the chassis as well. Seeking greater steering stability, front caster was increased by 2 deg. This was accomplished by placing shims between the front cross-member and the frame.

A side effect of this caster change was that front roll oversteer was diminished. To compensate, rear roll understeer was also reduced by changing the angle of the rear spring mounting points. As modified, the rear leaf springs were closer to horizontal than on the original chassis. With the new body, the lightweight 265 ci V-8 gave the 1956 Corvette a weight distribution of 52 percent front, 48 percent rear, excellent for a front-engine car.

Zora and Corvette Go Racing

Arkus-Duntov knew that the old maxim of Win on Sunday, Sell on Monday was precisely what the Corvette needed to stay alive as a General Motors car. With the V-8 in the Corvette, the potential now existed for some much needed competition victories.

His first plan was an assault on the Daytona Speed Week. He learned in 1955 that speed records and publicity are perfect mates, when he drove a Chevrolet sedan to a record time at Pikes Peak.

At that time, Austin Chenley, of Chevrolet's Campbell-Ewald advertising agency, thought it would be a great advertising gimmick for Chevrolet to break the existing Ford stock car record at Pikes Peak with a 1956 Chevrolet sedan. When W. R. MacKenzie, Director of Engineering Public Relations for Chevrolet, asked Arkus-Duntov if he would be interested in overseeing this high-altitude assault, the Belgian emigré said, "Splendid idea."

After convincing Chevrolet that an outside sanctioning body was a necessity for credibility, Zora dove into the technical aspects of the record attempt. NASCAR (National Association for Stock Car Automobile Racing), at that time a brand-new organization, was recruited to handle the stopwatch for the run, with Bill France personally overseeing the affair.

Arkus-Duntov checked into the Broadmoor Hotel in Colorado Springs, spreading the rumor that he was an eccentric millionaire who loved to see the sunrise at 3 A.M. on Pikes Peak. In fact he was learning the hillclimb road. This subterfuge was designed to keep Ford Motors from uncovering Chevrolet's intentions. Arkus-Duntov played along by speaking to clothing designer Oleg Cassini in French and Russian while he cast a sharp eye on Cassini's high-fashion models gathered around the hotel's swimming pool for a photo shoot.

On September 9, Arkus-Duntov got behind the wheel of the camouflaged '56 Chevrolet sedan and roared his way up the hill in a record-breaking time of 17:24.05 minutes, only five minutes longer than modern turbo rally cars take on the same roads.

Now a bigger mountain awaited him: Daytona Speed Week.

The Dry Sands of Daytona

In those days, Daytona Speed Week was a national rite of spring. Speed Week provided the chance for car makers to show what they could do. There were performance tests of all kinds, acceleration, top speed and others, conducted on the wide, sandy beaches of Daytona. Speed Week began a fascination with greater speed and improved performance that would not burn itself out until the mid 1970s. It also gave Detroit executives a great excuse to head for Florida in February, the meanest, coldest month of the midwestern winter.

In going to Daytona, Arkus-Duntov was taking a calculated risk. If the Corvette were to fall flat, it might be a death blow for the car. Clearly something special was needed. That something was another piece of Corvette legend, the Duntov cam.

The Duntov cam is not, as many still think, simply a high-lift camshaft. Not at all. It has slightly more lift than the stock cam, but actually less than the hot Power Pack cam. What Arkus-Duntov did that was so brilliant was to work backwards from the needs and characteristics of the valvetrain and the cylinder shape.

Starting with how he wanted to fill the cylinder, and taking into account the mass and leverage of the stock, stamped-steel rocker arms, he calculated the ramp and velocity of valve opening and closing for optimum high-speed tuning. He then translated his figures into a cam profile.

Other engineers at Chevrolet were not enthusiastic about the new cam and Arkus-Duntov had to spend some time on the phone from GM's Mesa, Arizona, test track before a prototype was ground

The first woman Corvette racer, Elizabeth "Betty" Skelton. Posing here next to a D-Type Jaguar, Skelton is wearing a chic racing outfit that's probably not made of Nomex. A daredevil stunt pilot, she also held several women's air speed records. Daytona Speedway

At the starting line at Daytona Beach, Betty Skelton prepares to launch her Corvette into history. This car is prepared differently than Fitch's machine, with snow tires at the rear for traction in the sand, and headlights and grille that are in stock trim. The fresh air scoops on the front fenders are taped over, however. Daytona Speedway

25

and sent to him. Once installed in his test "mule," the cam proved its worth, powering the test Corvette with 3.27 differential gearing to 163 mph at an engine speed of 6300 rpm.

If he was able to go 163 mph on a good surface, Arkus-Duntov reckoned that he could achieve 150 on the less-tractive surface of Daytona's sandy beaches.

This Arizona test mule was in fact an earlier Corvette chassis, modified to 1956 specs. It had conical fairings on the headlights, a fiberglass

This '54 Corvette also ran at Daytona but was not a factory car. It has a hard tonneau and racing windscreen. Daytona Speedway

Just before the start of one run, Betty Skelton puts on her cracked helmet while the starter cleans her goggles and the amazing Smokey Yunick hovers over the white and blue Corvette. Yunick was responsible for much of Chevrolet's stock car racing program, so he cast an expert eye over the Daytona Beach Corvettes. There are few engine builders in the world in a class with Yunick. Notice that the VW in the background has a "sports car" sticker on it! Daytona Speedway

cover or tonneau over the passenger's seat, a small windscreen and a large fin behind the driver's head, both similar to the D-Type racing Jaguar.

Confident that 150 mph was well within the car's performance envelope, Arkus-Duntov moved forward. The test mule was trucked to Florida in December of 1955 to make the 150 mph run under NASCAR supervision. Zora noted that the level of the tide, wind speed and wetness of the sand all had to be just right. But nature was not under the control of NASCAR, and he had to wait until January of 1956 before conditions were close enough.

Impatient, Arkus-Duntov chose a day when the sand was slightly dry, costing him some traction. But dry sand or not, the Corvette, with its godfather behind the wheel, made two passes before the clocks and came away with a 150.58 mph average, good enough for the record.

Because of this success, two more cars were delivered to Daytona Beach for Speed Week in February. The Corvette trio would be driven by Arkus-Duntov, in his 150 mph car, with John Fitch and Elizabeth Skelton in stock Corvettes. This would be the Corvette's first real test of speed.

Chevrolet Catches a Flying Fitch

John Fitch was an obvious choice as a Speed Week driver for Corvette; he was one of the leading sports car racers in the United States in the mid 1950s.

Born in Indianapolis in 1919, John Cooper Fitch came from a racing family. One of his earliest memories was hanging on for dear life as his father gunned a Stutz Bearcat around the Indy Speedway. After flying a fighter plane in World War II, Fitch

Skelton poses with the youthful John Fitch while a GM photographer rolls some movie film of the two racers together. The sand print on the front tires reveals just how small a contact patch these cars had in the late 1950s. It's amazing that they cornered at all. Daytona Speedway

Corvettes at the Sebring twelve-hour enduro occupy the first six starting slots. This picture dates from 1960, but the scene was almost identical in 1956. The cars are lined up for a Le Mans start, where the drivers run across the track, jump in their cars, fire them up and speed away. Dave Friedman

A few moments after the start at Sebring. The Corvettes are in the first seven starting positions. The drivers have gunned their V-8s to life and are roaring off to do battle. Dave Friedman

turned to auto racing, placing fifth in his first race ever, behind the wheel of an MG TC. Driving all around the world, Fitch raced for many teams, including the Mercedes factory, in their remarkable 300 SLR. In 1953, Fitch placed third at Le Mans in a Cunningham C5R. Flexible and talented, Fitch drove everything from an American stock car to a Formula 1 Grand Prix machine. By the late 1950s, he was widely considered one of the best competition drivers in the world.

In December of 1955, Fitch had written to Ed Cole expressing interest in the Corvette's future as a competition car. Fitch offered himself as a consultant for hire to aid in developing the Corvette's potential. In reply, Cole offered Fitch a ride in one of the three specially prepared Corvettes for Speed Week.

Sweating the Details at Sebring

When Ed Cole gave the go-ahead for a Corvette entry at the 1956 twelve-hour race at Sebring, he was buoyed by the genuine success of the Corvettes at Daytona and he had secret knowledge. The secret was that Zora Arkus-Duntov had taken his upfitted 1955–1956 Corvette mule to Sebring for some hot laps while he was waiting to make the 150 mph record run at Daytona Beach. While there, the Corvette mule ran like a real sports car and established very competitive times.

Although Cole's intentions were the best, to see a Corvette in the winner's circle at a major international race, he was asking the Corvette to

Corvette Women Racers

Elizabeth Skelton was one of the women daredevils of the 1950s. She was notorious as a stunt pilot and air racer, but she had also acquired a minor reputation for driving fast cars. She was the other of the 1956 Speed Week Corvette drivers to come from outside Chevrolet.

As David E. Davis recalled: "Betty was an aerobatic pilot and made quite a name for herself in the late 1950s. She was from Florida and she was one of those women that just came out of nowhere and established a name for herself flying the sort of airplanes that flew the Cleveland Trophy dash. And it became apparent to her that she wasn't going to make any money or achieve anything very spectacular if she limited herself to air races. So she got into making record runs with cars.

"She also worked for Campbell-Ewald and was involved in this kind of vague area where she was getting pieces to automobile racers and being Chevrolet's liaison with racers. And staging promotional events using various Chevrolet products. She had a very spritely personality and was very attractive in her younger years. Betty was petite and very cute and formed instant bonds with all of the people in racing that she came up against. She was their pal for life. Everybody loved Betty."

Skelton would continue racing and setting records for many years to come. In 1966 she took the women's Land Speed Record away from Paula Murphy. Driving Art Arfon's *Cyclops* at Bonneville she ran 277.62 mph, upping the record by 51 mph.

Zora Arkus-Duntov: A Legend

If it hadn't been for the almost magical appearance of a European-born, German-educated child of Russian parents, who knows what might have happened to the Corvette? It might very well have been dumped by General Motors, labeled an unpopular car by the press and vanished from life, except for rare and pathetic outings at Concourse d'Elegance.

But somehow, fate decreed that the Corvette would find a mentor, a benefactor, a godfather. His name is legend to anyone who has raced or loved the fast two-seater from Chevrolet: Zora Arkus-Duntov.

Arkus-Duntov was born in Belgium of Russian emigré parents, who moved back to Moscow when little Zora was only one year old. The boy's fascination with vehicles set a pattern that would govern his whole life. As a youth, Zora was captivated by anything that moved, " . . . rail cars, then motorcycles, anything." He learned to drive as a chauffeur's assistant in Moscow.

When his family moved to Berlin seventeen years later, Arkus-Duntov studied electro-mechanical engineering for a while, although it wasn't his cup of tea. After transferring to mechanical engineering, he acquired his own motorcycle, which he modified, as well as a Bugatti race car. His thesis from the university was on supercharg-ing to high-boost pressures. It touched off a super-charging fad in Germany in the early 1930s, so Arkus-Duntov claims.

As an engineer, Zora knew that the weak link of any engine is volumetric efficiency or breathing. The better an engine gets fuel and air in and exhaust out, the more power it makes. He discovered that his flathead could make much more power if it could open up its throat. His desire to have a more powerful version of the flathead Ford led to his designing the famous Ardun cylinder heads for the Ford V-8.

In the United States after World War II, Arkus-Duntov took a job with Fairchild Aviation, designing atomic hardware. Then one fine day, he visited the Motorama at the Waldorf Astoria hotel in New York City. There he saw the prototype Corvette and immediately fell in love with the car. He thought it was the most beautiful vehicle he'd ever seen and wrote a letter to Ed Cole, asking to work for Chevrolet. Cole politely sidestepped Arkus-Duntov's offer and told him to drop by if he was ever in Detroit.

Eventually, Zora was hired by GM, found his way to the Corvette and the rest is such sweet history.

In 1971, Arkus-Duntov retired from General Motors. His beloved Corvette today is better than ever, and is a dominant SCCA race car. Although advanced in age at this writing, Arkus-Duntov is still sharp, witty and outgoing. The Corvette was lucky to have him!

---

run before it could walk. What Cole created was a nightmare for John Fitch and a few odd mechanics. And yet, finally, with one respectable finish from a four-car team, they didn't do so badly after all.

The order was given with thirty-four days remaining before Sebring. The race was to be run on March 24. Due to a tantrum by Arkus-Duntov over the Corvette's questionable brakes, Chevrolet had hired Fitch to run the racing team. Fitch impressed ad agency and Chevrolet PR executives when they met him at Daytona Beach. Fitch was a fast driver, but he was also a hard-working, thoughtfully organized team manager.

Fitch would also be chief tester and development driver for the Corvette race cars. Arkus-Duntov would remain in Detroit, supervising the supply of parts that Fitch would need, flying down occasionally with a shipment of hubs, brake shoes, axle shafts and whatnot. To be eligible as production cars, the competition Corvettes had to be made from stock or RPO (Regular Production Option) items only.

In his book *Adventures on Wheels*, John Fitch tells how he quickly realized that the Corvettes supplied to him by Chevrolet may have been nice road cars, but they were by no means ready for the hardships of "big-league racing." Fitch fretted that he had very little time to work on them. But, somehow, it was done.

John Fitch writes that he had only one "poor orphan" Corvette. It was a 1956 body over a 1955 chassis with some experimental parts thrown in as well. But it was all he had to work with, so he ran lap after lap in it, waiting for the next thing to break. They had five weeks until the race.

Brakes were one problem that was never ironed out completely. They tried four different kinds of brakes for the cars and even the kind finally chosen—Bendix Cerametallix linings with wide, finned iron drums—gave problems with fade. The weight of the Corvette, although it was not overwhelming, was still high for an endurance racer. Whatever the reasons, Corvettes were very hard on brakes. Directing cooling airflows to the brakes, front and rear, became another major challenge for the Fitch team. The difficulty was compounded by the need to have an option part number associated with every development part.

Fitch records the struggle by saying that the car's handling was not controllable and predictable. They developed oil leaks, broke engine mounts and

A pair of Corvettes haul the mail down the pit straight at Sebring in 1961. These two cars are prepared differently: one has the headlight fairings and is using the front intakes for brake cooling; the other, on the right, has driving lights in the same spot, and exposed headlights. Both cars are struggling against Maseratis and other fast cars on the tough Sebring track. Dave Friedman

burned-up rear ends, which had the wrong oil in them. It was a tough time for all involved.

Three of the four Corvettes delivered to Fitch were fitted with stock high-performance 283 ci V-8s. The last one had a 307 ci motor, the result of a 0.060 in. overbore and a 0.20 in. stroke increase. This stroker motor also had large-valve heads. In addition, a German-made ZF four-speed transmission was installed just south of the clutch—which, it seems, was not perfectly mated to the pressure plate.

In the last days before the race, Fitch worked out his strategy for the four-car Corvette team. He planned to make a show of speed with the number 1 car, the one with the large engine in Class B. He wanted to give Corvette supporters "something exciting to say about the car."

He wanted to lap in the 3:45 range, which was pretty fast at the time. The three standard-engine Corvettes each had different options installed so each had a different personality. The car with the Duntov cam would be the rabbit for the other cars. If it survived, then the final two Corvettes could use all three of their gears for the latter half of the race. As Fitch noted, "We had a fast front-runner; we had quite a fast stock car; we had two steady performers tuned to go the distance."

The race began with a Le Mans type footrace for the drivers. Fitch saw the other three Corvettes make a clean start. He had taken the lead on the first lap for a few moments, when Mike Hawthorn, a former winner at Sebring and Le Mans, sped by in his D-Type Jaguar.

But on the second lap, Fitch's clutch began to slip badly on acceleration. He tried an old Le Mans trick, heating the clutch by slipping it with the pedal. That helped but didn't cure the problem.

Soon Fitch passed the number 5 Corvette, sidelined with an axle failure. An hour later number 7 was taken out with a blown engine. The remaining other Corvette was not sound either; it was having gearbox trouble, running with only third gear working.

The race strategy was changed. Both remaining Corvettes would limp around and try to finish. If they could finish, they stood the chance of proving something, and they just might win some prizes, too. Many other cars were dropping out from mechanical problems. That night, fate was kind and the two Corvettes managed to finish the race. Everyone was weak with joy. Well, not *everyone*.

Writing in the June 1956 issue of *Road & Track*, Jeff Cooper was remarkably unimpressed by the presence at Sebring of American-made sports cars in the GT ranks. Cooper declared, "The Corvettes, having the biggest engines were up at the head of the line-up. Several got good starts and

Fitch led under the bridge, but Hawthorn went through them like a shot into the first turn." And even more laconically, Cooper added, "Fitch, in the Corvette Special won Class B. His was the only Class B car in the program.

"The main impression left from the race were the awesome speed of the injector-Jaguar, the savage brilliance of Moss, and the genius of the grand master, Fangio."

Fitch was more enthusiastic, "What had seemed a dream a few weeks ago, and what had seemed impossible in the first hours of the race was now a reality! Two dirty, crippled Corvettes streaked and battered from their ordeal, roared into the pits from the darkness and were treated as if they had won the race itself. . . .

"Later we got the official verdict: winner in Class B, Corvette; winner of the production sports car prize, Corvette; winner of the team prize, Corvette. . . . We had stepped brashly into racing's biggest league and walked off with three prizes on the first try. It was less than we had hoped but more than we deserved."

As soon as Corvette began winning races, it became the subject of numerous ads, designed to boost disappointing sales. It was a crude approach, but it worked. Improved sales meant the Corvette was here to stay. Campbell-Ewald

Driven by Dr. Dick Thompson, the Corvette was poised to become the dominant force in American road racing. Campbell-Ewald

Corvette among the Big Boys

Despite a so-so finish on paper, the Chevrolet people knew that they witnessed history in the making. Corvettes had run on the same racetrack as Porsche, Ferrari, Jaguar, Maserati and Aston Martin and had finished ahead of some very fast and professional cars. The Corvettes had won the hearts of the crowd, and Chevrolet engineers had learned some very valuable lessons.

In fact, the tremendous excitement generated by Sebring caused Zora Arkus-Duntov to begin a much more ambitious racing project. He argued to GM management that many car companies, notably Jaguar, Ferrari and Maserati, had specially built competition cars, completely different from their production cars, which won the major victories—the overall wins at race meetings around the world.

That's what generated the valuable publicity, the overall wins in the big races. And if the other companies could do it, so could GM. Zora declared that he could build a competition car as good as anything on earth. It would be a car designed especially and purpose-built for racing but based on the Corvette: the Sebring Super Sport, or SS.

It wasn't always a happy ending. One of the first Corvette race cars was this effort by Bob D'Olivo and Racer Brown. Fortunately, fiberglass wasn't that hard to fix. Bob D'Olivo

Flush with the good advertising ink they had seen flow from Corvette's Florida adventures, GM management agreed to let Arkus-Duntov have his race car. But what management giveth, management can taketh away.

Dr. Dick Thompson at Sebring

Dr. Dick Thompson, one of the finest Corvette racing drivers of the 1950s and 1960s, was blissfully at home in a Corvette race car. Thompson was smooth but very aggressive. No one knew the early Corvettes as well as he did. And few drivers knew Sebring as well. It had been the location of Thompson's first race. Here he narrates one Corvette lap of Sebring, the old-style track. Join him for a hot lap.

"On your first lap, you go out much more cautiously than you might normally be because the pit stop has heated up all the coolants and maybe heated up the brakes and whatnot, and also cooled the tires. So, you have a different kind of car for that first lap or two. So you should be pretty cautious. Then you just get into a routine and usually you've decided pretty much on a lap time that you want to try to do. That may change as time goes on, but for the first five or six hours, you've got pretty much of a lap time you want to do.

"Coming out of the pits, you're on the airport part of the track and your next two turns are very easy turns. You have to be on the lookout for cars that are already up to speed and you're not. You have to take a little more cautious pattern through those first two airport turns. On the third turn, you turn into the road part and that's very narrow. You have to be very aware, because you're not into the flow of things yet, of slower cars you might encounter or the faster cars coming up behind you.

"So you're very cautious on that first half-maybe-whole lap, particularly until you get back onto the airport again. It's pretty narrow with crowned roads, and one very slow turn at the farthest point with sand banked up on the side that you wanted to stay out of if you could certainly help it. But if you had any problem with your brakes, why, that's where you'd have a real problem; you'd end up in that sandbank.

"Then you went up past what they called the Hanger Straight. Then you had a chicane that was maybe forty, fifty mile-an-hour turns; top end of second gear, bottom end of third gear. Then back onto the airport. Most of the airport turns were third gear; shift down once. Then the last turn on the airport before coming onto the pit straight was a big U-turn, also a third-gear turn.

"In one way, you had a very long turn and you could, if you tried hard, you could make up good time there because coming onto the pit straight, the higher speed you had, the better you went down that pit straight and the next two straightaways past the pits, when you're on the fly, is where you made up most of your time really.

"I still like the two turns past the pits; the two fast turns on the airport. They were the fastest point on the course, really. Most of the cars could just barely get through there flat out or maybe with just the slightest lift to the throttle without braking at all; just a little lift and then back on it. That made a more interesting part of it, I think. The square corners on the rest of the airport were kind of academic, not very interesting."

A Sebring Corvette, circa 1960. This sparkling roadster still has stock bumpers, headlights and lots of chrome. *The car is receiving a front-end alignment. The fuel injection is just visible in the engine bay.* Dave Friedman

Chapter 3

The Solid-Axle Years of SCCA Racing

But, oh, Jesus Christ, it was hard work to drive those cars! You could wear yourself out. You had to wrestle that son of a gun. But that's OK. Every time you overcame that, you were just a little bit taller. And that's what you were struggling for, to pass that guy, overcome those problems.

You were just trying to make it go faster and better. Comfort or anything like that really wasn't part of the consideration. If you could get a little better tire, or a little quicker steering or to hold better, that's what you were worried about.

—Dick Guldstrand, 1990

Corvettes and SCCA production class racing were made for each other like scotch and soda. What the SCCA wanted to encourage were safe, fast and affordable race cars. What Chevrolet wanted for Corvette was exposure to potential sports car owners and the healthy sales that racing wins generate. Now that John Fitch and Zora Arkus-Duntov had made the car into an able competitor, the Corvette was ready to stake out some territory of its own.

The entry of Corvettes into serious amateur racing in the United States was a historic moment.

Buford Lane, number 615, drove the Washburn Chevrolet Corvette after Bob Bondurant. Here, at Laguna Seca in 1959, Dean Geddes in number 213 comes barreling into a turn behind Lane. Both of these cars are V-8 powered, and number 615 uses the front side grille openings to flow cooling air to the front brakes. Dave Friedman

Corvettes were king on the West Coast. Races composed of all or almost all Corvettes charged up and down California. The cars competed on airports, old Army bases, city *streets, in parks. At Santa Barbara in 1958, Bob Dickson is leading Bill Gaskins in one of those races from the golden era in the Golden State.* Dave Friedman

You might almost call the 1956 Corvette the Model T of postwar racing in America. No large, V-8 powered car in motor sports history would compete in such numbers and with such verve as the legendary solid-axle Corvettes of the late 1950s and early 1960s.

Rise of the RPO Racer

One reason for the flood of Corvette racers was that Chevrolet made it easy to be one. All the car buyer had to do was pick the appropriate options at the dealership and when the new Corvette was delivered it would be a race-ready car.

In 1953, shortly after he joined the company, Zora Arkus-Duntov circulated a memo through Chevrolet saying that Chevy had a chance to unseat Ford as the king of hot-rod and speed parts.

At that time, hot rodders and racers of all kinds were partial to the Ford flathead V-8. While the engine was not very efficient, due to its side valves, it was big and made good torque, a must for good acceleration. It was also simple, had a large supply of speed parts in existence and provided a common language for tuners all across the country.

Arkus-Duntov maintained that with the introduction of the proposed Chevrolet V-8, it would be a good idea to offer factory-made speed equip-

ment as RPOs (Regular Production Options). As Corvettes went road racing at Sebring and elsewhere, all improved parts used on the race cars had to be available from the factory to justify the Corvette's classification as a production car.

Part of RPO lore is that Chevrolet engineering coyly labeled these items heavy-duty rather than racing. This was done partly to keep GM corporate off their backs, and partly to keep the competition at Ford guessing.

Such was the case with RPO 684. Developed for the B-Production race cars, RPO 684 was available to any Corvette buyer. Combined with RPO 579, the fuel-injected 283 V-8, and RPO 685, the T-10 four-speed transmission, these two packages would turn any street Corvette into a very competitive race car. RPO 684 included:
- Heavy-duty front coil springs.
- Heavy-duty rear springs (five leaves, up from the stock four).
- Larger front antisway bar.
- Larger, stiffer shock absorbers all around.
- A quick-steering adapter that lowered steering ratio from 21:1 to 16.3:1.
- Positraction rear end—a differential with two internal clutch packs that allowed power to flow to the wheel with traction.

•Heavy-duty brakes, four-wheel—a set of heavily finned aluminum brake drums, based on the Chrysler product, with Bendix Cerametallix lining pads, using five pads on the leading shoe, and three or four on the trailing shoe. Also contained within the brake drum was a disc of thin metal, stamped into a turbine fan. This helped to force hot air out of the drums.

At some time in 1959, the racing package became known as RPO 687 and added special rear axle ratios of 3.70, 4.11 and 4.56; fiberglass ducts to direct air to front and rear brakes; and LPO 1625, a 21 gal. fiberglass fuel tank, for racing only.

Pioneer Days

One of the very first Corvettes to be raced by privateers was the car of Racer Brown and Bob D'Olivo. At that time, Brown was technical editor of *Hot Rod* magazine, and D'Olivo was just starting his brilliant career as an automotive photographer. (Today he heads the photographic department for all Peterson Publications including *Hot Rod, Motor Trend, Sport Truck* and many others.)

Racer Brown had a 1955 Corvette that he had modified, and which he liked driving fast. Then D'Olivo and Brown heard that a Corvette would be racing at Pebble Beach. "It was going to be a so-called factory effort, but not publically known as such," said D'Olivo recently. "So we took Racer's 'Vette and drove up there, watched the race and saw the 'Vette get trounced pretty good. Later, we went over to the hotel where the Chevrolet people were staying. Zora was there and the people involved with the program at that time. We had a few drinks and told them that, if you want to see the car really run, give us a car.

"They didn't say much at the time," D'Olivo continued, "but about two weeks later they called and wanted to know where to put the car. Racer lived in an apartment complex at the time, and I lived in a house in North Hollywood with a normal, two-car garage. So, that's where they delivered the car. I moved my car out of the garage, which suddenly turned into a Corvette race shop.

"The first race was less than a week away, at Pomona. And we get this car—it still had the top on it, it still had the radio in it. Anyway, we didn't have time to do much to the car. Our problem was tires. We had Firestone Super Sport F70s, which were hard as a rock—and Pomona is not the course for that. We knew that Englebert was making some softer tires, but they were hard to get. Anyway we

The incomparable Jim Jeffords takes a corner at Road America, Elkhart Lake, Wisconsin, in 1959. Driving the Purple People Eater, *a beautifully bold Corvette, painted a wild purple color, Jeffords raced out of the Midwest to* become a two-time national champion. Jeffords was aggressive, completely confident, a naturally gifted driver. Dave Friedman

went to Pomona and got beat pretty good. And then we came back and really got serious with the car.

"We had the engine blueprinted. I started doing work on the suspension. Racer was doing all the engine work and I was doing the chassis work. Racer was basically a hot rodder; he goes fast in a straight line and that's all he knows how to do. But he knew about suspension too, we both worked on it. We had two or three stabilizer bars made up and tried the different sizes.

"We put an extra leaf in the rear springs. I tried to limit the travel in the rear suspension without being too obvious. There's limit straps on the rear axle of the Corvette—heavy canvas straps. I cut those, shortened them. And then I went to a couple of dealers and found longer rubber rebound bumpers they put up on the frame. And that limited upper travel.

"Everything that we would do suspension-wise, we'd take it out and run it until we started lifting the rear opposite wheel. When it started to lift, then we would back off. And that's how we would set our suspension.

"Unfortunately, Racer was a night person—and we both had full-time jobs. He would get to work at noon, and then show up at my house at eight o'clock and want to work till two, three in the morning!

"Edelbrock did all the blueprinting on the engine," D'Olivo explained. "To my knowledge, there was no cheating in the engine at all. Oh, maybe Racer did something to the carburetion, drilled some jets out, but the engine was absolutely stock.

"We ran it in the Cal Club races with Bill Pollock driving it, and we won every one of those. We even won the production class in one race and then changed the tires real quick and went into the main race with the modifieds and Ferraris and everything. And I think we got up into third or fourth place before Bill blew the engine. It was just kind of a joke to see what it would do.

"With the three-speed gearbox we were at a disadvantage on some courses with slow turns. So we asked Chevrolet engineering to build us a box with a higher first gear. They did that and we could then use first gear in the slow turns. About midway through the first season, SCCA said we could take the windshield off. Chevrolet engineering made up a little windscreen and we put it on.

"We only lost that first race. It won every production race, both Cal Club and SCCA. The championship came down to the last race at Palm Springs. It was us against the Mercedes coupes. And we happened to win that championship. Our car was the first one to beat the Mercedes coupes.

"After the car won the championship, there was one more race to go in Cal Club, out at Paramount Ranch," D'Olivo continued. "Bill was leading the race and the throttle stuck. He went around a curve, went up on the banks, came back down and went across the track and then down into a gully—and crashed the left front corner of the car, but not badly. So it came back to my garage and sat there for several months. I finally called Chevrolet and asked them what they wanted to do with the car."

Snaking through the treacherous esses at Riverside for a Kiwanis benefit race in July of 1959, Jim Jeffords in the number 1 Corvette sets up Skip Conklin (number 111) for a pass under braking. At the first kink in the esses, a Corvette has spun, narrowly missing an XK-120. Dave Friedman

Vince DeCarlo (number 300) was concentrating so hard on catching Bob Fletcher in his Mercedes 300 SL, number 166, that he spun his Corvette right around. That's Bob Dixon, number 166, in the white Corvette. The place is Paramount Ranch, the date 1957. At this point, Corvettes were still making a name for themselves; the glory days were still a couple of years in the future. Dave Friedman

The girls, the glory, the fun. Corvette racing in the early days was a magnet for good times. At Santa Barbara in 1958, Andy Porterfield tries to stay calm at the start of a race, despite thinking about the obvious talents of his companion. Dave Friedman

The fabulous Mr. Jeffords produces his patented victory smile at Danville, Illinois, in 1959. Note the cut-down windshield, permitted by the rules, and the neat roll-bar installation. Dave Friedman

The Chevy people asked if D'Olivo wanted to buy the car and all its spares, but after the whole season, he was aching to get his own car back into the garage before the sun burnt it up. He declined. The car was hauled away by a local dealer and then vanished, at least from D'Olivo's sight. There were rumors of the car racing the following year, and then nothing. Perhaps it had been crashed or sold out of state; no one knew, not even Chevrolet.

"The car didn't mean that much to me at the time," D'Olivo sighed, "but God, I'd like to have it now."

Weekend Warriors

In the late 1950s, Corvettes raced on weekends all over the country in Sports Car Club of America local, regional and national events. Crowds of spectators and race fans loved them for their dirt-tracking, four-wheel-drifting style of racing. Corvettes were felt to be the home team whenever they raced against foreign sports cars.

As word of their victories spread, the number of Corvette owner-drivers swelled. Corvettes were almost unbeatable in Class C Production at the beginning, with the 256 ci V-8 engines. Then, when the 283 came along, Corvettes moved up to B-Production and ruled the roost there too. By the early 1960s, many regional races pitted a sprinkling of other cars against a deluge of Corvettes.

Much of the racing action at that time took place on permanent road-racing tracks in Califor-

nia and on welcoming Strategic Air Command runways on the East Coast. The California tracks included such legendary names as Torrey Pines, Pebble Beach, Hanson's Dam, Palm Springs and Riverside.

In the East and Midwest sports cars diced and darted at Lime Rock, Watkins Glen, Elkhart Lake and of course, Sebring.

A Generation of Drivers

The Corvette became a cradle for American racing talent. Part of a generation of American race drivers—Bob Bondurant, Dick Guldstrand, Roger Penske, Dave MacDonald, Jim Hall and others—who took their early wins in Corvettes, went on to conquer larger and tougher races all over the world.

American amateur drivers were an amazing breed in those days. To hear about the exploits of those men and their fast fiberglass Corvettes is to long for a golden era, now past. Just imagine those hardy drivers in their short sleeves and chamber pot helmets, men who were their own mechanics and car owners.

And tough! Dick Guldstrand, whom you'll meet in a few pages, once broke his hand in a rollover during a Saturday Corvette race. Friends and competitors rallied to help him get the car back together. Then they taped his broken right hand to the shifter and he drove the Sunday race that way. Came in second!

These early racers earned little or no cash on their races, but theirs was the cosmic, palpitating,

Its day over, this Sebring Corvette was forced off the track by another car's spin and rolled several times. Despite the fiberglass being cracked like an eggshell, the driver was not seriously injured. What a sad sight for any Corvette fan. Dave Friedman

adrenaline high that goes with wheel-to-wheel competition. They struggled and raged against continual poverty, while lustily wheedling support from dealers and others. Yet, for a lucky few, there were secret supplies of parts and advice from the factory directly, if through clandestine channels.

What a time it must have been: going without sleep to party all the longer. Pushing your best friend off the track on the first turn and having him push you off on the last lap. Wrenching the beast at 4 am before race day. Driving your race car to the track, and then home again if it wasn't *hors d'combat*.

Imagine racing for fun, for the embraces of beautiful women and to show the world that this was your talent, your manhood, this was your car, your creation. As Dick Guldstrand said, "In high school, you had a hot rod or you were a candy-ass, one or the other."

The Flying Dentist and His Friends

The first golden era in the story of Corvette racers began soon after the Sebring experience of 1956. Chevrolet's executives realized that they had

At Road America in 1959, Jack Knab blasts his Corvette through the ess curves. He's hotly pursued by a Triumph and another Corvette. Dave Friedman

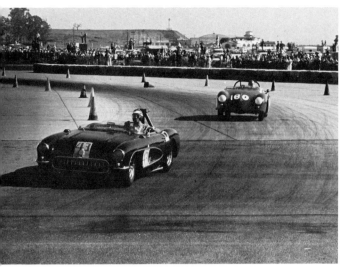

In the background, Don Yenko takes an unorthodox line in his number 1 Corvette, while, at the front, Bob Johnson in number 13 works to keep ahead of Doug Thiem in a Ferrari Berlinetta at Road America in 1962. Dave Friedman

Paul Reinhart, another West Coast Corvette ace, throws his car around a corner in Santa Barbara in September of 1961, chased by an oversteering Porsche 356. The Santa Barbara City Hall, visible in the background, looks the same today, but the racetrack is long gone. Dave Friedman

a potential race winner on their hands. They wanted to use that potential to communicate the Corvette's new, V-8 inspired performing talents to possible sports car buyers.

But, they had a problem. The factory could not race the car itself. The SCCA was for nonprofessional drivers. Chevrolet needed to find a weekend racer who could get the most out of the Corvette.

They found the ideal man in Dr. Richard "Dick" Thompson. Thompson's nickname, "The Flying Dentist," describes both his skill as a *pilote* and his full-time job. In the early 1990s, he is still a practicing dentist in the Washington, DC area.

"At Sebring of '56," Thompson recalled, "I co-drove a 300 SL with Paul O'Shea for the Mercedes factory. And through Paul I got the contact with John Fitch and GM, because they had just made the big effort at Sebring in '56. They wanted somebody to campaign the Corvette in SCCA that season."

Paul O'Shea proposed Thompson for the job. Later, John Fitch called and suggested that if Thompson were to buy the car, Chevrolet would deliver it at the first race. And then after that, they'd want it back after every race for teardown and evaluation, returning it before the next race. Thompson said it was " . . . the best deal I've had in a long time."

It was now four years after Dick Thompson's first race ever, in 1952. He and a friend had driven down to Sebring, Florida, in Thompson's MG TC for an AAA sports car race. Just sign on the dotted line and you were given a racing license.

"My friend and I both had MGs. We heard that there was a race down in Florida in the spring, at a place called Sebring. So we went down there and sure enough there was, so we just entered it and raced for twelve hours and learned a lot."

Thompson drove the MG until it was no longer competitive, then he bought a Porsche and raced it around the East Coast and Nassau in the Bahamas. After a hitch in the Marine Corps as a reservist, he drove the Porsche to a tie for the SCCA F-Production championship in 1954. Then he raced a Jaguar XK-140 until the Mercedes ride came along. Thompson's first race in a Corvette was at Pebble Beach, in Monterey, California.

Located at the head of California's spectacular Big Sur coastline, the Pebble Beach track was little more than a twisting serpent of blacktop near a world-famous golf course, just off Monterey Bay. Thompson's remarkable place in Corvette history was about to begin.

"At Pebble Beach in '56 was the first time I competed in a Corvette," Thompson said. "It was the first time I had really seen one. I literally took delivery from the dealer out there and drove it from the dealership to Pebble Beach.

"I was very pleasantly surprised. John Fitch and his people had done such a fine job down at Sebring. They had really revolutionized the car. It had obvious deficiencies, as we found out a little later. It was a good handling car. Better than the Jaguar of the time and better than the 300 SL of the time. Definitely better roadholding. It had one big drawback: it wouldn't stop!"

But the Corvette needed more than just better brakes for its first SCCA race of 1956. As Thompson remembered: "That first time at Pebble Beach we had two problems. One was brakes, the

other was that the carburetor floats kept fouling and it would starve out in the turns. We had a lot of trouble with that in practice. But Frank Burrell was the factory engineer who came along with the car. He solved that the night after practice, and it worked fine during the race. It was the fastest race car there for most of the race. And then it ran completely out of brakes.

"In practice I'd had a lot of trouble. I started about tenth, I think. Because we'd had so much trouble in practice, we didn't qualify well at all.

"At the first corner I knew I had the fastest car there. It was very obvious. I had no trouble passing the 300 SLs, about five of them, I guess. It would corner better, outaccelerate and for a while, stop just as well.

"And then of course, the brakes got worse and worse and worse. Until, on the last two or three laps, there were literally no brakes. And at that time we only had a three-speed gearbox, so you couldn't use that too well [for braking]."

Bob Bondurant was certainly as fast as the Playboy *rabbit in a Corvette. Here he's just passed Vince Mayell on the outside and is preparing to drift the car to the apex of the corner. Both cars have cut-down windscreens and headlights taped over to keep glass off the track. This is from Del Mar in 1959.* Dave Friedman

There were as many driving styles as there were Corvettes. Here Andy Porterfield leads a bunch into a difficult turn at the Paramount Ranch in 1957. Porter- *field's car is nicely turned out with a trick fairing instead of a windscreen and a chromed roll bar.* Dave Friedman

Now, Thompson was driving a fast car without brakes through a forest. "Pebble Beach was a very terrifying kind of course. It went through the woods. There were trees three feet off the edge of the course, so you had to have confidence in the car. That was the day Ernie MacAffie was killed there by going about two feet off the road," Thompson recounted.

When the race began, Thompson gunned the Corvette down the straight, toward the first turn. He passed most of the other cars right there. When Chevrolet ad rep Barney Clark, standing along the track farther into the woods, saw that the Corvette was leading the race he whooped happily. The racing program was in part under his supervision, since racing was being used as a sales tool.

Thompson drove like a virtuoso, in complete control. But the twisty nature of the Pebble Beach Circuit ate into his brakes. Several laps from the checkered flag, a 300 SL passed him and took the win. Except for this nagging problem with brakes, the Corvette would have won its first SCCA race! Arkus-Dunkov and company were in heaven.

Stop Me If You've Heard This One

Dick Thompson was thrilled about finishing second on the first time out with a new car but had one big reservation about the Corvette as a racer: "Actually, the brakes were so bad that when the race was over and I pulled into the pits, I had to leave it in gear and stall it to get it to stop. There were literally no brakes at all. The problem was that the return springs on the brake shoes would lose their temper from the extreme heat. Everything would just destroy itself.

"At the end of the race, Frank Burrell pulled a wheel and pulled a drum and all the parts fell out on the ground. It was just all melted and destroyed. They improved the quality of the return springs and that helped the situation somewhat. But they were limited in those days because the specifications were very rigid for a production car, and there wasn't very much they could do.

"That whole season we had continuing trouble with the brakes, but after a while we learned what you could do and what you couldn't do and we just

On a B-Production grid at Cumberland in 1959, Jim Jeffords prepares to devastate the field once again. His mechanic is buttoning down the Rochester fuel injection that made early Corvette V-8s so competitive. Dave Friedman

Jeffords in close-up. One of the best Corvette drivers of the late fifties and early sixties, Jeffords was an advertising man from Milwaukee, Wisconsin. When a Corvette dealer asked Jeffords what he could do with good sponsorship behind him, Jeffords immediately replied: "Win the championship!" Dave Friedman

Jeffords at speed. A few months later, the Purple People Eater had a tiny windscreen, and the rollbar had been chromed. In his second championship year, Jeffords raced with an effortless grace that effectively masked his aggressive driving style. Dave Friedman

Another Corvette racing master, Bob Bondurant. Nothing's so sweet as victory. Bondurant has just won at Del Mar in Long Beach, California, in 1959. His Corvette shows some crude touches like the angle iron on the windscreen and the extra instrument mounted above the dash. No matter, the car was fast. Dave Friedman

raced around that problem. Fortunately the car would outaccelerate the 300 SLs, which were the main competition—the Jaguars just weren't fast enough.

"Down at Palm Springs I finally got the brakes to last until the last lap. And then I had quite a battle with one 300 SL on the last lap because I then had no brakes, same old story. Fortunately enough, I was able to win.

"That was on an airport," Thompson added. "It's a lot easier on an airport when you don't have brakes because you can always say the hell with it and drive off. From then on we knew what we had and I would baby the brakes the whole race to get them to last, if I could. It was the same car I took to the championship that year."

And take the championship he did. The final points total for Class C Production in the 1956 season was Dick Thompson 10,000; Harry Carter, driving a Jaguar, 5,500; and Dick Kessler, also with

Bondurant at speed in the same Corvette, here at the Kiwanis Grand Prix at Riverside Raceway in California, in 1959. His claim was that the Corvette was much faster if driven smoothly. His winning record seems to bear that out. Dave Friedman

Jim Jeffords and His *Purple People Eater*

One of the most flamboyant, aggressive and successful Corvette racers of the late 1950s was Milwaukee, Wisconsin, advertising executive James Jeffords. He came out of nowhere and became one of the leading amateur drivers in the United States. He was soon dicing among the top professionals and vying for national championships.

Jeffords first raced his own XK 120 Jaguar at Wilmot, Wisconsin, in 1954. He finished second there and went on to win fourteen of his next seventeen events in 1954 and 1955.

"In 1956 Chevrolet started their factory racing team," Jeffords said. "I called Ed Cole, who at that time was chief engineer for Chevrolet. I ran an advertising agency in Milwaukee. I told him, 'I hear you're starting a Corvette racing team and I'd like to be part of it.'"

Cole said that he had heard of Jeffords, and he gave him Dick Doane's number, who along with Indy winner Jim Rathman was doing some undercover work for Chevrolet.

Eventually, Jeffords was sent to Caracas, Venezuela, with the Corvette team to race, but the dictator there, Jiminez, kept the cars for six months, driving them himself. In 1957, the Automobile Manufacturers Association (AMA) factory racing ban took Jeffords off the Corvette team and he raced Ferraris and Porsches for other owners.

In 1958, Jeffords got a call from Lionel Lindheimer, sales manager for Nickey Chevrolet in Chicago, a large and prosperous dealership. Nickey wanted to sponsor a Corvette and they wanted Jeffords to drive it.

"I was interviewed by the owner and he asked me what would happen if they sponsored me," Jeffords recalled, "and I said, 'I'll win the national championship.' I was very modest in those days." Jeffords

stipulated that the car would be maintained by his racing mechanic only, that he would hire and run the crew, and that he would be in charge of the racing program. They said yes.

Jeffords continued: "So they agreed to that and I hired this wonderful mechanic, Ronnie Kaplan, and we won the national championship in 1958 and again in '59. I think we won 90 percent of the races we started in those cars.

"In those days there was a song on the radio: One eyed, one-horned people eater, and I said that if they really wanted to get their money's worth in promotion, they should paint the car some garish color. So we painted the car purple and just about that time the song came out. So they wrote 'Purple People Eater' on the car and that's how it all started."

After a casual dinner with Lance Reventlow, millionaire playboy and creator of the Scarab sports racer, Jeffords bought one of the front-engined Scarabs for the bargain basement price of $17,500, on the condition that he campaign it as aggressively as he had driven his purple Corvette. He did, but problems at the sponsoring dealership caused them to withdraw from racing, and Jeffords was on his own again.

In 1960, Jeffords drove a Camaradi Corvette at the race in Havana, Cuba. In 1959 Fidel Castro had briefly kidnapped Juan Manuel Fangio, but in 1960 he tried, unsuccessfully, to stop the race itself.

Jeffords won the International GT race in the Corvette, while Stirling Moss in a Camaradi Maserati Birdcage won the feature race, the next day.

"They put Castro's son, who was then twelve years old, in the car with me for a victory lap. They had tanks there and soldiers with rifles in every pit. They gave me a whole floor of the Hilton Hotel for winning the race. It was kind of a wild place," Jeffords said. That was the last time he raced a Corvette.

Jaguar, 2,000. Clearly the Corvette had been more than just dominant, it had ruled the racetracks.

In 1957, Thompson once again trumped the roost, this time in B-Production, with the 283 ci motor. Thompson recalls that the 1957 Corvette was a much better race car.

"The next year, 1957, they made very definite improvements; they got a limited-slip rear axle, which helped. And a four-speed gearbox, and the fuel injection. That cured a lot of the other problems we had, but they didn't do much for the brakes. But by improving the other portions of it, we didn't have to use the brakes so much to get the same or better performance out of it."

In 1958 and 1959, Chicagoan Jim Jeffords took the B-Production crown, also by sizable margins. Jeffords drove for Nickey Chevrolet, a large Chi-

cago dealership, whose logo featured a backward K, for name recognition. Jeffords' car went by the colorful name of the *Purple People Eater*. Although in truth, it was more of a Corvette eater, triumphing over seventeen other Corvettes for the national points championship in B-Production both years.

Yenko—Another Corvette Stalwart

Although Dick Thompson returned to take the A-Production championship in 1961 and 1962, with Don Yenko winning the B-Production title, by 1963 the first two places in A-Production were taken by Cobras. Dick Thompson finished a competitive third and Don Yenko was back in eighth place.

Don Yenko had a Chevy dealership in the town of Canonsburg, about thirty miles southwest of Pittsburgh, Pennsylvania, also the hometown of

Hourglass Field in San Diego was one of the airport tracks where Corvettes raced. There it was all hay bales and pylons, and may the best Corvette win. In this 1959 race, number 13, driven by Dean Geddes, with the spiffy matching car, helmet and roll bar shows the fast way around the track to Tony Settember in number 58 and former stock car racer Buford Lane in number 614. Dave Friedman

Bobby Vinton and Perry Como. He began by racing a small-block '61 'Vette in B-Production.

Bob King of Goodyear said of Don Yenko: "Yenko was pretty spectacular in the B-Production Corvettes in the early to mid-sixties. I saw him several times at VIR [Virginia International Raceway] during that period. VIR was an extremely difficult 3.23 mile racer's circuit with every imaginable corner configuration and two blazing straightaways. Yenko ran a rain race at VIR in 1963 or '64 on a set of Michelin street radials he borrowed from a spectator, and he buried the big-bore field."

Yenko went on to offer specialized versions of the Camaro and Corvair throughout the 1960s and into the 1970s, calling some of them Yenko Stingers perhaps after the Sting Ray. He was killed in an airplane crash in the 1970s.

Corvettes Own California

In the sunny climate of California, in the late 1950s and early 1960s, Corvettes established complete dominance of amateur racing in the top production classes. Due to the availability of used Corvettes, their relatively low cost, and the grow-

Below the ocean cliffs of Del Mar, just north of San Diego, was a perfect place for sports car racing. In the parking lot of the fairgrounds, a nice, but tight racecourse was set up by the SCCA. At this race in 1960, Bondurant leads Tony Settember in number 58 and the hard-charging Dave MacDonald in number 00. Dave Friedman

ing body of knowledge on tuning and speed secrets, a Corvette made a perfect beginning race car for the serious amateur and the up-and-coming professional racer.

Dick Guldstrand was a California hot rodder who was struck by lightning, and destiny, when he saw his first Corvette.

"I got out of the service in '52 and right on top of that I saw my first 'Vette. And I went crazy! I just couldn't believe that Americans had built a car so impressive. Cause we'd all seen Porsches and Ferraris, Maseratis and all the other stuff that had been around. But, man, there was an American car. So, I dug and scrounged and finally by probably '58 or '59 I bought a '56 and I just had to go try it out.

"I mean, the first thing you'd do, of course, is you'd take it all apart, right? Because I had no problem building cars. And I did a lot of the trick things that they had back then, the special brakes and the four-speed and the injector; I learned all about that and put all that on this little '56."

In his "other" profession as an aerospace engineer, Guldstrand had learned a few high-tech things to augment his natural nuts-and-bolts approach to racing. He wanted the best car possible.

"I found some really grim front springs and put two sway bars on it. And re-did, re-arched, the back springs, lowered and de-arched them, put an extra leaf on it, really got it tightened up—because I was finding out that the tracks we were running on were pretty flat. And you had to really dirt track it. There was no way of just driving it right around the corner.

"So everybody kind of developed a style, and that style would determine how you would develop the car. And in most cases, the stiffer the better; you could slide it around corners and it was predictable and stable. You got away from the inherent understeer that was built into the thing, because the front geometry was awful. You couldn't let it move."

Guldstrand explained: "Actually it was the lack of camber gain that caused the understeer. It wouldn't gain any camber, and the roll centers were way too low. Way below ground level. So it was just awful; it would take a horrendous spring just to hold the car up because it rolls around that center and the higher rate the spring is, the more it holds it up. But then the more it pushes [understeers] because you're loading the hard side tire, and there's no way around it. So we made it slide around. There was nothing you could do to redesign that. We lightened them up as much as we could, light body parts, and we did a lot of work on the engine.

"Look at any of the pictures from that era and you can see the fast guys were actually drifting 'em. Because number one, the tires weren't that good. God help you, the tire was, what, five inches wide and it was a little treaded nothing, a recap.

"So you learned to keep up the momentum. And, coming from sprint cars and midgets, you could dive into a corner and throw it sideways, gather it up and stand on it. That carried momentum through the corner and out the other side. You didn't have to stop it and try to turn the corner and all that. A lot of powersliding, you know. A lot of car control, which you had to learn.

"You taught yourself to drive. There were maybe a couple of classes from the SCCA, but that was just to see if you didn't have a death wish. It had little to do with your driving ability or your education. It was rules and flags, you had to learn all that stuff. It was more to sort out somebody who had an ego problem than any kind of education.

One lonely Ferrari GT surrounded by all those Corvettes at Road America in 1962. Bob Johnson in number 13 leads the way. Dave Friedman

It's Corvette and Ferrari again, a battle that raged loudly in the early 1960s. The number 4 Corvette of Johnson and Morgan prepares to pass the 250 GT of Hamil and Serena. Dave Friedman

Corvettes leap into the lead at the start of the Sebring twelve-hour in 1961. Yenko and Moore are in the number 1 car, Kilborn and Rairdon in number 2, Robertson, Warren and Burroughs in number 3, and Johnson and Morgan in number 4. Various Aston Martins, Ferraris and smaller cars such as Triumphs and Lotuses are also having a good start. Dave Friedman

Trouble with the diff! This Sebring Corvette needs a new differential because the wrong lube was used, or because the gears were not worn-in before racing on them. Dave Friedman

Still running after a major front-end misunderstanding, the Yenko and Lothar Corvette limps around Sebring in 1962. Dave Friedman

And you sorted yourself out: how fast you wanted to go, how hard you wanted to push."

Some of the other outstanding drivers of the California Corvette scene in the late 1950s and early 1960s were Andy Porterfield, the brilliant Dave MacDonald, Paul Reinhart, stock car racer Buford Lane, Tony Settember, Doug Hooper, Joe Freitas, Red Farris and Bob Bondurant.

Of all these drivers, Bondurant certainly went furthest, winning the World GT Championship and the Manufacturers GT Championship for Carroll Shelby in 1967 in the Cobra Daytona coupes. After many more victories in a number of formats, Bondurant opened a competition driving school. He's currently the leading teacher of fast driving and car control in the United States, with pupils including Al Unser, Jr., Rick Mears and Bill Elliot. Bondurant stresses smoothness to all his driving students, and bases his instruction on what he learned as a practicing, and winning race driver.

Sadly, by the beginning of 1963 the glory days of the solid-axle Corvette as the dominant SCCA production racer were coming to an end. Two new cars which appeared at the end of 1962 would completely overshadow the live-axle Corvette. One was a reptilian creation from Carroll Shelby, the other was the evolution of the Corvette itself, the magnificent Sting Ray.

The mouse that roared. Ready to go racing, this fuel-injected 327 ci small-block engine made 350 hp and survived race after race. Ed Cole's V-8 had become Zora Arkus-Duntov's masterpiece by the early 1960s. Chevrolet

Keeping ahead of a Porsche RS Spyder and a Lister-Jaguar is not as easy as Bob Bondurant makes it look. Driving his favorite Corvette, the number 614 Washburn Chevrolet car, Bondurant shows the style that would make him a champion in Europe a few years later. This race is at Santa Barbara in 1961. Dave Friedman

Although Dr. Dick Thompson is driving, this '62 Corvette has some odd touches, like the kid's horn on the hood. It also has brake cooling scoops everywhere, big, rectangular ones in front and a smaller version under the rocker panel for the rears. Note the asymmetrical windscreen. Dave Friedman

47

It's colder 'n hell at Pikes Peak, but Corvette racer Al Daniels smiles despite a rear deck full of snow. Corvettes have always done well at the Peak due to their fuel injection and low center of gravity. Dave Friedman

Get on those brakes! Joe Fretias puts the boot to his number 77 Corvette at Pomona in 1962 while Dave MacDonald, his car still wounded in the right front, runs right in with him. It was a matter of honor not to brake for a corner first. Drivers often ran each other off the road waiting for the other guy to brake until it was way too late to make the corner. Dave Friedman

Of the California wild men, one of the fast ones was Dave MacDonald. At Riverside in 1962, MacDonald has the rear of his Corvette hung out, while the Ferrari behind him bides its time. MacDonald was regarded as one of the best drivers in the United States until he met his death at Indy. Dave Friedman

Bob Bondurant: From Corvettes to Cobras

Bob Bondurant rose to prominence as a racer by driving one of those old solid-axle Corvettes. He went on to beat Europe's best on their own turf driving Cobras for Carroll Shelby. Talking to Bondurant today, you become aware that the Corvette taught him much of what he learned about racing. But you also notice that the man has a remarkable ability to understand vehicle dynamics, coupled with a powerful ego and a dynamically competitive nature.

He tells the story like this:

"You learn to control the weight transfer of the vehicle with the throttle and the brakes. Half- and quarter-mile dirt ovals, you don't have brakes. You controlled it all with the throttle. It's all weight transfer control and you can do the same thing with a car. Plus you run handlebar to handlebar, wheel to wheel with someone.

"When you got in a car you had fenders and four wheels. And it's nothing to be sliding through the corner and runnin' wheel to wheel. And so [for] a lot of people who have never done that, it's a little scary the first time they do that. It's all vehicle feel.

"1958 is when I first started driving Corvettes. I never drove one on the street. Number one, you can never afford race cars, so you figure out what you can buy or finance or sponsor or whatever. So I bought the 1957 Wayne Corvette that Jerry Austin drove. C. S. Means Chevrolet agreed to sponsor me with parts. They helped me get started."

Bondurant continued: "My first race was at Santa Barbara and I had a neat car. It handled like the Triumph; it was a straight-axle car and you'd power slide that around. And you power slid the Corvette around. Sort of like bikes: you're wheel to wheel, fender to fender. I was right at home there, right away.

"Skip Hudson at that time was *the* Corvette driver. Bob Dickson was winning things in those days, Andy Porterfield, of course, was winning everything. All of a sudden, I'm in a race with these guys, and Tony Settember. I go down the back straightaway and I came out of the corner a little bit quicker, so I'm passing them one by one. I got about midway through passing and I thought, 'You can't pass these guys.' They were guys I idolized. I realized that I was talking to myself and I said, 'Bondurant. Stop it and go!'

"So I passed Bob Dixon going down the straightaway and I was way over my head. I did the biggest 720, that's two 360s, and stuck it back in gear and I still finished fourth. That was Saturday. Then on Sunday I settled down a little bit and I ended up second.

"So I scrounged around and got just enough money to get some support from C. S. Means Chevrolet; they helped me with parts, he built the motor and got us going. So, I won the next race.

Then we needed some more horsepower and the engine built a little better, so Don Nichols, 'Dyno Don' as he is called, dialed our motor in, and I won eighteen out of twenty races.

"I won the B-Production championship of 1959 and I got Best Corvette Driver of the Year from Valvoline, the trophy. Then I sold the car and started driving for other people."

Caught in the bitter Cal Club–SCCA feud of those days, Bondurant was banned from racing for six months. He refused to take it lying down. He spent his free time learning to fly helicopters.

One day, he got a call from Shelly Washburn telling him that the only way Chevrolet would sell him one of its new Sting Ray Corvette race cars was if Bondurant would drive it in the *Los Angeles Times* Grand Prix in November of 1962. Bondurant agreed and came out of retirement. Although he did not win that day, he loved the handling of the new Corvette Sting Ray.

Yet, at that very same race, the Shelby Cobra made its debut. Bondurant and others realized that the Cobra was light enough to run away from the Sting Ray. Some of the best Corvette drivers, Bondurant included, switched to Cobras because they wanted to drive whatever was fastest, so they had a valid chance of winning races.

Bondurant did very well as a Cobra driver. His smooth style and careful car control made him very fast in the light but tricky Cobras. As Carroll Shelby turned his eyes toward Europe and the GT championship, Bondurant elected to go with him.

"The next year, '64, two Cobra Daytona coupes came along," Bondurant said. "Dan Gurney and I came together at Le Mans, Jochim Neerpash and somebody else in the other car, and Dan and I won. We finished fourth overall and first GT. But all the years driving the Corvette, driving sideways, all the way back to Nick Pastor's Triumph which had a locked rear end, going back to that and the bikes, all that was preparation."

Bondurant commented on the Corvette's handling: "The way you would make a solid-axle Corvette handle is to drive it sideways in a four-wheel drift. Again, steering it with the throttle, just like I did with the motorcycle. And it would come in the corner and the back would come out; the back would want to come out but you'd steer into it.

"After I lost the back end, I realized that this was neat. You can really—if you run it in deep, what we now know as trail braking—ride the brakes in real light to keep weight on the front tires so it steers where I want it to go. Then when the back end would come out, I'd steer it with throttle. This way you kept the motion of the car going, the speed of the car and a faster cornering speed. Not knowing or understanding why, you just did it."

Another Corvette stalwart, Dick Guldstrand. Known as Goldie, he was a skinny aerospace engineer who had an overwhelming love of Corvettes and a heck of a talent for racing. Guldstrand was a master of tuning the car and developing it. At Riverside in 1962, Guldstrand applies a touch of countersteering as his Corvette rockets out of a turn. Dave Friedman

Later in 1962, Guldstrand had sponsorship from Hy Baher Chevrolet in Hermosa Beach, California. Now the car has a trimmed-down windscreen, fabric cushions taped over the headlights, and is missing a few teeth. Dave Friedman

Despite the funny roll bar, Paul Reinhart was a fast and stylish driver. The Porsche behind him seems to be driving a different track entirely, so unlike are their racing lines. Dave Friedman

Charging ahead of Paul Reinhart is the formidable Dave MacDonald. Here you see MacDonald at his ultimate: in control even if the car is out of control. Dave Friedman

Dave MacDonald had an 8/10s Corvette body made in fiberglass and mounted it on a custom-made frame. Three of these bodies were made, the second one going to Jack Lufkin's Bonneville Corvette, and the third van-

ished. MacDonald soon switched to Corvette Sting Rays, then Cobras and then went to Indy with Mickey Thompson, where he was killed at the very start of the 500 in 1964. Dave Friedman

Chapter 4

Real Racers: The SR-2
and the Sebring Super Sport

Jerry Earl bought a Ferrari, and his father didn't like it. It was too foreign and too fast. So we designed a special car for him, a Corvette. I stretched the nose out ten inches and we put a fin behind the driver's head for stability. Because, of course, nobody really knew about aerodynamics then; you just made a shape and that was all.

—Bob Cumberford, former GM stylist

The experiences at Chevrolet engineering at Sebring in 1956 had taught them a number of lessons about racing the Corvette. First, the Corvettes had winning potential. Second, they could not be in the hunt for overall victories; those prizes were reserved for the sports racers or specials driven by the finest drivers in the world.

Bud Gates drives the SR-2 at Nassau in 1960. Although the car looked great, thanks to GM stylists like Robert Cumberford, it was never seen as a competitive race car.

Perhaps since it was built for Harley Earl's son Jerry, the idea was to keep it from being too fast. Dave Friedman

It seemed clear to Zora Arkus–Duntov that Chevrolet needed to develop a flat-out race car based on the Corvette, which could conceivably win at Sebring, Daytona and even at European races like the fabled 24 Hours of Le Mans. Yet, the first Corvette factory racing special had its origins on a much more personal level, with Harley Earl's son, Jerry.

As Bob Cumberford, then a GM stylist, remembers it, "Jerry Earl bought a Ferrari, and his father didn't like it. It was too foreign and too fast. So we designed a special car for him, a Corvette. I stretched the nose out 10 inches and we put a fin behind the driver's head for stability because, of course, nobody really knew about aerodynamics then; you just made a shape and that was all."

This special was known as the SR-2. The earlier Corvettes from Sebring in 1956 had been called Sebring-Racer-1, or SR-1. The original SR-2 was built for Jerry Earl, but when it first appeared, racing at the 1956 Road America June Sprints at Elkhart Lake, Wisconsin, it was being driven by Dr. Dick Thompson, who was not thrilled with the car. The SR-2 was mostly an experiment with the Corvette body. It did have the RPO racing parts, but it was heavier than the stock Corvette and had even more brake problems than the stock cars.

About that fin behind the driver's head. Didn't it look familiar, like directly off the Jaguar D-Type race car? Bob Cumberford said in an interview, "We weren't copying the fin on the D-Type Jaguar, because ours was exactly the same line as the fender line of the '57 Chevy. If you look, you can see that it's the same line."

Underneath that custom bodywork, red paint and white accents, the SR-2 was all Corvette, even if many parts were the RPO items which had been developed for Sebring in 1956. One system that was subject to constant improvement was the brakes. If there was only one complaint from Corvette road racers it was that the 'Vette's brakes were not ready for prime time. The SR-2's brakes were heavily finned, wide aluminum drums which were recessed completely into the front wheels. Each brake assembly had an internal fan for cooling. It was a good idea, but still not enough.

Said Cumberford, "The SR-2 used Chrysler brake drums—about four inches wide—with conformable shoes. The shoes had a rib on the back which allowed them to flex. Even if the drums were a little out of round they wouldn't squeak or pulse. But they would engage smoothly."

The Corvette SR-2 had its competition debut at the Daytona Speed Week of 1957. For Daytona it also had a plexiglass bubble roof for streamlining, pants to cover the rear wheels, also for low drag, fairing cones for the headlamps and a plexiglass cover for the grille, to allow only a small center opening to cool the engine at speed.

At Daytona's Speed Week in 1957 the SR-2, with its fuel-injected 283 ci engine tuned for 310 hp, running on open pipes, won the standing mile speed run, at an average of 93.04 mph. It also took second place in the flying mile at 152.86, just behind a racing D-Type Jaguar. The SR-2 was driven by stock car ace Buck Baker.

Dr. Dick Thompson drove the SR-2 in a few races but didn't think there was anything remark-

The SR-2 at speed. Although it was really a standard RPO racing Corvette, the SR-2 had an aggressive and international bodystyle that recalled the Jaguar D-Type. Dr. Dick Thompson, the driver in this photo, wasn't crazy about the machine, saying it had all the faults of a stock Corvette and was heavier to boot. Chevrolet

Legend has it that Zora Arkus-Duntov bought a Mercedes 300 SLR like this one and stripped it to this condition so that he could directly adapt the Mercedes space frame to the Corvette SS. True or not, the SS did have a tube space frame which closely resembled the Mercedes. Mercedes-Benz

able about it. He claims that the handling and accleration were about the same as his B-Production SCCA racing 'Vette. After a while, another SR-2 was built as a showpiece and gift for Harlow Curtice, then president of General Motors. It was a less radical car than the Jerry Earl version, with less of an extension in the front end and a lower, centered tail fin. You might say that this car was a bribe, so that Curtice would look fondly on Chevrolet's racing activities. But ironically, it was Curtice who championed the AMA ban on factory involvement in racing, which was just a short time away.

Establishing a pattern for the future, the Jerry Earl SR-2 was pensioned off to Bill Mitchell, Harley Earl's successor in the Styling Section. Mitchell would go on to race the car for fun, supporting it out of his own pocket. After its competition career was over, the SR-2 hit the auto show circuit and became famous for sitting still.

Corvette Super Sport

Perhaps he was frustrated by the failure of the SR-2 as a racing machine, or perhaps Jerry Earl wanted a more prestigious race car of his own. For obscure reasons, Harley Earl acquired a Jaguar D-Type race car, in bright yellow, from Jack Ensley of Indianapolis. Ensley had raced this D-Type at Sebring, bringing the car in for a respectable third-place finish. This was in the spring of 1956, after the first modest Corvette victories at Sebring.

Earl smuggled the D-Type into the semi-secret Studio Z at the Styling Center and told his men that he wanted the car reworked to take a Chevy small-block motor.

Bob Cumberford recalled: "Harley Earl brought in a D-Type Jaguar—that was on Styling's budget; that's how they could do it. And he wanted us to put a new front on it and a new rear. We wanted to keep the Jaguar's oval sides, they were good for cross-wind resistance. But the D-Type had a front subframe that mounted the engine and it was too narrow for the Chevy V-8."

Even though Zora Arkus-Duntov was on vacation with his wife Elfie in New York, he heard about the D-Type conversion and hated the idea. Responding that Chevrolet should make a new race car of its own, not a shotgun wedding of Chevrolet and Jaguar, Arkus-Duntov pleaded with management for a chance to design and build at least one prototype. That was the birth of the first Corvette SS or Super Sport. Management said yes.

Now Arkus-Duntov had the kind of freedom he had been aching for, and the kind of challenge he wanted. The racers from Chevrolet were going to get on the track with Mercedes-Benz, Ferrari, Maserati and Aston Martin and show the big boys who was really fast. But as with the Sebring effort, there was so little time. Less than six months

would elapse between the clean sheet of paper and the race at Sebring.

Fortunately, Styling had a jump on the game. Harley Earl had been playing with various Corvette designs for some time, just to express himself. One of these design studies, called the XP-64, would be just right for the proposed SS. Its streamlined sports racer body looked a little like the D-Type Jaguar, but it was lower and wider. And, in place of the Jaguar's rear fin, the XP-64 had a conical headrest for the driver which tapered for low wind resistance.

This headrest was called the "flying football" by Styling staff insiders. At the rear of the body, the rear deck slid down flatly to meet the upswept underbody. The effect was more than a little like the back end of Bill Mitchell's Sting Ray racer, a descendant of this very design.

Inside the Corvette SS

When the Corvette SS was approved, Harley Earl had his staff create a full-size clay study of the XP-64, so that Arkus-Duntov and his engineers could see what they had to use. No one understood the importance of downforce in those days, so if the body was aerodynamically clean it was pronounced fine. In fact, the Corvette SS had several major problems with cooling airflow, but they were not discovered or even imagined at this early stage of construction.

Arkus-Duntov and his team set up shop in one walled-off corner of the technical center and went to work on the Super Sport. The first thing they needed was a frame. Here Zora wanted lightness and strength, a state-of-the-art approach. Based on the best technology available in 1956, he chose a round-tube space frame. It would be both light and strong. But tube frames needed development time, and Arkus-Duntov didn't have it.

To speed up the process of frame fabrication, he simply bought a Mercedes 300 SLR and stripped it down to the frame. Then, as Bob Cumberford remembers " . . . he copied the frame in wooden dowel rods around a Chevy small-block engine. So the chassis of the SS was really as good as anything on the road at the time."

Then the Duntov frame was carefully welded out of thin-wall 1 in. chrome-molybdenum steel tubing. The frame consisted of a triangulated segment around the engine and another at the rear of the car. They were tied together by two trussed sections along the doorsills. The front end used a massive, 4 in. wide, rear-pointing, U-shaped tube to take much of the front suspension stress and to serve as an engine mount. Front suspension geometry was conventional. Twin upper and lower A-arms were fabricated from steel. The off angle A-arms aided in combating squat during acceleration and dive under braking.

This is how the Mercedes looked with its clothes on. Although the Corvette SS had similar proportions to the 300 SLR, it was a much more expressive shape, including *the famous "flying football" behind the driver's head.* Mercedes-Benz

The rear, de Dion axle had a unique locating system, partly due to a suggestion by Maurice Olley. There were three kinds of locating points. One was the attachment end of the coil-over shock as it mounted to the hub carrier. This point served to stabilize the axle in the vertical dimension. Next was a pair of trailing arms, made from the same light but strong tubing as the frame, which also attached to the hub carriers. These two parallel links ran from the frame to points above the axle centerline on the hubs, acting to counter axle rotation and reduce toe-out on cornering.

The other two links were set low. They ran below the de Dion tube. They pointed inward from the frame and located the axle horizontally with the shocks. They also inhibited squat and had the effect of raising the rear roll center, but reduced the need for hard springs and shocks. Unfortunately, the rubber bushings used to mount these links would prove to be their fatal flaw.

Chevrolet engineering made its own rear-end ring-and-pinion gears. They were precision machined and subjected to shot-peening for greater surface strength. Ratios from 2.63 to 4.80 were available; a 3.55 rear end was chosen for Sebring.

Arkus-Duntov had chosen the de Dion rear axle because it was well known from an engineering standpoint and would need little development time. He also had in mind that the de Dion would give the Super Sport great stability at high speeds on the bumpy Mulsanne straight at Le Mans, at that time a four-mile-long roller coaster of small and large bumps, to be taken absolutely flat out for twenty-four hours.

Arkus–Duntov: Rebel with a Cause

Arkus-Duntov wanted an overall win at Le Mans, which he never had as a driver, for the Corvette SS. Sebring was to be just a rehearsal for the French race in June. Not only would a Le Mans victory satisfy him personally, it would also make the entire European racing community take instant notice of the Corvette, and it could stimulate sales like nothing else.

In one of his typical underground moves, Zora also got permission to build a mock-up of the SS chassis, to get the bugs out before they built the race car frame and chassis. As the development chassis was completed, it was fitted with a fiberglass mock-up of the final magnesium panel body.

As soon as it was driveable, Arkus-Duntov got in it and began flogging it, looking for flaws and design errors. He is said to have put over 2,000

Women say that men never grow up, it's just that their toys get more expensive. Here's Zora Arkus-Duntov posing with the SS before its one and only race at Sebring in 1957. Sadly, the experience was a disaster for Zora, Corvette and Chevrolet. By the time he returned to Detroit from vacation, the SS program had been canceled. Chevrolet

miles on the test mule while the race car was being completed.

In testing, the mule behaved beautifully. Zora was getting more excited day by day. He knew a good race car when he drove one, and this Corvette Super Sport was looking like a champ.

It had plenty of advantages: the frame based on a Mercedes 300 SLR, the potent small-block V-8, excellent front and rear suspension, Arkus-Duntov's loving care at every stage of construction, a show car body and interior, and good handling right out of the box.

After driving substantial test miles in Milford, Michigan, some of it in cold weather, Arkus-Duntov and the SS mule went down to Sebring to continue shaking down the design. Things were already very different from the hectic factory effort of the year before. This time the Chevrolet people were calm, confident and composed. They were expecting to do very well, perhaps even win the race, an outrageous assumption for a brand-new

race car. But they had seen fast times on the stopwatch and their hopes were not all pie in the sky.

Shakedown at Sebring

John Fitch was already at Sebring with a three-car team of production Corvettes. Fitch had kept in touch with Chevrolet after the 1956 race at Sebring, and once again he had been given the title of team manager for Corvette. In his book, *Adventures on Wheels,* Fitch mentioned his response to driving the mule around the Sebring track.

"The firewall was made of one-inch plywood, and a great thickness of fiberglas[s] was clearly visible through the many gaps and omitted parts . . . Despite a pronounced roll and a feeling of too-soft suspension, and without stretching anything, I was able to break the Sebring record unofficially after three laps on my first time out with the car."

To anyone who knows motor sports, such an accomplishment is not just remarkable, it's darned near a miracle. Granted that Fitch was a superior driver and that he knew the Sebring course very well. Still, the mule was a cobbled-up version of the final SS, and it was several hundred pounds heavier than the final SS would be.

At this point various accounts of the events at the 1957 Sebring differ. Fitch says that he was hired to drive the Super Sport, from the beginning. Others, including insider Karl Ludvigsen, believe that Stirling Moss and Juan Manuel Fangio were engaged to drive the SS, but that the car was not ready in time for the race, so both Moss and Fangio took other rides, the SS reverting to Fitch by default.

According to Bob Cumberford, one of the stylists working on the SS project, "The SS came out of the styling department, and they should have been less concerned about making it a show car, not caring if it gets a few chips from rocks in that beautiful blue paint. If they were going to have raced the car for twelve hours they should have run it for twenty-four hours at full speed to see what would break."

However, Fitch says the SS couldn't be fully tested because the brakes hadn't been seated and the engine was not ready to be run at 100 percent power.

Whatever actually happened, the SS race car was not driven by Moss and Fangio, the mule was. When Fangio went out in the mule, he loved it. After warming up, Fangio broke the track record by a full two seconds! When he came in he grinned and said, "Fantastico!" Fangio gave the impression that there was even more speed in the overweight mule, but he hadn't pushed it. No matter what the pre-race understanding, Fangio and Moss left to drive for Maserati.

John Fitch dices with a Maserati 450S driven here by Jean Behra at Sebring in 1957. The crowd loved the Corvette SS and was heartbroken when the car retired. If this car had been given a chance, Chevrolet might have won Le Mans in a few more years, a goal which Zora Arkus-Duntov was never to realize. The number 20 car is a Maserati 300S driven by Stirling Moss. Chevrolet

Writing about the race for *Road & Track*, Bernard Cahier said, "Undoubtedly the main attraction was the new Super Sport Corvette to be driven by Fitch and [Piero] Taruffi, who was specially flown from Italy at the last moment. Low and very pretty, the fuel injected SS Corvette was a much different machine from previously known Corvettes. The light chassis was of the multi-tubular type and the dry weight of the machine was only 1,850 lbs."

Later in that same article, Cahier wrote, "The Americans could well cheer about that performance, since Fangio had proven to them that, if masterly driven, the new Corvette could hold its own with the best from Europe. Fangio and Moss were equally pleased with the performance of the Corvette. Especially praised was the road handling of the car, its brakes and comfort. Fangio even told me that it seemed he could drive this car comfortably at high speed for 10 days if he had to!"

On the morning of the race, Fitch got in the SS to sort out some braking problems. Front wheels were locking up randomly under hard braking. Fitch tried heating up the brakes but it didn't help. At the last minute, a piece of brake plumbing was removed from the mule, whose brakes were very good, and grafted onto the SS. The problem was still there.

What seems to have happened was that the mule developed into a good race car, but the magic didn't transfer over to the SS itself. Now Fitch was out of time. The race would begin in fifteen minutes and he had no more quick fixes. He'd just have to make do with bad brakes.

After a Le Mans start, Fitch roared away in the SS to a rousing cheer from the crowds. The car was still not good under braking but it was fast enough to put Fitch sixth at the end of the first lap. At that point, he was behind only Ferraris and Maseratis driven by Peter Collins (world champion at the time), Stirling Moss, Jean Behra and Masten Gregory. Arkus-Duntov's Corvette SS was living up to its promise.

The brake problem grew worse as Fitch tried to wring every bit of performance out of the SS. He wanted to put it into the lead. By the third lap, the front end of the SS was uncontrollable. Fitch darted into the pits and shouted at Arkus-Duntov that he needed new tires. One of the fronts was worn down to the fabric because the brakes had locked so often.

With fresh rubber Fitch rejoined the race, a lap down. He passed everything in sight and was soon closing on the leaders again. Suddenly, silence. The engine had died. Fitch was able to coast into the pits. A long stop ensued. Finally the engine's coil was replaced and the motor fired up.

Fitch squealed out of the pits and worked his way around the track. The car was feeling good. Again the engine quit. Fitch jumped out and worked on it himself, with officials crowding around, making suggestions for repairs. Again he sped back onto the track. When the crowd saw the Corvette SS back in the race, they roared. Spectators and fans waved to Fitch so wildly, he thought they were warning him of danger, but no, they were just thrilled to see him back in the fray.

For a while, the brakes worked perfectly, but then Fitch could feel that something was coming undone in the suspension. The car's rear end was all over the track. It took everything Fitch knew to keep the SS on the road.

And the heat had been rising unmercifully. The engine was not cooling itself despite the car's large mouth. Oil temperature read 300 deg.; water was at 225 deg. Fahrenheit. The magnesium body was not allowing air to flow through the car. Again, the lack of full-scale testing showed crucial flaws, yet ones easily fixed, pre-race.

Fitch resigned himself to defeat and rolled the car into the pits. Piero Taruffi was persuaded by Ed Cole to go out in the car, with cooling holes quickly cut in the doors. The Italian returned after just two laps, saying the SS was unmanageable, even dangerous. And so the Corvette SS's day was over.

It was discovered later that one of the rubber bushings on the four-link de Dion rear suspension had been broken on installation, overtorqued and split down one side. It was only a matter of time until it failed completely, and yet, here was another problem that could have been easily solved in testing before the race.

It was a sad day for the Corvette team, even though one of the stock cars won the Production GT class by finishing twelfth overall. The other two Corvettes came in fifteenth and sixteenth, although they ran steadily and consistently.

Exhausted and bitterly disappointed, Arkus-Duntov took a vacation. While he was away from Detroit, the roof fell in.

The AMA Racing Ban

At this same time, Ford and Chevrolet had discovered that NASCAR stock car racing was a boon to car sales, and the two factories had been running racing programs in NASCAR through their respective advertising agencies. Chevy had just upped the ante with fuel injection and Ford was countering with supercharging. The private racers in NASCAR were being squeezed out. When NASCAR complained to Detroit, they didn't know what they had started.

In June of 1957 the AMA, a group composed of CEOs from the Big Three car companies (GM, Ford and Chrysler), and others voted to ban factory involvement in racing. The resolution recommended to members that they "not participate or engage in any public contest, competitive event or test of passenger cars involving or suggesting racing or speed, including acceleration tests, or encourage or furnish financial, engineering, manufacturing, advertising, or public relations assistance, or supply 'pace cars' or 'official cars,' in connection with any contest, event, or test, directly or indirectly."

When Arkus-Duntov returned from his vacation, the two SS Corvettes which were to go to Le Mans had been sent to a warehouse, and Chevrolet was out of the racing business. Humbled, Zora returned to the production Corvette and began thinking of ways to violate the AMA recommendation. It wouldn't be easy, since GM president Harlow Curtice had signed the agreement, but then Arkus-Duntov was used to hard problems—he was an engineer.

In wrapping up the career of the Corvette Super Sport, John Fitch wrote, "The Corvette SS didn't really disappear with Sebring '57. Despite the crippling ban imposed by Detroit on its own racing activities, the SS is still alive in many fine Corvette-powered privately owned Specials now active on US circuits. Lance Reventlow, the young California millionaire, utilized many features of the SS when he and his expert staff designed and built the remarkable Corvette-engined Scarabs."

Chapter 5

The Sting Ray Racing Years of the Sixties

I had done pretty well with my little solid-axle, you know, and I got a guy named Hy Baher, of Baher Chevrolet, to sponsor me in about '62. And he said, what do you think of the new Sting Ray? I said,

"Well, I haven't seen one yet." So he takes me down there and shows me one, and I about had a spasm. I had never seen anything so beautiful.

—Dick Guldstrand

The parking lot for Dodger Stadium in Los Angeles was briefly used as a road-racing course. Here, in 1963, Bob Bondurant leads the roadster of Dick Guldstrand, and the number 00 car, formerly piloted by Dave MacDonald, now driven by Ronnie Bucknam. Dave Friedman

Only an asshole would drive an old Corvette if he could get ahold of a Sting Ray.
— Fritz Voight, Mickey Thompson's mechanic

If you like automobiles, the first time you see a brash and beautiful new car like the Corvette Sting Ray, it makes your eyes bug out and your knees go weak. To someone who is sensitive and aware of cars, the Sting Ray made an impact like a nuclear warhead. Nothing quite like the Sting Ray had been seen on the street. Only about enough people to fill the Astrodome had ever watched Bill Mitchell's Sting Ray race.

With its closely coupled shape, streamlined rakishness and aggressive, masculine appearance, the Sting Ray was a huge hit with the sports car crowd. Long past were the days when the pukka purists turned a collective nose up at the Corvette. With its new 327 ci small-block, the Sting Ray was the fastest and best-handling Corvette so far. No more an ugly duckling, the Sting Ray was the most beautiful swan Chevrolet had ever put on the road.

Many Corvette racers, like Dick Guldstrand, simply went wild over the new Corvette. So exciting, so sleek and powerful looking was the new Sting Ray that to see one was to want one.

Bob Bondurant was in frustrated retirement, like Ajax in the Trojan War, learning to fly helicopters when fate decided that he would be one of the first racers to experience the new Sting Ray. In fact, Chevrolet wouldn't sell a Z06 Corvette to Washburn Chevrolet unless Bondurant would be in the driver's seat.

Bondurant recalled, "Shelly Washburn called me up and said, 'I have an offer from Chevrolet to buy a new Sting Ray. They're building four race cars, and I can't buy it unless *you* drive it. So if you would do me a favor and come out of retirement and drive one race at Riverside, then I have the car.' I thought about it and I said, 'OK, forget all the petty politics, the bullshit you went through; go ahead and run it for Shelly.' And that's what I did. And that got me back racing again."

Bondurant went on: "Chris Coghill and Davey MacDonald and Allan Grant and I flew back to St. Louis, to the Corvette factory, picked them all up and we headed out to California.

"Now going from the solid-axle Corvette to the swing-axle, the car handled better. It didn't have as good of brakes at first, although we didn't have the brake problems that everyone else had because I used the brakes more lightly. Doug Hooper had tremendous problems. All the other guys did. I just gave a talk the other night and Doug was telling about how bad the brakes were, and I said, 'I don't remember that.' And I didn't think about it at the time I was talking to him.

"But you could take the new Sting Ray and go a lot quicker. It had the 327 engine in it and a little more sophisticated suspension, better aerodynamics and the power worked great. Bob Johenks was the guy who really made the car work, maintained it well. You could eat off the floor in his shop. I always felt a hundred percent confident with him. Shelly Washburn was a great guy to drive for. A nice person. He understood racing and you didn't make any money, but he was paying your expenses and giving me a hundred dollars a race."

Design and Development of the Sting Ray

For racing car fans in the United States, the 1963 model year would go down in history as the debut of the Corvette Sting Ray, one of the most exciting and successful sports car shapes in history. Produced as a roadster and the infamous split-window coupe, the 1963 Corvette Sting Ray set enthusiasts' hearts on fire. The shapely Sting Rays represented a new generation of hope for Corvette fans that their favorite car would race to wild new heights.

Designed by Bill Mitchell with important contributions from Larry Shinoda and others, the Sting Ray had its origins in several different internal Chevrolet projects. First, there was Mitchell's Sting Ray racer, which he liked to say "Looked more like a shark than a grouper."

Ultimately a re-body of the Sebring Super Sport mule chassis, the Sting Ray racer was Mitchell's private project. However, he could only field the car for one full season, due to the high cost of running a race team out of his own pocket.

The beautiful, streamlined body of the Sting Ray racer was tamed and modified into a study for the short-lived Q Corvette. The Q was a dead-ended design exercise in the late 1950s when it looked like the whole of Chevrolet was going to get a new powertrain item, a rear transaxle, to better balance the weight of its cars.

Arkus-Duntov and some of the other Corvette engineers liked the transaxle and wanted to design a special Corvette to make use of it. The project they completed was known as the Q. It would have been a sharply styled Corvette coupe, very similar to the Sting Ray, but slimmer and less muscular looking.

The Q transaxle project was canceled, however, when unit costs could not be kept down, resulting in a domino effect: the Q Corvette project collapsed, leaving Zora and company with a lot of development work on their hands. It also left Chevrolet with a provocative new look for the Corvette. In his typical fashion, Arkus-Duntov applied much of this engineering to the new-generation Corvette, due to bow in 1963.

The new-generation Corvette would be known as the Sting Ray. For the first time, there would be an all-new Corvette, rethought and reengineered from the ground up. It would have a completely new

The roller skate on Dick Guldstrand's roll bar is part of Corvette legend. After finishing several races upside down, Guldstrand was presented with the roller skate to *make it easier for him to keep rolling after he flipped the car. The roller skate was never given an RPO number.* Dave Friedman

chassis with a clever and compact independent rear suspension, using the stubby axle halfshaft as one of the lateral suspension links.

Even with his extensive experience as a suspension engineer, Dick Guldstrand was impressed. "Duntov did a superb job. He knows what he's doing. He generated all the right numbers. Way ahead of anybody else. And if you understand what a tire requires, to survive, to do the job for you, to gain maximum lateral control and stability, then you can work around it. And he worked a lot with the tire people. You don't just design a suspension; you go with what works for the tire. How do you keep a tire happy, that's the bottom line. And he knew that, he understood that."

Another innovation of the Sting Ray Coupe was its use of a steel "birdcage" which surrounded the driver and passenger with a solid structure, especially in the coupe. Similar to a section of unibody, the steel birdcage gave the new Corvette much greater stability and rigidness of frame than the previous car. It also increased occupant safety by a huge margin. This birdcage structure is carried through into the present Corvette. It also forms the basic structure which many builders use as the foundation for their Corvette race cars. The birdcage is often beefed-up or connected with a tubular roll cage for added strength and safety.

Bill Mitchell was a styling master who developed the Sting Ray design theme in his 1959 Sting Ray race car. He then transferred the design, with the considerable help of Larry Shinoda and others, into the shape of the production Sting Ray in 1962. Mitchell loved racing and wanted every car he designed to look sharp and predatory, not soft and slack. He succeeded Harley Earl as GM vice president of Design, and head of the Styling Section. Chevrolet

A Sting Ray challenges the lonely curves and awesome drops of Pikes Peak in 1966. To drive a roadster up this course takes plenty of courage. Dave Friedman

Sting Ray Technology

While retaining the same basic layout as the earlier Corvettes, the Sting Ray had a more sophisticated chassis, with the rear differential bolted to the frame, and with a single, transverse leaf spring serving both rear wheels. It was an elegant and clever independent rear suspension which saved weight and substantially increased available traction and cornering force.

The new vehicle would also feature an improved and enlarged 327 ci small-block motor as its main powerplant, with the hot, fuel-injected engine option L84 capable of well over its advertised 360 hp.

Despite its controversial split rear window in the coupe, the Sting Ray was an incredible success. Corvette sales soared and the Sting Ray name entered the popular imagination. Sting Ray songs by the Beach Boys and others hit the charts. Before long, the whole nation would be celebrating the Sting Ray's good looks on television's popular series, "Route 66."

Racing prospects for the new Corvette looked great. The Sting Ray should be fast and nimble.

In this close-up, Tom Jamison uses the power of the 327 engine to bring the back end of the car around at Pikes Peak, as he sets up, rally style, for the next turn in 1963.

The Peak is a never-ending series of tight switchbacks and treacherous closing radius turns. Dave Friedman

Unknown to the rest of the world, Zora Arkus-Duntov was secretly working on a lightweight version of this new Corvette, to be called the Grand Sport. Chevrolet had even prepared a special racing package, RPO Z06, which made the stock Corvette into a competitive production race car.

There was only one little problem, Carroll Shelby's brand-new Anglo-American Cobra. The Cobra showed up at Riverside, California, at the end of 1962. It was raced at the *Los Angeles Times* Grand Prix, a sports car race which the Corvettes were expected to win. Chevrolet had sold the first six Z06 Corvettes ever made to well-established racers for them to run in this event. There was only the one competition Cobra in existence at the time, and it didn't win the race due to a broken rear hub.

But no matter. Feather light and powered by its own V-8, the Cobra was simply faster. Even at the dawn of a new age for Corvette, the sun was beginning to set. Cobras, not Sting Rays, would be the racing champs of the early 1960s. And although many Corvette stalwarts such as Dick Guldstrand stuck with their favorite, the national championships for the next half decade invariably went to Shelby's quicker cars.

The Cobras

Corvette veteran Dick Guldstrand commented: "The handwriting was on the wall. I don't think it won the first race, Doug Hooper won it in the Corvette. But it made no difference that the Cobras had some troubles because it was obvious that the Corvette was completely outclassed and that Shelby had really pulled one off. It had more to do with rules and acceptability, because you know anybody could have built a real barn burner that wasn't a production type car, and that's what Shelby did. If you could con the SCCA into accepting it as being homologated, boy you got it wired."

Bob Bondurant wasn't all that impressed with the Cobras at first. He passed up driving the first Cobra to take a ride in the Z06 Corvette at Riverside. As Bondurant remembers: "Carroll was after me to come out of retirement and I said, 'Well . . . OK.' We went to three races, and the car wasn't ready. Then Shelly Washburn called me and told me about the deal with the Corvette, so I went with what I knew would work.

"Then Carroll called me and said, 'Well, you made the wrong mistake! We got the car ready for Riverside.' And I said, 'Well maybe I did, Carroll, but if it works out, well, maybe down the road we can work something out.' At the time I had no idea it would be good and I would be driving for him later.

"Kraus [in the Cobra] blew us off the track. The car broke, I guess a halfshaft or stub axle, but the handwriting was on the wall. So then I went back into racing full time. For Shelly. I mean full time as an amateur. And I was the only one that could stay with the Cobras, but I couldn't beat 'em, because he could outbrake and outaccelerate me, but I could out-corner him."

Still, one appearance by the new Cobra was chilling but not conclusive. Guldstrand and the others like Dr. Dick Thompson got in their Sting Rays and loved them. They proceeded to get out on the track and make mincemeat out of the rest of their competitors, including the solid-axle Corvettes.

A solid-axle Corvette and a Ferrari Berlinetta dice it out at Monterey's Laguna Seca, while, overtaking both of them is the future—a Sting Ray. To see the solid-axle car in the same shot as a Sting Ray is to appreciate just how far GM design went in a few years. Dave Friedman

The debut of the Sting Ray as a race car took place at the Los Angeles Times *Grand Prix in October of 1962. Unfortunately, it also marked the first race for Carroll Shelby's new Cobra. Here, the superb Dave MacDonald does his best to stay ahead of Bill Krause driving the first racing Cobra ever. Dave Friedman*

Snake in the Pass

The mystical sorcerer Don Juan, in Carlos Castenada's novels, talks about every man's need for a "worthy adversary" to bring out the best in him. As race cars, Corvettes had many adversaries, but their number one competitor was always the Shelby Cobra. From its first race at the end of 1962, the Cobra delivered notice to the Corvettes that their time as the big dogs of club and semi-pro racing was over.

Even though the first Cobras were fragile and hard to control (they were *always* hard to control), they were fully a thousand pounds lighter than the Corvettes and that is a differential which simply couldn't be overcome by horsepower or handling.

The whole thrust of the Grand Sport program was to develop a "lightweight" Corvette that could meet the Cobras head on. But Chevrolet and GM politics killed the Grand Sports before they had a chance for factory development.

For a while, in the early 1960s, it was a rout, an exodus. Many of the best Corvette drivers such as Dave MacDonald, Andy Porterfield and Bob Bondurant defected to the Cobra team, or simply bought Cobras and raced them independently.

Yet, by the end of the 1960s, the wheel of fate had turned and the Cobras were fading, even though the last version of the Cobra, the 427, was a remarkable machine, a rocket capable of 200 mph, according to some. But, as Corvette racers found out, corporate Detroit has its own agenda, and racing is but a small part of it. Near the end of the sixties, Ford cut Shelby loose, having achieved its goals in racing both in the United States and offshore. It should be remembered that Shelby's own personal goals took him and the Cobra team to Europe where the Cobra Daytona coupes had made magic and taken the international GT crown away from no less a competitor than Enzo Ferrari.

When Ford withdrew its funding and backing from Shelby's racing operations and the manufacture of Cobras, that was the end for Shelby's cars. By the very end of the 1960s Cobras were sitting in dealer showrooms, without buyers, for as little as $6,000 to $9,000. If only we had known then what we know now!

Sting Ray Handling

Dick Guldstrand, commenting on the Sting Ray's handling capabilities, said: "The whole car was lower, the mass centroid was down, the engine was down considerably. And that was a very significant breakthrough. Duntov did a superb job. He knows what he's doing. He generated all the right numbers. Way ahead of anybody else.

"The front suspension on the Sting Ray was not at all like the solid-axle car. They'd raised the roll centers. They'd developed a lot of camber gain. They'd taken some of the bump steer out of it, not enough, but they'd taken some out of it.

"And of course you had a much better steering system. They had the track rod, the relay rod—idler arm, Pitman arm—was super, and they had trailing links. It was a major improvement.

"The heart and soul of the Sting Ray rear suspension is unsprung weight. The whole point of

A victory on its maiden voyage! Doug Hooper brings one of the four Sting Rays in first at the Times *Grand Prix. The Cobra broke that day, but Corvette drivers knew that they were no longer king of the hill. Still, they enjoyed the victory while they could. Dave Friedman*

In the Mickey Thompson pits before the Times *Grand Prix in 1962, Dave MacDonald, in the unzipped driving suit, prepares to do battle with the rest of the world. These first Z06 racing Sting Rays had massive brake problems, and a few other small flaws. The small flaws were soon corrected, but brakes remained a major fault for years. Dave Friedman*

Also at the Times *Grand Prix in 1962, another of the four Z06 Sting Rays is made ready for battle. This number 614 car is the second-generation racer from Washburn Chevrolet. The guys in Detroit wouldn't sell dealer Shelly Washburn this car unless he could talk Bob Bondurant into driving it. Washburn brought Bondurant out of early retirement, and set him on the second phase of his racing career. Dave Friedman*

The Dave MacDonald Sting Ray gets gassed up during a pit stop in the Times *Grand Prix of 1962. Note how the flanges for the rear bumpers are cast into the Corvette's fiberglass in back. Also, the car is racing on ordinary stamped steel wheels. Dave Friedman*

eliminating that huge mass of the solid-axle differential housing to the unsprung element, is brilliant. You know, that's what they tried to do with the de Dion and all the rest of them was to get rid of that unsprung weight. What it tells you is that with the right springs and shocks, you can keep the tire on the ground a hell of a lot better than with this huge mass underneath the car [solid axle] trying to throw itself off the ground.

"But the problems with it were again with real high control situations you had a lot of toe change. You created toe steer or roll steer. You can kind of envision what's happening to that wheel and tire going through those two geometric changes; you can see how there's one big arc that's created by the halfshaft and another smaller arc, but lateral with the trailing arm. So what it does is it generates toe change, which is steering the car.

"So then they had to do a lot of stuff in front with sway bars and so on to create roll understeer. So you didn't have the terrifying possibility of power oversteer. With an engine like they had, my God, they were putting out 365 hp in those things, the fuel-injected 327s. An incredible piece of equipment."

The Rough Racers

Dr. Dick Thompson would take the SCCA A-Production championship in 1962 after a season-long battle against two Ferrari Berlinettas, and Don Yenko would take the B-Production champi-

This time it's race winner Hooper in the Mickey Thompson pits. That's Thompson himself at the rear right corner, checking a tire pressure. Thompson was prepping and dialing in these cars till the last minute; that's why the number is painted on so crudely. Some engine cooling and handling problems had been fixed, but brakes remained a challenge. Perhaps this car won because driver Doug Hooper saved his brakes better than the other Sting Ray pilots. Dave Friedman

onship. But from then on, A-Production was the domain of the Cobra. By 1965, the B-Production class was won by a Shelby-prepared Ford Mustang GT 350, driven by Bob Johnson, a former Corvette racer.

Despite the hard times, Corvettes raced on. Although Bob Bondurant and Dave MacDonald, two gifted and very competitive drivers, had defected to the Cobra team, many of the old guard such as Thompson, Guldstrand and Yenko continued to race against the odds, sometimes conjuring a surprise victory when the Cobras broke or got cocky.

Most racers simply ordered the RPO Z06 package and then personalized their cars, bringing forward many of the tuning tricks they had learned on the solid-axle cars. Some racers ordered their Sting Ray Z06 with the heater for heat during the chilly nights of endurance racing, or just for the extra cooling capacity. Bumpers, headlight globes and other bulbs were removed, carpet was torn out; engines, transmissions and differentials were blueprinted. Interiors were sometimes stripped. Since these were production classes, not too much changing from an "as delivered" condition was allowed.

The condition of these new Sting Rays seemed to have varied substantially at delivery. While customers for Sting Rays on the street were beginning to find some minor and some major flaws with their Corvettes, racers were doing the same thing.

At the start, the biggest complaint was brakes. From their first race onward, the Sting Ray Z06 cars were hard to brake smoothly. Until the brake drums were heated up, they would pull sharply to one side or the other, making it hard for the driver to set up a corner properly. Then, when the brakes

The Corvette Sting Rays were running in a special category at the 1962 Times *Grand Prix, XP or Experimental Production. They had not been formally introduced to the public, so they weren't, strictly speaking, production automobiles.* Dave Friedman

Bob Bondurant returned to racing after he had quit in anger over the feuding between Cal Club and the SCCA. When Bondurant returned to motorsports he did it in a Corvette Z06 sponsored by Santa Barbara Chevrolet dealer Shelly Washburn. Just like the pretty blue solid-axle car, this Corvette Bondurant raced in 1963 carries number 614, the address of Washburn's dealership. Dave Friedman

You can't see his face, but that's A. J. Foyt driving the number 5 Sting Ray at Sebring in 1963. By now, the Corvette had been enthusiastically received by the public, and orders for Z06 race cars were pouring into Chevrolet. But the Cobras were finding their stride also, making it increasingly difficult for the Corvettes to finish on top. Dave Friedman

When brilliant Corvette driver Dave MacDonald defected to the Cobra camp, other Corvette racers grimaced in pain. MacDonald's hard-charging style suited the Cobra's light weight and touchy handling. Here, MacDonald is setting up to pass Bill Sherwood in the number 83 Corvette at Del Mar in 1963. Dave Friedman

were at working temperture, they didn't last very long. For several races, brakes were the Sting Ray's worst feature.

Engines also had some variation. But in the case of a racing motor, it was automatically stripped down and balanced at the start. One of the country's leading Corvette tuners and engine builders at that time was Bob Johenks of Santa Barbara, California. Johenks began by blueprinting the cylinder decks and the crank bore. Then he would get the heads on a flow bench and make sure that the engine could breathe. What Johenks claimed as the secret of a powerful small-block was good breathing and careful attention to details. Heads were given trick valve jobs, performed by Johenks' son.

At the start, few engine builders did as much, so Johenks' cars, including the number 614 solid-axle and number 614 Sting Ray, were race winners. It was the strength of the number 614 Sting Ray that launched Bondurant's racing career in Europe.

Yes, Corvettes still oversteer. Here, the Allen-Stevens Sting Ray comes a cropper at Sebring in 1963. Dave Friedman

Don Yenko, a Chevy dealer and a leading Chevrolet tuner, raced his Sting Ray up and down the East Coast. Although he was better known for his Yenko Stinger Camaros and Corvairs, Yenko was a hot Corvette shoe as well. Here, Yenko leads Allen Wylie's number 16 Corvette at Bridgehampton, New York, in 1963. Dave Friedman

Paul Reinhart was another solid-axle guy who made the switch to Sting Ray power. At Riverside in early 1963, Reinhart leads the good-looking roadster of Dick Guldstrand into the tricky turn seven. Dave Friedman

Grady Davis, who would soon be a part of the Grand Sport story, leads another Corvette around Road America in 1963. The Davis Corvette, number 2, is cornering in a neutral attitude and is just about to clip the apex of this curve. Dave Friedman

After its brief shunt in the dirt, the number 6 Corvette of Allen-Stevens is back in the hunt at Sebring in 1963, but about to be overtaken by its companion car, driven by Grant Campbell. Dave Friedman

The classic Sting Ray side exhaust pipes were actually developed by Junior Johnson and Smokey Yunick, stock car racers. Here they are visible on the Foyt-Hurtubise number 5 and the Salyer–Kumnick number four. Dave Friedman

69

The Faithful Carry On

Dick Guldstrand remarked: "All the other guys had coupes, but I wanted a roadster because it would have a lower center of gravity and the car was lighter. And, see, you don't go at top speed that often. They thought I was crazy to have a roadster, and they all had coupes for the aerodynamics, but I figured out mathematically that the roadster would be much faster overall.

"We couldn't get a roadster with the Z06 package which was all the trick stuff, so I had to build it. So I got the roadster, it was a dark blue '63, that we got late in '62. And I must have put a thousand miles on it right away. I had never driven a car that I was so impressed with. Then I took it back to the shop and took it all apart. There it was, a brand-new Corvette, the only roadster in this part of the country and it was in pieces all over the garage.

"So I looked it all over and figured out the spring rates and shock absorbers and I lowered it way down and put a roll cage in it—all the stuff you did with 'em. And we went out and really did well. But the problem was that now, the Cobras were there.

"Everybody wanted to go with the Cobra team, Dave MacDonald, Bob Bondurant and Ken Miles

Dick Guldstrand, one of the greatest Corvette drivers, tuners and partisans. Here Goldie is wearing a Shelby American T-shirt to puzzle and vex the competition. The Cobra guys sure as heck weren't wearing Sting Ray shirts! Dave Friedman

Battle of the roadsters, at the Times *Grand Prix of 1963. A year after the Cobra's debut, it had become a competent racing machine. Here, Guldstrand throws his Sting Ray around a corner, desperately trying to stay ahead of Bob Bondurant in the number 99 Cobra. Guldstrand is driv-* *ing a car that's 800 lb. heavier and it shows in his oversteering attitude. Bondurant in the Cobra is cornering neutrally, and looks as though he's setting up a pass on the inside.* Dave Friedman

Dick Guldstrand figured out that a Corvette roadster was lighter, lower and had a lower center of gravity than the coupe, making it a good choice for a race car. This lesson spread quickly and lots of roadsters became impromptu racers. Chevrolet didn't originally offer the Z06 racing package for roadsters, so the cars had to be converted one at a time. Here Gene Cormacy leads a Corvette coupe at Road America in 1964. Dave Friedman

Another roadster at speed. In what seems like an uneven contest, Red Faris jumps into a corner in much better shape than Joe Fretias in his 1956 drop top. The low center of gravity in the Sting Ray becomes obvious when compared with the older Corvette. Dave Friedman

At Sebring in 1964, this Hudson-Grant Corvette shows some Grand Sport touches, but it's a production racer. Notice the plexiglass headlamp covers, rear brake cooling scoops and the large rear tires on mag wheels. Dave Friedman

Don Yenko at Sebring in 1965. Complete with windshield wipers and truck running lights on the roof, this Sting *Ray shows a rear fender flare to accommodate the ever-widening racing tires of the period. Dave Friedman*

was with them then. So I became the ol' underdog. Not that I wanted that but it was what I could do. And I did pretty well. I won the Cal Club regional championship three years in a row, '63, '64 and '65. But I never won a national championship because our points didn't count. We weren't offered points in the national scheme of things. But I couldn't have cared less. We were winning races. And that little roadster did well, extremely well."

Carroll Shelby himself once said to Dick Guldstrand, "You kept us honest," meaning that the racing Corvettes kept the Cobras on edge. One wrong move or lapse in development and the Corvettes were there, hungry, waiting to snatch the win away from them. This *was* an underdog role, one which the Corvette racers were not used to playing, but in the end they filled it well.

Back in the Saddle Again

Corvette fans would have to wait until the last gasp of the psychedelic 1960s before Corvettes were once again in the winner's circle in SCCA Production racing. The power behind the throne of this comeback was the superb Mark IV porcupine head big-block engine, affectionately known as the Rat Motor.

In 1957, Chevrolet began manufacturing a large-capacity motor for use in medium-size trucks. Known as the W engine, it displaced 384 ci and had a bigger brother, the 409 ci. While these

engines were fine for heavy-duty applications, they were not popular with the performance crowd because the combustion chambers were too tilted in relation to the top of the block and their own cylinder heads.

During 1962, Semon "Bunkie" Knudsen was moved from Pontiac to Chevrolet as the new chief engineer. Ed Cole was now president of the division. Knudsen gave his staff the green light for a new, racing engine based on the W block. Engineer Dick Keinath began with the bore centers from the 409 and designed a more modern engine around them from the bottom up. He repeated many of the strengths of the small-block, but on a slightly larger scale.

But the big news about this motor was its cylinder heads. To give the engine better airflow and more horsepower, Keinath developed a unique head with valves canted off the vertical. Intake valves were cocked at 26 deg., and exhaust at 16 deg. This innovation became known as the porcupine engine, from the way its valve stems bristle out from the cylinder heads.

This new motor, in 409 and 427 ci displacements was known internally as the Mark II, the original W being the Mark I. The engines were powerful in testing and even found their way into a Junior Johnson race car for one Daytona 500 in 1963. But Chevrolet found out about the secret project and clamped down on it, since racing was still verboten.

Due to all the subterfuge surrounding this powerplant's development, it was also known as the Mystery Engine.

A production version of this same engine came to be known as the Mark IV. It was tooled in 396 and 427 ci sizes and became available in the Corvette in 1966. The Turbo-Jet 396 engine made 425 hp and 415 lb-ft of torque with one four-barrel Holley carburetor, on premium gasoline. Compression was 11:1. A stock Corvette could do 0-60 mph in 5.7 seconds.

The 427 would be available in the Corvette the following year, and its derivative the RPO L88 aluminum head engine shortly thereafter. Much of the development work on this motor was done on Roger Penske's Sunoco Corvette which Dick Guldstrand drove in the 1966 Daytona twenty-four-hour race. Despite a shunt into the wall overnight, the Sting Ray finished twelfth overall.

As the aluminum big-block engines began appearing in Corvettes near the end of the decade, the Cobra's stranglehold on road racing began to slip. Soon, the plastic sports car would again strut across America's racetracks, undisputed champion of Production class racing.

Dick Guldstrand puts the moves on an XKE at Laguna Seca in 1965. The E-Type has either moved over to let Goldie by, or it can't get enough grip to find the apex of the corner. Guldstrand has the rear of his hood open a bit to improve cooling. The roller skate is there, but it's lost in the white line at the edge of the track. Dave Friedman

It's not a good idea to have a Ford GT 40 on your tail, no matter how fast you are. At Daytona in 1966, the Corvette of Guldstrand, Wintersteen and Moore roars around the pylons, waiting for the Ford to make its inevitable pass. *Dave Friedman*

One Lap at Riverside with Dick Guldstrand

Dick Guldstrand narrates a lap executed in a Corvette at Riverside Raceway, near Los Angeles:

"I think we'll drive the long course, because that one was really awe inspiring. There were two elements to Riverside. One was the really high speed stuff and the incredible rhythm of it. It was a ballet. It was almost ⅔ of a mile long, that back straightaway. And a really high speed banked corner, 120, 130 miles an hour.

"You'd go through the kink in that Corvette roadster at close to 160 miles an hour. If you didn't have an 'oh shit' every lap, you weren't really trying.

"So you give yourself about half a lap or a lap to be sure that everything's warmed up and up to speed. And then you always reach over with your left foot and touch the brake pedal just to be sure that it was OK before you got into turn nine. What if it went to the floor just as you committed to the turn? No brakes and you're dead. And it wasn't the brakes, it was *death*! Lots of people died in turn nine, let me tell you. So you reach over and touch the brakes just to make sure that it's got pedal. Turn nine was that really high speed right-hander that was banked and you came flying off the banking into the short straightaway, which is the start-finish straight; then you had to pull it way over to the start-finish tower on the right side, almost touching the wall, to get it set up for turn one—because if you did it right, you could go through turn one flat out. And I mean absolutely flat out, and that was as fast as you were going down the back straight, 150 miles an hour, something like that.

"You come out of the pit area and up past turn one and enter the track towards turn two. That's the way you got on, you always had to stay over to the right for the traffic to go by and you kinda wiggled your way through turn two and then you were starting to get up to speed in turn three and turn four. You're usually warming up the car and wiggling it around to be sure that the gears and everything is working. So it was imperative that you used every bit of track that was clear over to the starter's stand, all the way over to the apex of turn one and then let it drift out to the center of the track again and move it back to the left to start picking up turn two. You could see turn two coming up.

"Turn two was an absolutely blind, very high speed right-hand kink. It wasn't really a full turn, but it was the one that feeds you into the esses. And that's where the rhythm comes in. The way that you set up for turn two and the grace that you entered and exited two *completely* set up the rest of the esses. If you were off line or rattled or something coming out of two you'd never gather it up till you crashed in six. And I know; I've done it! You'd be gathering that mother up all the way till you hit the wall at six.

"So it was that rhythm. But once you established it coming into two, and you slid over into the little kink, approaching turn three which was a right-hander, you had to keep that rhythm up. You could almost make it flat out, and I think that a number of times I'd make it flat out. You didn't lift up through there, and it was everything you could do. But that rhythm is absolutely essential.

"Turn six is the end of the esses where you climb up the hill through five, which is a left-hand corner that then set up to go up the hill into the right-hand, sweeping turn six—which was actually two turns in one. You apexed on the entrance, let it slide out into the middle, turned it back into the corner, down right, got back on it again and let it slide out to the outer edge as you exited turn six, heading down the 'whoop de doos' to turn seven.

"And then as you approached turn seven, you would accelerate up the slight grade and there was a slight hill at the top of the entrance to turn seven. So you'd let it go up the middle of that and let it just flop over the top and get a lot of left-hand lock because seven was a left-hand turn, and just let it kind of slide down into the corner.

"One time Carroll Shelby and John Timmanus were out at Riverside running one of their driving schools and I was out there testing for Goodyear, and Shelby said that Corvette probably went through turn seven faster than any car they'd ever seen.

"It was just a matter of that rhythm where you dropped it over the top and gathered it up, back on the power, just clip the edge on the inside left as you exited going up toward turn eight, which is a disaster because you can do nothing with turn eight except screw it up. There is no fast way through turn eight. It's a dead slow, diminishing radius, hard right-hand buttonhook. And it was awful; more guys went off there. It also had a decamber to it. It cambered to the outside in exactly the wrong place and it would slide you off into the dirt.

"There was a lot of finesse to that corner, and God, if you did it right . . . that could just *shoot* you down the straight. In the Can-Am cars I drove there we did 200 miles an hour down the back straight into turn nine. And then of course you just buckled up your seatbelt and checked your gauges, scratched your nose and looked at everybody."

Dick Guldstrand and George Wintersteen, both very experienced and talented Corvette pilots, drove for Roger Penske at Daytona in 1966. Penske was a new team owner at this time, having left the driver's seat for the captain's chair. In this pit stop, Wintersteen is climbing out of the car as Guldstrand, in the black helmet, rushes in to take his place. Dave Friedman

Chapter 6

Rise and Fall of the Corvette Grand Sport

They were a reasonably good compromise, for a car that was based on a lot of production components. The cars did everything quite well. Acceleration was very, very strong. The engines in the Grand Sports originally had the sidedraft Webers on them which tended to flood out or starve out in the corners and that was something that needed to be solved on them. But with the Corvette, you lighten it up and put that engine in it and good brakes and bigger tires and it made a pretty good race car.
—Jim Hall, of Chaparral fame

Daddy, Daddy, what's a lightweight Corvette? Shut up and keep sanding.
—Joke from the 1960s

Roger Penske puts the hammer down at Nassau in 1964 on his way to victory in this Grand Sport. Note the odd fittings in the right B-pillar. Penske added this special hardware for the air jacks and for adding coolant in the pits. Dave Friedman

The Corvette Grand Sport is another odd and frustrating saga in the story of Corvette racing. Only five of the potent, hand-built Grand Sports were ever made, and to own one today is to be guaranteed a secure retirement.

Meant as an endurance and GT racer, the Corvette Grand Sports came closer to showing what a competition Corvette could do than any car that came before it. They represented the very limit to which the technology of a stock-based Corvette could be pushed. The Grand Sports were meant as a direct answer to the Shelby Cobras, and many car buffs think that they could have emasculated the Shelby roadsters, had they been supported by the factory.

Raced by such great names as Roger Penske and Jim Hall, the hulking, mile-wide Grand Sports had a brief moment of glory before the GM corporate steam roller squashed them flat.

The Weight Issue

Talk to old-time Corvette people or Chevrolet insiders about the Corvette Grand Sport and you'll hear them refer to it as the "lightweight Corvette."

That's because the concept of making everything as light as possible was central to the 1962 Grand Sport project, the first full-bore Corvette racing specials to come from the Chevrolet factory since the ill-fated Corvette Super Sport of 1957.

Lightness was important because production Corvettes couldn't simply be stripped down to race car weight. It took a more aggressive approach than that—it took a redesign. Furthermore, there was a rule change in international racing for the 1962 season, doing away with displacement limits for GT cars. That meant the Corvette could compete in international races such as Le Mans with a chance of winning, thanks to its big, powerful, dependable engines.

Enter the Sting Ray

In November of 1962 a race of historic, perhaps cosmic significance took place on the West Coast, near Los Angeles. It was the *Los Angeles Times* Grand Prix at Riverside Raceway, a popular sports car enduro that always brought out the southern California car guys in droves.

This Grand Sport, driven by Roger Penske, Jim Hall and Hap Sharp, shows the progression of the car's development. New fender flares have been added to hold even bigger racing tires, and rear brake cooling scoops have appeared on the rear fenders. In this photo, Roger Penske lowers the car's nose with brakes before entering a hard left-hand corner. Dave Friedman

For this particular race, the Chevrolet factory had a big suprise ready for the competition, the all-new Corvette. With its 327 ci motor, new body, new chassis and independent rear suspension, the Sting Ray represented a new era for Corvette. And once again, the racing elves at Chevrolet had cooked up a hot competition package for the Sting Ray, called RPO Z06. This was the Sting Ray equivalent of RPO 685 from the solid-axle years. By every possible calculation, this car should have been unbeatable.

In fact, Chevrolet stacked the deck by insisting that only well-known racing organizations, such as Mickey Thompson, could even buy a Z06 Corvette,

and further, the factory wanted to have approval of who would be driving each car.

There were four Z06 Corvettes entered in the *Times* Grand Prix, and one of them won. It should have been a great day for Chevrolet, but it wasn't. It was a disaster and they knew it. The *Times* Grand Prix had been the first race for the hand-built Ford-powered Shelby Cobra. And, while the Cobra survived, it had flat run away from the Corvettes.

Zora Arkus-Duntov and others at Chevrolet, and the whole California racing community knew in short order that the Cobra had gone so far beyond the norm in power-to-weight ratios that no one could catch it.

The Corvettes had plenty of horsepower, good handling and tuning. But the Cobras were a thousand pounds lighter, and they drove like it.

Lightness in a race car is a primary virtue. It was the secret magic of Colin Chapman of Lotus. If the overall car is light, then the engine can be smaller, the brakes smaller, the suspension lighter and smaller and so on. The lighter car accelerates quicker, and takes less time and distance to slow before a turn. Light cars are easier on their brakes and tires throughout a race.

While the Cobra wasn't a world beater in its first race, it clearly upped the ante for sports car racing in the United States. Up to 1962 if you wanted to win the top production categories as a pro or amateur, you got a Corvette. After 1962, you got a Cobra or ate dust.

Zora Takes a Shot

The beautiful and tremendously powerful Corvette Grand Sport race cars form a second layer in

Corvette Grand Sport number 2 is more than three seconds a lap faster than a racing Sting Ray. In these early races the Grand Sport was being sorted out, while Dr. Dick Thompson lost valuable championship points in A-Production. Here, the car is about to win at Watkins Glen, New York, in 1963. Chevrolet

In December of 1963, Corvette Grand Sports landed in force for Speed Week at Nassau in the Bahamas. Although there were some fast and some odd cars in these races, the Corvettes scored their first convincing wins here. Competition includes Cobras, Ferraris, Volvos, Porsches and others. Roger Penske is out in front here in his number 50 Corvette. Dave Friedman

Carroll Shelby is hopping mad as he examines the Grand Sports on the docks in Nassau. Driver Ken Miles joins Shelby for his walkaround, although Miles wears a smirk compared to Shelby's frown. The Grand Sports gave Shelby's Cobras a licking in the Bahamas. Dave Friedman

Zora Arkus-Duntov's continuing desire to capture a win at Le Mans as well as other significant international tracks. The first layer was his purpose-built Corvette Super Sport, whose one-race career was a tragedy no one at Chevrolet, Zora included, wanted to repeat.

Still, they had been winning on both sides of the equation. Chevrolet hadn't been officially involved with motor sports since the 1957 racing ban of the AMA. But, Chevrolet, through its ad agency Campbell-Ewald and other outlets had been shoveling money and parts into the programs of many private racers who used Chevrolet power or cars.

While this operation satisfied some inside Chevrolet, Arkus-Duntov wasn't one of them. He didn't like having to pretend, he didn't like standing at a distance while others did the racing. And he really didn't prefer working on projects, such as CERV I which were meant for the test track only.

Then, in 1962, the French-based Federation Internationale de l'Automobile, or FIA, allowed production-based GTs to compete without a displacement limit in the World Manufacturers Championship. This meant that American V-8s would be allowed as racing motors.

Zora realized that here was his next shot at a Le Mans victory. So he was inspired to design an ultralight version of the upcoming Sting Ray.

The idea this time was not to make factory race cars, but to create limited-production cars that were race-ready from the factory. Then private racers, with secret factory backing, could run the cars to glory all over the world. Semon "Bunkie" Knudsen, now head of Chevrolet, thought they could get away with it, so the project was a go. Plans were to build 100-125 Grand Sports so they could be homologated, or certified for racing as a production car, not a prototype.

An irony about the Cobra is that Carroll Shelby went to Chevrolet first with his scheme to plant an American V-8 in a European Sports car. Apparently, Shelby talked to Ed Cole, then head of GM, who reasonably responded that they already had the Corvette, so they weren't interested in Shelby's dream car.

When Shelby went to Ford, they didn't really have a performance car, so he got his V-8 motors and the rest is not just history but legend.

Grand Sport Generic

Beginning from the ground up, Arkus-Duntov needed a new frame for the lightweight. He was looking to drop over 1,000 lb. from the Sting Ray's weight. That meant drastic measures and a start-from-scratch attitude.

The Grand Sport's frame was designed and put together by Walter Zeyte, a Chevrolet engineer who contributed to the independent rear suspension of the production Corvette. It consisted of two

John Mecom rolls one of the Grand Sports off the docks at Nassau. Note the large hood scoop, designed to feed air to a new cross-ram fuel-injection manifold. Dave Friedman

parallel, wide-diameter tubes, fabricated from seamless steel stock, in a ladder pattern.

Four cross-members connected the two main-frame tubes. The front cross-member was huge, 5.0 in. in diameter, compared to 4.25 in. for the long tubes. This front member dipped down in the center to clear the engine and was made extra strong to handle front suspension loads without deforming. The next cross-member, the smallest at only 4 in. wide, came behind and supported the transmission. A third cross-member was right behind the driver and held various body and rear suspension mounting points; then the ladder frame tubes kicked-up in the back where the final cross-member connected them. The rear differential was mounted between these last two crossbars, with the Corvette transverse semi-elliptical leaf spring mounted below the differential, much like the stock vehicle.

Front suspension A-arms, upper and lower, were similar to the production pieces, but were much lighter than stock, and hand fabricated. Front ball joints and steering knuckles were of a rare chrome-nickel-molybdenum alloy, a metal so tough, it couldn't be machined on regular equipment.

While this frame lacked the sophistication of the Corvette Super Sports' space frame, it was

79

Roger Penske was still a young whippersnapper when he drove a Grand Sport Corvette to victory at Nassau in 1964. That tall fellow next to Penske is Texan Jim Hall, another American racing legend in the making. Like Penske, Hall would retain close ties to Chevrolet over his racing career. In Hall's case, this led to the development of the Chaparral racing cars. Dave Friedman

Changed again, this Grand Sport was driven by Penske and Hall at Sebring in 1964. The car's dangerous, nose-high racing attitude is clear in this view, as Hall accelerates out of a corner, raising the 'Vette's prow. The bulging hood scoop has been replaced with a more streamlined power bulge. Dave Friedman

Penske dices with Ken Miles in a Cobra at Nassau in 1964. Speed Week in the Bahamas was one of the high points in the Grand Sports' racing history. The car's front suspension is hard at work as Penske charges toward the apex of this turn. Dave Friedman

simple to make and repair and achieved its targets in weight and torsional stiffness.

In fact, the first Grand Sport frame that was made, was put together 0.25 in. too short, making it useless for racing. Chevrolet engineers hooked the frame up to a huge stroking machine which bent and pumped it like a torture device. The frame passed with high marks for stiffness and, with all its strength, was still much lighter than the stock unit.

Brackets and other pieces mounted on the frame were drilled for lightness. To save more weight, pieces such as an aluminum steering box and aluminum differential were used. Standard 15x5 in. wheels were also lightweight magnesiums from Halibrand with knock-off centers.

The two mainframe rails were too close together to put the driver down between them. This meant that the driver must sit above the level of the frame rails and the car's center of gravity would be high.

The real advantage of the twin frame rails was that they also allowed the body to be lifted off very easily and quickly for racing setup and repairs.

The body of the Grand Sport was a hand-laid, full-size Sting Ray body, which had the glass fibers running in the right directions for strength. It was 0.04 in. thick. The birdcage or center steel shell of the production car was hand assembled, lightened and reshaped. The fiberglass body pieces, like all Sting Rays, were then bonded to and around this steel armature.

Also, in front, the flip-over headlamps of the Sting Ray were replaced with focused units behind clear plexiglass, in the same body contour. The new headlamps gave the car a walleyed, hammerhead shark look, an ominous, predatory appearance.

Beneath that highly vented hood was to be a special engine, but like most everything else about the Grand Sport program, this dream miscarried a bit. Still, the promise was there.

Arkus-Duntov planned for an all-custom motor, based on the small-block. It would be an aluminum alloy casting, a powerful and advanced twin-spark engine with hemi heads, big valves and the latest high-performance cam. Based on the 327 production engine, this 377 ci screamer was designed to produce 550 hp at 6400 rpm and 500 lb-ft of torque at 5200 rpm, both monstrous numbers for a pushrod motor. In racing trim, the alloy engine would be about 75 lb. lighter than the cast-iron V-8. With that kind of power on tap, the Grand Sports would be able to accelerate like they were shot from cannons.

Stopped Short

This was getting exciting, some real race cars were taking shape in the Chevrolet technical center, and they looked impressive. A Corvette Grand Sport mule was taken down to Sebring for some pre-race brake tests. The idea was to learn from previous mistakes and sort the brakes before race day. A modified Sting Ray was present as well for these tests, which would also evaluate tires. Dick Thompson would be one of two drivers, pro-racer Masten Gregory the other.

Intense secrecy was the order of the day. Sebring had actually been rented by Mickey Thompson, to test his big-block Sting Ray and to create interest in his name-brand line of Chevrolet speed equipment. The factory tests of the Grand Sport would be camouflaged under Mickey Thompson's schedule. Arkus-Duntov and Corvette race drivers Doug Hooper and Bill Krause drove the Mickey Thompson Corvettes, evaluating brakes for those cars. The production Corvettes, even the race cars were still way too heavy for the disc brakes that existed at that time: Girling, Lockheed or Kelsey-Hayes.

When Gregory went out in the Grand Sport mule, he was very fast. Immediately, he was within a second or two of the lap record, and this was in a brand-new race car, on its shakedown cruise.

While tests showed that the brakes were not awful, the rotors overheated badly. In fact, the rotors glowed cherry red when Gregory pulled into the pits after his hot laps. Still the Grand Sport was fast. Everyone had reason to feel good—the Grand Sport program was on course and Christmas was near. And yet, Scrooge had one surprise left for the Corvette and its people.

Someone, either a GM insider, a reporter or some corporate enemy of Chevrolet, made sure that word of the test session reached Frederic Donner, GM's chairman of the board. While Donner may have sympathized with the goals of better publicity and recognition for Chevrolet, he was a company man, and he was not interested in his employees getting too big for their Dearborn britches.

Donner called Bunkie Knudsen on the carpet and insisted that he completely dismantle the Grand Sport and any other racing programs inside

Back in Detroit, in a secluded part of the Styling Section, a Grand Sport roadster prototype was under construction. Lighter and faster, the roadsters were the last flourish of Grand Sport performance. This prototype has a front grille, another variation of the big hood scoop and a truncated A-pillar. The coupe top was simply cut off with a hacksaw and the holes glassed over. The nicest thing about the car is its streamlined roll bar. Dave Friedman

When Penske switched over from driver to team owner, he ran this Grand Sport, and hired Dick Guldstrand and Dick Thompson, two of the most experienced Corvette racers ever, to drive it. This car is nose high while it's standing still! Here the car awaits tech inspection at Sebring in 1966. Dave Friedman

Chevrolet, or he could forget about his job. The cars were to be disposed of in any way, so long as it was soon.

Arkus-Duntov and the others were enjoying their Christmas vacations when they got the news that the Grand Sport was dead. At that time, it would be possible to build five complete cars, from parts that already existed.

Zora tried to look at the upside. They had always intended to sell the cars anyway, so they would do it now, rather than later. Plans for the 100-125 cars needed to homologate them for racing were out of the question now, but five winning Grand Sports would still make an impression.

Zora and the other Chevy engineers called two racers they knew and asked if they might be interested in the loan of a new, supersecret, Cobra-killing Corvette Grand Sport.

The two, Dick Doane and Grady Davis, both had large, private racing operations and were respected by Chevrolet as folks who could get the

job done in racing. Doane was a Chevrolet dealer in the Midwest, and Davis an executive with Gulf Oil.

Although both teams were excited to get a shot at the Grand Sport Corvette, neither was able to do much with their car in 1963. Doane's car was sidelined for most of the Road America 500 at Elkhart Lake, Wisconsin, in September. Davis entered several more races with his car, although he wanted to win the A-Production division with his Z06 Sting Ray, driven by Dr. Dick Thompson. It didn't matter, the 1963 A-Production champ was Bob Johnson in, you guessed it, a Shelby Cobra.

Race Premiere

The racing career of the Grand Sport Corvettes is not as distinguished as we might like it to be. While these cars were fast and mean looking, they were never developed to the extent that Arkus-Duntov and the others planned. When Frederic Donner padlocked the Grand Sport program, engines and other components were nowhere near ready to race.

But, the hardy privateers went forward, their banners flying.

In its first race ever, at Marlboro Raceway in Maryland on April 7, 1963, Corvette Grand Sport number 004 stalled on the grid, an injector clogged.

Here's the Penske Grand Sport during the early-going at Sebring in 1966. Dick Thompson makes a valiant effort, but the GT class was won by teammates Moore and Wintersteen in their Grand Sport. Dave Friedman

The Moore-Wintersteen GS at Sebring in 1966. On their way to winning the GT class, this Grand Sport raced for twelve hours straight, but spent some time in the pits near the end of the race for rear-end problems. A Ford GT40 Mk II at left is about to blow by the Grand Sport. Dave Friedman

Its driver, Dr. Dick Thompson, pumped up for the race, fumed in the pits for twenty minutes before the car was ready to go out again. Since they were out of direct competition, Thompson drove the car as fast as it would go, trying to establish some parameters for its performance.

The trick, all-aluminum engine was not available for these races; it wasn't ready yet. With a production 327 motor delivering 360 hp, the Grand Sport was about three seconds a lap faster than the Z06 Sting Ray, and about the same amount slower than Roger Penske's little Cooper-Climax. Since the Grand Sports were not going to be made in large enough numbers, they had to race in the SCCA Modified class, the stomping grounds of purpose-built race cars, many of them running Corvette powertrains.

At a later race at the Meadowdale, Illinois, Dick Thompson had his first flying lesson. The Grand Sport made so much front-end lift that the car got airborne over a bump and landed so hard it broke its shock mounts! About this time, a new twin-throat fuel-injection system was added and the hood was given a tab spoiler and a large vented bulge to clear the new fuel injector.

Thompson finished fourth at the end of the season, including a win at Watkins Glen, New York, in a car that was coming much closer to being competitive. But it was a hard season for all involved. The Dick Doane car managed only two races, scoring a sixth in one and a DNF in the other.

Clearly, the Grand Sports were not making the waves they had been designed to create.

Arkus-Duntov was keenly aware of all this and he brought the two race cars back to their home base in Warren, Michigan. There, much of the technology of the two veteran cars was transferred back to the three that had sat in the shop.

John Mecom, Corvette Teamster

While in the garage, the Grand Sports received some important changes. For one thing they got bigger tires, a change that would turn out to be a genuine improvement. They went from a 6.5x15 in. wheel to 9.5x15 in. in front and 11 in. in the rear.

Fender flares were added to cover the wide tires and several other changes were made to the bodies. Holes were drilled in the rear fascia of the cars to exhaust hot air from the differential area, and permanent cooling ducts were cut in the front and rear fenders. The headlamps were covered with a fiberglass piece in body color.

But most importantly, the Grand Sports were finally fitted with the engine they had been meant to carry, the all-aluminum-alloy 377 ci small-block. Although there wasn't time to produce the twin-spark heads for these engines, as delivered they still developed 485 hp at 6000 rpm, and 435 lb-ft of

84

The Penske Grand Sport at Sebring in 1966 is in good shape while a Shelby Mustang GT 350 understeers its way off the track. Dave Friedman

Prova, indeed! That's the Italian word for prototype and it's seen on the license plates of upcoming Ferraris and other experimental cars in Italy. Simple and unadorned with scoops and other devices, this Penske Grand Sport ran a superb Sebring and took home a first in the GT class, and a ninth overall. Dave Friedman

torque at 4000 rpm. Special equipment included four Weber 58 mm DCOE twin-throat carburetors mounted on a lightweight alloy cross-ram manifold, the first of its kind for the small-block.

Chevrolet then decided to send the cars to Nassau in the Bahamas. The sunny island of Nassau had a Speed Week every year in December, to provide some racing in the sun during the depths of winter. There was an FIA-sanctioned sports car race, and some other races supporting it. Viewed as a sportsman's race, wealthy owners and drivers brought some of the best cars in the world.

To serve as the camouflage for their efforts in Nassau, Chevrolet picked Texan John Mecom's racing team. Mecom's outfit was world-class, if privately run. It would have the three updated Grand Sports, car numbers 003, 004, and 005, to run at Nassau.

Mecom was a no-bull young man with big Texas oil money to stand behind him. When Mecom decided that he wanted to go racing, he did everything first-class, and often won. His first race car was the Cooper-Zerex Special, driven by Roger Penske. This tiny car raced in the sports car classes, but it was a center seat rule-bender built from a Cooper Formula 1 car.

At Nassau in 1963, Mecom also entered a Ferrari, a Corvette-powered Lola GT coupe (the ancestor of the Corvette GTP of the 1980s), the mid-engine Scarab and Penske's Cooper-Zerex Special.

By the end of 1963, Carroll Shelby thought that he and the Cobras had seen the last of the Grand Sports. The Grand Sport coupes had raced against the Cobras several times, always losing, except for Dick Thompson's win at Watkins Glen.

So, you can imagine how shocked he was to discover those three Grand Sports on the dock in Nassau. Shelby climbed all over, and under, the Grand Sports wearing a frown like the Grand

Canyon. He noticed that they looked more powerful than previously. Shelby driver Ken Miles smiled in delight as Roger Penske walked up, to wax eloquent on the speed and power of the new, improved Grand Sports. Suddenly, Shelby wasn't looking forward to race day as much.

Now on his own with the Grand Sport, George Wintersteen and co-driver Welch tackled Sebring again in 1967. Their number 4 GS has made a very good start, quicker than the Ferrari P3 that's in front of it. Chances for an overall win were slim due to the amazing competition at the top of the field. Don Yenko in another Corvette took the GT win in the over 5000 cc class that year. Dave Friedman

85

CERV I and II

Although the Chevrolet Engineering Research Vehicles (CERV) numbers I and II never saw any form of competition, they are a part of the Corvette racing story because they were built as potential racing machines, and so deserve some mention. CERV I was crucial in learning about how the new ultrawide racing tires behaved in action, and CERV II was in many ways the cousin of the Chaparral 2 which rewrote the books on chassis design and aerodynamics in the late 1960s.

CERV I came to be in a round-about fashion. After the Sebring SS program, anything with a hint of racing was definitely out for Chevrolet. Arkus-Duntov had done some work developing the Corvair, so he was thinking of high-performance rear-engine applications. At the same time, he was reminded of how hot it was in the Super Sport and how placing the engine behind the driver would ease that problem.

There was simply no way that he was going to get permission to build a single-seat, rear-engined race car. Unless, of course, he could prove that it would sell cars and make money for the corporation. The agenda for the trim vehicle which became known as CERV I was to establish a definitive record at Pikes Peak and possibly to compete at Indianapolis. Wheelbase was 96 in., track 56 in. and overall length, 172 in.

As a hillclimb car, CERV I would have been a natural. It had a very light tube space frame of chrome-moly steel, with trapezoidal bulkheads at front and rear, and large triangular trussed sections on either side of the driver, holding two custom-made fuel cells. The driver sat in a fairly upright position and had the use of two brake pedals, one to the left of the clutch for left-foot braking.

For power, Arkus-Duntov cooked up a remarkable, all-aluminum alloy motor. Using the form of a typical small-block, this engine was cast completely from aluminum; it used no iron liners, although it ran standard Corvette forged pistons. Most accessories such as water pump and starter motor were also of aluminum. Although some parts, such as the bellhousing, clutch and fuel-injection manifold, were of magnesium for an even greater strength-to-weight ratio.

From 283 ci, this engine produced about 350 hp, but it weighed only 350 lb. That's an even horsepower per pound. With a total vehicle weight of 1,450 lb., there was only 4.14 lb. for each horsepower to accelerate.

With GM management again forbidding any competition activity, CERV I was drafted as a tire-testing vehicle. It contributed substantially to Chevy engineers understanding the new wider racing tires. As a last gesture, in 1964, with a new body that helped streamline the exposed front suspension and a Corvette Grand Sport 377 ci motor, CERV I ran 206 mph at the GM Milford Proving Grounds high-speed track.

CERV II suffered a common fate of several Corvette factory race cars: it was in the wrong place at the wrong time. Although CERV I had been very useful, racing technology, indeed the frontiers of all automotive technology were advancing at a breakneck pace. The increasing use of computers in engineering design and the increase in racing tire widths (by four or five times what they had been a few years ago) both made CERV I an instant antique.

Arkus-Duntov set about designing a car to meet the 4.5 liter FIA rules for endurance racing; it used a 92 in. wheelbase and 56 in. track. Unlike CERV I, the number two machine would be a sports racer, low, wide and with two seats.

Although it was planned for a tube space frame, CERV II was built with a central tub made from boxed sections of aluminum. A smaller box carried the front suspension, while the rear suspension was mounted on the engine block and transmission housing.

One of the most interesting technologies CERV II would explore was high-performance four-wheel drive. All-wheel drive was a part of the CERV II concept from the beginning. In his usual fashion, Zora found unique and imaginative solutions to his problems.

Unfortunately, says Chevrolet development engineer Paul Van Valkenburgh, CERV II was not as fast as a standard, rear-wheel-drive Chaparral 2, so it was put out to stud as a tire and suspension test vehicle. Later, the CERV II was fitted with a semi-automatic transmission which became the object of much controversy when it was used on Jim Hall's Chaparrals.

Both CERV I and II had been in the Briggs Cunningham Museum in southern California for years, on loan from Chevrolet. When that outstanding collection of cars was broken up, the two CERV vehicles became the center of a legal firestorm. The vehicles were sold at auction as part of the Cunningham collection, then after the sale, Chevrolet claimed that it had only "loaned" the CERVs to Cunningham's museum and they had no right to sell them.

The new owners claimed that they had bought the cars legally and weren't going to give them back.

A Pain in the Tailbone

In the first qualifying race, the Grand Sports ran beautifully, filling the front of the grid for the Tourist Trophy race the next day. But in the race itself, the Grand Sports showed up a weak spot—their differentials. Both cars left the race with differential failures. One Chevrolet engineer in Detroit diagnosed it as the use of fresh gearsets, rather than those which had been broken in.

Mecom's crew quickly fabricated differential lube coolers from transmission oil coolers. They mounted them on the cars' back decks, under a body-colored hood of thin metal. For the moment, the differentials were under control.

In the Governor's Cup race, the Grand Sports of Penske, Augie Pabst (of the famous Milwaukee brewing family) and Thompson placed third, fourth and sixth, respectively. In the featured Nassau Trophy race, the Grand Sports showed a new bug in their battle with the breeze. At high speeds, so much air pressure developed under the hoods of the Grand Sports that they broke the fasteners at the cowl side of the hoods.

Both cars in the race did the same thing and both had to come into the pits to get their hoods taped down so they could continue racing. In this race Dick Thompson finished fourth and John Cannon eighth. Penske's third place overall was also a first in the prototype class, a victory of sorts.

When the Grand Sports returned to Warren, Michigan, they were given new hoods, with some vertical louvers to help hold them down. In preparation for Sebring of that year, the remaining two Grand Sports had their tops chopped. They were made into roadsters so they would have less frontal area and could run faster in a road race. Also the

experience of Dick Guldstrand in California in his red Sting Ray roadster had shown that the topless car had a lower center of gravity and less drag.

The three coupes were ordered to be sold by General Motors brass. Jim Hall bought one, and John Mecom the other two, although he later sold one of the coupes to fellow Texan Delmo Johnson, who raced it without success.

Jim Hall said of the Grand Sports: "They had some front-end lift and at high speeds they got a little light. I didn't compete in the car enough to analyze and say, 'Jeez, here's something we ought to fix on these cars.' Had I been campaigning the car on a week-to-week basis I'd be more familiar with that, but I just didn't run it enough. Besides Nassau, where my car had some trouble, the only races I was involved in were endurance races. So, it wasn't really a flat-out deal; you set the pace and conserve the car a little bit and go to the end."

Sebring—March 1964

All three Corvette Grand Sport coupes qualified for Sebring in March of 1964. They were driven by Delmo Johnson and Dave Morgan; Jim Hall and Roger Penske; and John Cannon and A. J. Foyt. This was not going to be their finest moment.

Johnson and his car were never competitive. Foyt and Cannon had a steady but unspectacular run in the top ten until a broken wheel retired them. Then, the Hall-Penske car, which had been running close to the front, broke a halfshaft. In a moment that will live forever in Corvette racing lore, Hall and Penske "borrowed" a stock halfshaft

It's hard to keep cool at Sebring with your mirrors full of world-class Ford GT40 Mk IV. Wintersteen pushes his GS as hard as it will go to stay ahead of the furious Ford. The Grand Sport's large-diameter tubes right below the grille send air to the front brakes. Dave Friedman

Although Ford GT40s dominate the grid at Sebring in 1966, the Corvette GS of Dick Thompson and Guldstrand makes a good showing on the second start of the race. Roadsters were easier to get into than closed coupes, so they made faster starts at Sebring. Some drivers would wait several laps before they actually buckled their seatbelts together. Dave Friedman

from a spectator's Corvette parked nearby and grafted it into their Grand Sport. It was a perfect fit and they finished the race on it. They wound up eighteenth.

After a rebuild which included a big-block engine swap, Delmo Johnson continued to race his car through the mid 1960s. Roger Penske bought Jim Hall's Grand Sport and had it rebuilt as well. The car was stripped of its onboard jacks and a system that added cooling water under pressure. Frank Coon and Jim Travers of Traco refreshed the aluminum small-block engine. The rear end was rebuilt and strengthened. Penske won the 1964 Nassau Tourist Trophy race in that car, beating Ken Miles in the first 427 Cobra and Mecom Grand Sport. Then Penske sold that coupe to George Wintersteen who raced it at Sebring in 1965 and sold it.

Penske soon bought the last two Corvette Grand Sport roadsters from Chevrolet. He hired Dick Guldstrand to drive for him. One of the cars was upgraded to a Chevy 427 engine, with big-valve iron heads. Later it had one of the first versions of the L88 aluminum big-block engines

installed. Guldstrand drove that car at Sebring in 1966 with Dr. Dick Thompson. They were fast during the race but hit the wall overnight and finished twelfth.

The two Grand Sport roadsters were campaigned for a few more years with 427 ci engines, although it was already too late. The era of the mid-engined sports car had begun and big, front-engined roadsters, like the Corvette Grand Sports, were sadly on their way out of the winners' circle for all time.

While the Grand Sports had their moment in the sun, we'll never know what they might have accomplished had the Chevrolet factory been allowed to support and develop them in the open. With factory support there might have been wins at Sebring, Daytona, perhaps even Arkus-Duntov's dream of a win at Le Mans. We'll never know.

This much is certain, the five extant Corvette Grand Sports are among the most expensive and desirable cars on the collector market in the 1990s. For a car that was frustrated so much, the Grand Sport is finally getting the acclaim and respect it always deserved.

Zora Arkus-Duntov poses with CERV I, an open-wheel car designed to serve as a high-speed testbed for Corvette components. Zora originally planned to race the car at the Indy 500, but Chevy's nonracing policy dashed any *serious competition efforts for this car. It was fast at Pikes Peak, but a misreported time relegated it to the test track.* Chevrolet

Chapter 7

Corvette-Powered
Racing Specials of the Sixties

The Sting Ray was a great car. It was my favorite Corvette race car. It was the prettiest race car I ever saw. But in addition to that, it was a very honest car. It did what you asked with no vices. We won the Championship that year against some very tough competition. Scarabs, and Cunningham had three or four cars. Maseratis and D-Jags and whatnot. And did this without any brakes!

—Dick Thompson, Corvette racer extraordinaire,

It didn't take a genius to see that one of the Corvette's best features as a race car was its dependable and powerful engines. From the first Corvettes at Sebring, through the SCCA championships of Dr. Dick Thompson, Jim Jeffords and Don Yenko, through the first angry meetings of the Corvette and the Cobra, engines were there for drivers; flexible, strong and getting better with every day of development.

The Sting Ray always looked just right. Proportions, shapes and visual excitement are what this car is all about. Dick Thompson eases the car into a turn under mild braking at Nassau in 1959. Dave Friedman

Dick Thompson on the grid at Riverside for the Los Angeles Times *Grand Prix in 1960. Across from the Sting*

Ray is perhaps a Devin SS or other road-race special of the period. Dave Friedman

The tremendous racing success of the simple pushrod, small-block motor led to the creation of the Mark II large-displacement or Mystery Engine, which was also raced with great success. Its successors, the Mark IV production engines, known as big-blocks or Rat Motors, provided Corvette racers with yet another powerful lightweight motor that they could ride into victory lane.

From the first 256 ci motors of the '56 to the wonderful 327 in the Sting Rays, to the 396 and 427 big-blocks, the Corvette engine was always well prepared for race day. And a steady stream of improved speed parts came from the factory with bulletins announcing the proper RPO number. This was due, in part, to Zora Arkus-Duntov having a special high-performance engine development group within the larger Chevrolet engine development department.

Furthermore, it was pretty obvious that Zora had a great idea when he put his hot engine in a purpose-built chassis and called it the Super Sport. When his own competition activities were so rudely curtailed by Chevrolet, other racers were not reluctant or slow to copy Arkus-Duntov.

You may recall a quote from John Fitch's book *Adventures on Wheels* cited a few chapters ago which said that the spirit of the SS was alive in the Scarab, a privately built racer that used many of the Super Sport's principles and some of its technology.

Due to the complete shutdown of Chevy's factory racing program, which included stock cars and other forms of competition, there were a lot of frustrated engineers at General Motors who were interested in sharing their talents with successful privateers. In the case of Jim Hall's Chaparral cars, this aid became unwritten factory involvement.

With racing specials such as the Chaparral, Cheetah, Devin SS, Scarab, Lister-Corvette, Bocar and others, Corvette technology and Corvette-developed engines and speed parts were powering drivers to victory. It wouldn't be right to call these cars Corvettes in the strict sense, but they are part of the Corvette racing story.

Mitchell's Sting Ray Roadster

One privately financed, SCCA Modified race car had more claim on the Corvette name than any other. It was the first car ever called a Sting Ray.

When the AMA racing ban shut down Arkus-Duntov's highly visible racing operation, other GM racing fans, such as Bill Mitchell, who had by now succeeded Harley Earl as head of Styling, were frustrated too. Mitchell loved motor sports long before he came to GM. After having a great time with the SR-2, Mitchell was looking for something a bit wilder. He got it with the car that would carry the most magical of all Corvette names, the Sting Ray. Here's how that car came to be.

It is the end of 1957. The AMA racing ban is in effect at GM. Under pain of firing, GM employees, especially those associated with the Corvette, are to stay away from motor sports.

At Chevrolet, the Sebring Super Sport program has been shut down tight. The two SS racing chassis are securely stored in a warehouse, but the bucks, tooling and spares for the cars have been destroyed. Ed Cole, Zora and others still want to race. They have plans for an underground railroad to deliver parts to privateers around the country. Time passes. One day, Bill Mitchell meets with Ed Cole. Mitchell persuades Cole to sell him the SS mule chassis for five hundred bucks. Why Cole agrees to this, no one knows, but Mitchell may have voiced his plans to race a private car in SCCA, and Cole may have agreed on the condition that Mitchell take the heat if the corporation didn't like his plan.

Mitchell then has the bare chassis delivered to his mysterious, highly secret Studio X in the Styling Center. There Mitchell, Larry Shinoda and other designers create a car of supreme beauty. It will be clearly a Bill Mitchell design, with sharp edges, large flat surfaces and a quality of tautness—like skin stretched over a skeleton, or the shell of a sea creature.

At the same time the design reminds you of the P-38, one of Harley Earl's favorite planes. Known as the Lightning, the P-38 was a big, twin-engine fighter plane with the pilot in a central pod thrust forward from the center of the wing. It was a fast, hot-rod plane whose sleek, lightweight design gave it outstanding air mobility and aerobatic poise. It was a hell of an aircraft.

Only in the Sting Ray's case, the P-38 theme of three pods connected by a curved, winglike surface, is brought into the jet age and radically streamlined. The rest of the body echos the Corvette SS

with its side-exiting exhaust, tapered tail and headrest *cum* fairing. Below the beltline, the car is very quiet, with all sides bending in and under on large radius curves.

This design was essentially a roadster version of the canceled Q Corvette, a proposed car that would have had a rear-mounted transaxle and inboard rear brakes. The hardware was meant for all Chevrolets, but the transaxle was scrapped and the rest of the project collapsed without it, Corvette included. For Mitchell's Sting Ray, certain measures were taken to ease the scorching heat

Good times under the golden Nassau sun. From left to right, Dr. Dick Thompson, Dick Constantine and Bill Mitchell. Thompson and Mitchell were in Nassau to race the Sting Ray prototype, based on the discarded frame of a Corvette SS, with a striking new body by Mitchell. Little did the world know that the Sting Ray would become the next and most famous Corvette. Dave Friedman

The celebrated Chevrolet small block engine, Corvette style. This engine was immensely popular in racing specials thanks to Duntov's insistence that speed parts be widely available. Road & Track

Low, sleek and menacing, the Sting Ray raced in C-Modified most of its career. Note the mesh in the hood and the side exhaust, two items eventually seen on the production Sting Ray a few years later. Dave Friedman

At the Nassau garages in 1959, the Sting Ray gets some needed prep before the race. Note the mag wheels with their three-lobed knock-off spinners, and the Sting Ray logo on the side of the car. The fish part never made it into production, but the name stuck. Dave Friedman

Sebring drivers had felt in the SS. The firewall was insulated and two panels were cut in the hood to exhaust hot air from the forward raked radiator.

The Sebring Super Sport chassis remained as before: 1 in. tube space frame, fabricated double A-arms, with coil-over shocks in front; and the four-link de Dion axle at the rear with inboard brakes. The complex braking system remained also.

A mercury switch set at an angle would cause the brake-line pressure to the rear brakes to hold at a certain level of braking g's. Front brake-line pressure could continue going up as the driver pressed the pedal harder, but the rears would maintain their set level. This system may sound good on paper, but it never worked on a track for the SS or Sting Ray. After four races with unpredictable front-wheel lockup, the system was replaced by a typical racing setup of big finned drums all around, biased toward the front, but controlled by pedal pressure only.

The Scarab, seen here in a rare, unpainted shot, was a full-blown racer that built on the bedrock of the Corvette engine and used some of the leading chassis technology of the era. Road & Track

Lance Reventlow was the passion and bankroll behind the Scarabs. Here he details a tire on one of the later, front-engine Scarabs, with his split-window coupe sharing the driveway. Road & Track

Under the hood was a race-prepared 283 fuelie making 280-300 hp. It used the Duntov cam and aluminum heads. The headers were the prototypes for the famous side pipes of the street Sting Ray, a four-into-one design.

In its first race, at Marlboro in Maryland, the bright red Sting Ray placed fourth behind two Porsche RS Spyders and a Lister-Jaguar. But Dick Thompson had driven an excellent race. He was in the lead from the start, however, the wet April racetrack made his already strange brakes even more treacherous. A spin late in the race put him back in the pack, but he had regained fourth before the contest was over.

Thompson charged so hard late in the race he was suspended for ninety days by the SCCA and Fitch drove the next couple of races. The same brake problems surfaced with Fitch at the wheel, until the refit occurred. Brake problems aside, the last races of 1959 saw a much improved vehicle.

As Dr. Dick Thompson said, "The Sting Ray was a great car. It was my favorite Corvette race car. It was the prettiest race car I ever saw. But in addition to that, it was a very honest car. It did what you asked with no vices.

"We won the Championship that year against some very tough competition. Scarabs, and Cunningham had three or four cars. Maseratis and D-Jags and whatnot. And did this without any brakes!"

With a highly improved braking system, lightened body and stiffer coil springs all around, Thompson did take the C-Modified championship in 1960. For those races, they mostly used 7.10 Firestone racing tires on 5 1/2Kx15 in. Halibrand mag wheels and a welded differential.

Augie Pabst in the Meister Bräuser Scarab gave Thompson a tremendous mid-season chal-

The Chaparral 1 sports racer was a graceful, powerful and reliable car. In various paint and team colors a brace of Chaparrals dominated modified racing events in the late fifties and early sixties. Here, the Chaparral is painted as a Meister Bräuser team car and is blowing by an Allard. Only a decade separates the two cars! Road & Track

lenge and beat him several times. At Sting Ray's final race in 1960, its braking problems couldn't be overcome and led to the car's retirement. Walt Hansgen, an aggressive driver, slipped in front of Thompson just as they had to brake hard for a corner. As usual, Thompson had little or no brakes left so he piled right into Hansgen's Maserati, heavily damaging his car's front end.

By the end of the season, championship or no, Bill Mitchell had to plead poverty. Racing out of his own pocket was hurting him, especially with so many people on the payroll and the cost of travel all across the country.

Jim Hall had a close relationship with Chevrolet throughout his racing career. Hall was one of the most gifted driver/engineers to ever compete in motorsports. Along with Mark Donahue, Hall redefined the nature of professional racing, combining a racer's guts with the analytical mind of an engineer. His Chaparral cars were the most innovative and exciting racing hardware of the sixties. Road & Track

In 1961 the refurbished Sting Ray became a show car, testing the waters for the debut of the production Sting Ray at the very end of 1962. The car continued on the show circuit for years, receiving some custom bodywork and a variety of exotic show engines. Mitchell personally restored the car to its silver, as-raced condition and let it reside at the Indianapolis Motor Speedway museum.

In 1987, the year that Chevrolet was honored at the Monterey historic races in California, and again in 1989 at Lime Rock in Connecticut, Dick Thompson got to drive the Sting Ray once more, now fitted with disc brakes.

"It was," he said enthusiastically, "just ever so much fun to drive. I got fifty laps in it at Lime Rock. I would like to see that car have more of a career in vintage racing right now. It would be quite competitive, I think."

From Super Sport to Scarab

Start from the position that you have all the money in the world and you are young and excited and you want to build race cars that will run with anything. That position is where Lance Reventlow found himself in the 1950s. He was the heir to a fortune, Woolworth department stores, and he had access to some of the nation's best racing builders in California.

Dick Troutman and Tom Barnes, both stars from Frank Kurtis' garage, did the body and frame for the new cars. Warren Olson was the straw boss, Ken Miles assisted with design and Chuck Daigh was the driver. Jim Travers and Frank Coons built and tuned the Corvette small-block engines. They would later branch off and open shop under the Traco name.

The car they produced was known as the Scarab, named after a mysterious Egyptian beetle, and was painted a rich, sapphire blue, similar to the Sebring SS.

Indeed the whole Scarab project was similar to the SS. The Scarab used a tube space frame, twin A-arm front suspension, a de Dion rear axle with Watts linkage, and coil-over shocks all around. Up

The number 7 Lotus leads Bob Bondurant in his solid-axle Corvette in 1959. The Corvette's Chevrolet small-block V-8 was plugged into several race specials such as the Cheetah, the McKee and the Lister-Corvette, which enjoyed SCCA race success in the late-fifties. Dave Friedman

front was a 300 hp Corvette 283 engine running Hilborn injection, although the motor was ultimately bored out to 339 in. Individual headers fed into side-mounted exit pipes. After competition tuning, the motor was making 375 hp on racing gas.

The Scarab body was sleek and good looking, something of a mid-ground between the SS and a Maserati Birdcage in appearance. It was fabricated, mostly by Emil Deidt, from thin aluminum sheet.

The McKee sports racer, later known as the Chevette, was a practical and speedy creation. One of the first good mid-engine cars from America, it had Corvette power and a very good transaxle designed by Bob McKee, the car's overall creator. Road & Track

Bob McKee at his drafting table. He went on to sell his transaxle to a large number of racers. His race car was very competitive and made formidable use of its Corvette engine. Road & Track

One way the Scarabs differed from the Corvette SS was in brakes. The Scarabs used the best racing brakes they could find, huge NASCAR stocker drums, 11 in. units from the Mercury Turnpike Cruiser.

Scarabs began hauling their shells around racetracks in mid 1958 and immediately ruled the competition. Driven by Chuck Daigh and Reventlow himself, the Scarab team began beating Ferraris, Jaguars, Maseratis and other racing specials in its second race.

Several more Scarabs were built and raced by Reventlow's team until he decided to move into Formula 1, and he sold the Scarabs to Harry Heuer and other customers. Heuer was the son of a Chicago brewery owner, maker of Mëister Brau beer, hence the name Mëister Brauser racing. Augie Pabst drove the Mëister Brauser Scarab to a number of national race victories in the early 1960s.

Driven by Pabst and former SR-2 racer Jim Jeffords, the Corvette-powered Scarabs were outgunning everything Europe had to offer, even the Bill Mitchell Sting Ray racer driven by Dick Thompson. Thompson's national championship in 1960 in the Sting Ray was a testament to his remarkable skill and daring as a race driver. When the brewery was sold, new owners didn't want to race and the Mëister Brausers were finished. Ultimately, the switch to mid-engine sports racers in the next few years made these fast blue cars obsolete.

From Scarab to Chaparral

Texan Jim Hall was a young man with barrels of family oil money behind him when he began

A Devin chassis. With Corvette power, a fiberglass body handmade in California and a chassis designed and built in Scotland, the car was an international vehicle. Note the A-arm front suspension and the large inboard rear disc brakes. Road & Track

racing as a teenager. Like another young millionaire, Lance Reventlow, Hall proved to be a superior driver. By 1960, Jim Hall had run third in the US Grand Prix at Riverside in his own Lotus GP car.

After being a business partner with Carroll Shelby in a Dallas sports car dealership, Hall became a well-known racer around the United States. He hired Troutman and Barnes, of Scarab fame, now on their own. The car that emerged from this joint venture would be known as the Chaparral.

Troutman and Barnes built the Chaparral as a refinement of the Scarab. The Chaparral was smaller, lighter and better suspended than its predecessor. It used a Corvette 283 motor, opened up to 318 ci, with three two-barrel carburetors. At only 1,479 lbs. and with 325 hp, the Chaparral had a tremendous power-to-weight ratio; it would be fast and nimble.

The Chaparral used independent rear suspension, not too different from the Lotus Formula 1 car Hall had driven at Riverside, and beautifully fabricated twin A-arm front suspension, with the A-arms enclosing coil-over shocks. There were Girling disc brakes all around and they were much more successful than the best drum units of the Corvette SS and the Scarabs. Weight distribution was an exact 50:50 front and rear, giving the car a precise balance that a driver could work with, not fight against.

In the hands of Jim Hall and his friend Hap Sharp, the Chaparrals were mighty race cars but they were born just as the mid-engine revolution hit road racing in the United States. While several more Chaparral 1 race cars were built, for a total of six in all, they were soon outraced by Lotus 19s and Cooper Monacos.

Sold to the Mëister Brauser team, a Chaparral 1 driven by Harry Heuer blazed its way to the SCCA National C-Modified Championship in both 1962 and 1963.

In the meantime, Jim Hall kept busy driving the Corvette Grand Sport for Chevrolet and private owners. When that car's racing career was over, Hall and Sharp got together on a new contender, the Chaparral 2, a vehicle that would be one of the first high-tech racers.

While it would run contrary to established fact and historical record to call the Chaparrals in any way Corvettes, there is a powerful connection between a development car within GM known as the Corvette Grand Sport II and the Chaparral 2C.

Chevrolet engineers had been creating test vehicles to explore vehicle and suspension dynamics. The information from these programs

A Devin SS, on the beach but fully clothed. This model is nicely turned out with wire wheels, outside exhaust and a frameless windshield. A light car, its performance on the street was sparkling but it was just not hot enough on the modified racing circuit. Road & Track

Bill Devin works on one of his fiberglass body molds, this one for his famous coupe. Devin's cars are becoming popular again in vintage racing, where they look good and sound great. Road & Track

would be used to design better suspensions and chassis for all Chevrolets and GM cars, or so the engineers said. The vehicles they built to assess these dynamics just happened to be exotic mid-engined race cars.

One vehicle was known as the Grand Sport II. It used an all-aluminum alloy 327 engine and one-speed automatic transmission; this drive train was "loaned" to Jim Hall for use in a Chaparral 2. It won its first race, with Hall lapping the field all the way to the third-place car.

Thus began a highly secret relationship between Chevrolet's engineering and R&D departments and Chaparral racing. The outcome was the introduction of the front of "chin" spoiler, the rear inverted wing and the remarkable Chaparral 2J "sucker" car.

The 2J used sliding skirts to seal the car to the track surface. Then, two high-efficiency turbo fans in the rear of the car sucked out the air beneath the vehicle. Normal, ambient air pressure pressed it fiercely down onto the track surface, with no penalty in drag. Traction and cornering speeds were unbelievable. With other builders tearing their hair out, the car was ruled illegal.

Jim Hall shifted into single-seat racing at Indy, but retained his close ties with Chevrolet engineering.

Bocar

Bob Carnes was a racing enthusiast from Denver and an aerospace engineer. He named his car after himself, using the beginnings of his first and last names. Carnes understood engineering well enough to know that the current hot sports car racing setup wasn't that hard to build. You took a tube frame, a Corvette engine and some suspension components, put a fiberglass body over them and presto, a sports racer.

Carnes designed his own chassis, used Porsche trailing arm front suspension, with the Corvette solid axle in back. One classy element in the chassis layout was the 1.5 in. right-hand offset of the engine, designed to balance the driver's weight in a left-hand seat. The Bocar's roadster body was high waisted and had a swoopy kit-car look, a small grille and angled quad headlamps. By 1959 the XP-4 and XP-5 had sold a few vehicles each. With the XP-6, Carnes took a radical step toward challenging the faster, lighter Scarabs. He stretched his 90 in. wheelbase 14 in. and fitted a GMC supercharger to the front of the Corvette engine, with Potvin drive off the crank.

This arrangement never paid off. The XP-6 had a mediocre record as a racer, although it did win a few pole positions. A fire at the Bocar garage and factory suddenly put an end to Carnes' support and manufacture of the car. They were raced for a few more years and then vanished.

Cheetah

The Cheetah was supposed to be a Corvette-powered answer to the Cobra. Designed for limited production, the Cheetah was meant to be a race car, not a street GT. Light in weight and ready to unleash near 400 hp, the Cheetah always suffered from a lack of development.

Dave Thomas was the principal behind the Cheetah. He had been a California hot rodder and had raced solid-axle Corvettes. He did some fabrication of stunt cars for Hollywood and dabbled in other forms of racing. Then, Thomas got together with Don Edmunds, a former Indianapolis driver and a gifted sprint car builder.

That's also why the Cheetah has been described as a sprint car with a coupe body—the frame and suspension is directly related to sprint car, or simply *is* sprint car.

There was a beefy tube frame with a roll cage that wrapped up around the driver. Front suspension was Corvette, as was the rear, although the Corvette's transverse rear leaf spring was replaced by a pair of coil-over shocks.

The Cheetah used a 327 ci Corvette motor with Rochester fuel injection. The engine was essentially stock, but with 11.25:1 compression. There was actually no driveshaft in the Cheetah. The engine was so far back in the frame that the transmission linked directly to the differential with a U-joint.

The early cars all had alloy bodywork; they were meant to be works racers driven by Thomas and others. The later cars had fiberglass bodies which were a little heavier.

The bodies were shaped very aggressively. The driver sat just in front of the rear axle and there was almost no rear overhang. This gave the Cheetah a 45:55 weight balance, which should have been good for racing. But the car was not easy to drive. It had massive oversteer and had trouble with front-end lift at higher speeds.

Without the right, magic combination of car and driver, the Cheetah never was a threat to the big names of its day, like Scarab, Chaparral, Lotus or Porsche.

Lister-Corvette

The Lister-Corvette was another example of a special frame and body utilizing the reliable and torque-rich power offered by the Chevrolet Corvette small-block engine.

Brian Lister was British and liked motor sports. He eventually built himself a lightweight car to take a Jaguar XK inline six motor. For those who may not know it, the XK was a superb engine, designed for strength at the bottom end, with hemi-heads, big valves and cross-flow breathing on top and dual overhead cams. It was a fine piece of technology in its day.

The Formula 1 Scarab. After tremendous victories in the Corvette-powered Scarab road racers, Lance Reventlow decided to tackle the big boys in Europe. He got creamed and returned to the United States with broken spirits.

The old saying that to make a small fortune in racing you have to start with a large fortune might have been coined from Reventlow's experience. Chevrolet

Similar to the small-block, the XK engine was continually bored and stroked for more displacement and more power. It began life as a 3.4 liter sedan motor, but by the 1960s the same engine had been opened up to 4.2 liters and made well over 200 hp on the street, in the wonderful E-Type.

With all the experience Jaguar had running at Le Mans and other endurance races, the XK engine was well sorted out by the mid 1950s and was dependable as well as powerful.

Lister-Jaguars were not too expensive, either, at about $8,000 ready to race. With a twin-tube frame, disc brakes and thin aluminum body, the Listers were certainly competitive. The famous "trick" of the Listers was to use a low-profile body with a huge power bulge covering the engine. This gave the Listers a low frontal area, and yet stayed faithful to the rule book. It made for odd-looking cars, but they went fast and couldn't be protested.

Listers did well in SCCA racing at the end of the 1950s but many of their drivers were looking for still more power. When a Corvette engine was transplanted into the Lister, it made a fast car even faster, but some say, the engine overpowered

the thin front A-arms and de Dion rear axle suspension.

Briggs Cunningham bought a couple of the Listers for his racing team, but he preferred the new smooth, aerodynamic body made especially for the Corvette-powered cars. Walt Hansgen was once SCCA C-Modified National Champion driving the aerodynamic Lister-Corvette.

McKee

Like many of the Corvette-powered specials, the McKee began with a talented craftsman realizing that he could put together his own race car based on what he already knew, with a little judicious copying from the right sources.

Bob McKee ran a machine shop in the Midwest. He had worked at Indianapolis as a tuner and mechanic and there met Roger Ward. One day Ward called wanting McKee to install a Buick V-8 in a Cooper Monaco sports racer. McKee did the conversion, including designing and building a transaxle from the gearbox and differential components of a Corvette.

99

Then Dick Doane, a Chevrolet dealer in the Chicago area, asked McKee to build a whole car that would be Corvette powered and race under his own sponsorship. McKee did it, copying the Cooper's strong but light tube frame, and adding an improved version of the McKee transaxle. The rear suspension used a number of Corvette parts and the front suspension was a mixture of Chevelle, Buick and import parts. Because the car was often called a Chevette, it is easily mistaken for the subcompact that Chevrolet would sell years later.

The McKee Chevettes were adequate cars for their day. They were popular with those who wanted to compete with the foreign cars using an American product, but sadly, they were only as good as, and not better than most of their competition.

Devin SS

One of the reasons someone races a car is to draw publicity and media attention to a vehicle that is planned for production. If you don't have a huge budget to promote your products, just let them win races and everyone will come to your door. That's what Chevrolet itself planned with the Corvette in 1956.

Bill Devin is a perfect fit for the mold of the entrepreneur, the maverick, the dirty fingernails and hands-on, garage engineer kind of guy. And, eventually, he made a pretty darned good car, too.

Devin got out of the Navy after World War II and began playing with cars, tuning racing engines for several Chevy dealers who sponsored race cars. Devin liked the small-block motor. After a few years, he began experimenting with fiberglass bodies for sports cars and racing specials. At first, these were for rear-engine cars on the VW platform. Once, Devin got ahold of some Porsche engines and put them in a number of cars; but great sources of engines and other parts were hard to find and easy to lose, according to Devin.

Devin offered as many as twenty-seven different body variations, to fit everything from a Triumph to a Thunderbird. All of them were sports roadsters with a design that used the Italian GT style on a slightly larger scale than an MGA.

When Malcolm MacGregor, a wealthy Scot, wrote to Devin that he had a sophisticated tube frame that he'd like to cover with a Devin body, Bill shipped him several bodies and a Corvette engine.

Later in England, Devin drove the car and loved it. With its light weight, rigid frame and Corvette engine, the vehicle was fast, cheap and easy to love. By the end of the 1950s, Devin claims to have sold 3,000 sports car bodies but only about fifteen of them were the completely assembled, top-line Devin SS.

This car, with its 92 in. wheelbase, would be called the Devin SS. Bill saw it as his move from kit cars to limited production. The SS would have the MacGregor frame, Devin's latest bodystyle, a slim and pretty roadster, Corvette engine, Girling disc brakes, rack-and-pinion steering and a de Dion rear axle. The MacGregor frame was welded from 3 in. steel tubing in a style that mixed a pure space frame, such as the Maserati Birdcage, with the ladder-tube style of the Corvette Grand Sport.

The frames and chassis would be made in Ireland and shipped to Devin's factory in California, where the engine, interior, wiring and body were installed. Price was about $10,000. Performance was impressive for the price: 0-60 mph in under five seconds and 0-100 in just twelve seconds. The Devin SS would race in either B- or C-Modified, depending on whether it carried a 283 or 327 ci motor.

In the late 1950s through about 1963-1964, Devin SS drivers did fairly well in SCCA racing. None of them ever won the championship in their class, but they had a lot of fun, and got plenty of bang for the buck. In the main, they competed against the whole spectrum of Corvette-powered specials: the Scarabs, Bocars, Listers, McKees, Sadlers and the Devin-bodied Echidnas from Minnesota.

The lack of an ongoing development program or a budget for top engineering talent doomed the Devin SS to also-ran status. But, interestingly, the rare Devin SS is once again seen on racetracks as vintage racing rejuvenates many racing specials from the 1950s and 1960s.

Bill Devin himself notes with some bitterness that Lance Reventlow's people kept calling him up while they were building the Scarab, asking for parts and advice. But a year earlier, when Devin had needed financing for a project, Reventlow had left him high and dry.

By the mid 1960s, the Devin SS was underpowered and needed more aerodynamic downforce. The cars finally disappeared as mid-engined sports racers began to dominate competition.

Chapter 8

Racing With the Ponies,
Corvettes in the Seventies

It was a stable car. You felt safe as hell in it. Directional stability was terrific. Where it felt uncomfortable to me was when we were going those extreme speeds at Le Mans. It felt like it was dancing. The thing seemed to work, like flex. And not the chassis, the body. It would shimmer at that speed. On a normal track, like Brainerd or Sebring, it was like a rocket. It was just terrific. And Sebring is a rough track.

—Dick Smothers

For Corvette racers, the start of the 1970s meant that things were back on track. The menace of the Cobras had faded with the 1960s as Ford shut down its Total Performance program and cut Carroll Shelby loose. Now, Corvettes were once again winning national racing championships. This revitalization actually began in 1965 with the big-block engine for the production Corvette and continued strongly in 1968, with the introduction of the Mako Shark style, fourth-generation body. In

By the end of the 1960s, the Corvette had recovered from its dose of Cobraitis and was ready to charge to the head of the pack again. The Corvette also received a big-block engine with enormous power and a slippery new, Mako Shark style body. The race was on. This Johnson and Johnson Corvette at the Watkins Glen six-hour in 1968 has it all—disc brakes, big-block power and superior aerodynamics. Dave Friedman

Everybody loves Corvettes. After movie star Jim Garner made the racing film Grand Prix, *he went on to help boss a racing team of Corvettes. Known as American International Racing, the honchos were Garner, Guldstrand and*

Bob Bondurant. After a couple of unlucky races the group disbanded. This is one of the team cars at Daytona in 1968. Dave Friedman

SCCA A-Production racing, Corvettes of the Owens-Corning team and ones driven by John Greenwood won national championships in 1969, 1970, 1971 and 1972.

All in all, the turbulent "Me" decade of the 1970s was a wild time for Corvette racing. Professional motor sports benefited from a flood of serious corporate sponsorship money. Even the better amateur racers needed sponsorship and product subsidies to help pay the escalating costs of turning wheels in anger.

The emphasis both in the press and in the talk of barbershops across the country, was shifting from the hearty amateur driver-owner who worked on his own car to that of the pro, the hired gun, who drove for the big bucks and owed no loyalty. Racing had grown up and changed since the days of the brilliant young Corvette hot shoes. Gone were the likes of Dave MacDonald, flinging, sliding and dirt-tracking his number 00 solid-axle Corvette around the regional tracks of California in the early 1960s.

Owens-Corning Corvettes Insulate against Defeat

The swinging Corvette 1970s actually began in 1968 with the emergence of the powerful Owens-Corning team. Composed of drivers Tony De-Lorenzo and Jerry Thompson, this team had a remarkable string of seventeen victories at the end of the 1960s, two national championships, and wins at Daytona and Sebring.

DeLorenzo was a brilliant racer who worked his way up from the amateur ranks and became one of the leading Corvette drivers of his era. He began racing in his late teens, after seeing a Troutman and Barnes Chaparral race at Meadowdale, a regional track outside Chicago.

DeLorenzo commented: "My brother and I talked my dad into getting a Corvette for a company car, in 1964. He got a black fuel-injected coupe, with all the heavy-duty options. And at the time, I got a call from Zora Duntov. He said it had come to his attention that my father had ordered this car. The only racing option that wasn't on this

When Tony DeLorenzo got the Owens-Corning Fiberglass company to sponsor a pair of Corvettes, history was made. The team ran wild at the end of the sixties, taking two *national championships, with Delorenzo emerging as the dominant Corvette racing shoe at that time.* Dave Friedman

car was the 37 gallon gas tank, and he wanted to know who would be driving the car. I told him it wouldn't be my dad, it would be me. And he said OK, that's all he wanted to know. We took delivery of the car and I immediately started stripping it down to be able to take it to driver's school at Watkins Glen."

DeLorenzo began racing with his own car, a 140 hp Corvair Corsa, in what eventually became the Trans-Am. He ran at Nelson Ledges, Wilmot, Wisconsin, Watkins Glen, Lime Rock and a distance race at Marlboro, Maryland, which turned out to be one of the early Trans-Am races. When he earned enough points to go to the runoffs in 1966 but couldn't afford to make the trip to Riverside, California, his brother lectured him on the pressing need for sponsorship. Soon, with backing from Hanley Dawson, DeLorenzo obtained a brand-new 1968 L88 Corvette, spares and a station wagon for a tow car.

"The first race we entered with the car, at Wilmot again, we won with no trouble. The second

race was Elkhart Lake and several things happened there. That was the first time I drove a car over a hundred and fifty miles an hour, and it was the first race my dad ever went to.

"So in '68 we met up with Jerry Thompson and he said we had an opportunity to be involved with the Sun-Ray DX Corvette team, and the start would be at the Daytona twenty-four-hour for the 1968 season.

"In the winter of '67 we built a car out of parts, a 1968 Corvette roadster. And it was a great exercise in futility. But we built this car and got it ready and we were part of the Sun-Ray DX team at Daytona. A pretty august group, I might add. Don Yenko and Peter Revson, Jerry Grant and Dave Morgan, and Jerry Thompson and myself.

"That year there was another big Corvette team there: Dick Guldstrand's team, that was owned by Jim Garner. They had a three-car team also. We found out just about everything that you could break on a new Corvette. We broke transmissions, we broke driveshafts, halfshafts, front spindles, we broke steering relay rods. Chevrolet engineering, Corvette group, was designing and building new parts as fast as we were breaking them."

DeLorenzo continued: "Don Yenko was clearly the main factory connection, and also my partner, Jerry Thompson. He was an employee at Chevrolet engineering and he was a good friend of Yenko's. They basically were the factory connection.

"We had two '67 cars and the '68 at that first race at Daytona in February of '68 but strangely enough, it was the '67 car with Jerry Grant and Dave Morgan that actually won the GT class.

"Then the team broke up. Yenko went on with one of the cars to run national races, as did the third car; it ran some races in the Southwest. And Jerry and I resurrected the '67 car and attempted to run it in C-Production and my car in A-Production, as a team.

"I won the central division A-Production championship in '68 and '69, as I recall. But we had nothing but trouble with engines in Jerry's car. That was the small engine, a 327. That should have told me something but it didn't, to my everlasting regret, about how important that part of the equation was. And where you go to get good engines and how much they cost. I just assumed that was just part of the group, so to speak. Our guys were competent engine builders but they were not for development. We built good engines but when the horsepower race started, that's where we fell short.

"At the runoffs that year, I raced tooth and claw with Don Yenko and Don dropped out for some reason, I forget what, leaving me in the lead. I had a 22 second lead and then there were two caution periods. They were just local cautions on one corner. The rule was that when you saw the yellow, there was no passing. And as luck had it, in both instances, I got stuck behind a much, much slower car. Long enough to evaporate my 22 second lead to zippo. On my tail was Peter Consiglio in a 427 Cobra roadster. Peter was quick, but Yenko and I ran off and hid. But that was when Riverside had a 4,000 foot straightaway, and every lap he just went in deeper, till he passed me and I couldn't find a way around him. The margin of victory was 0.4 seconds."

Next, DeLorenzo began his relationship with Owens-Corning fiberglass. Late in the summer of 1968, DeLorenzo was looking for a sponsor because Hanley Dawson needed to withdraw. Dottie Cole, wife of Ed Cole—at that time president of General Motors—said that she wanted to take one of his racing proposals to a friend of hers, Curtis LeMay, Owens-Corning chairman of the board.

As DeLorenzo recalled: "She marched into his office in New York and said, 'I think you should do this,' and handed it to him. At the time I was working for the automotive division of Rockwell; I joined them when I got out of school, in February of '67. I was at my desk one day in early summer of '68 and a man by the name of Spiff Caravin called me up and said he was from Owens-Corning. So I went to Toledo and talked to their public relations man

The Sun-Ray DX battery team of Corvettes was a powerful force in the late 1960s, with drivers such as Tony Delorenzo and Don Yenko onboard. Here, one of their cars is prepped for the Watkins Glen race in 1968. Dave Friedman

Owens-Corning pit action. Note the ram air hood, wide rear tire and, what's that, a manual lug wrench! Even in endurance racing quick, accurate pit stops are crucial to victory. Dave Friedman

whose name is legend to those who know him, Roger Haliday. He's a transplanted Britisher whose father wrote for several motorcycle magazines. I think he helped perfect the art of racing public relations.

"And I negotiated a deal with them that was very modest, I think $25,000 for the whole season. But that would get us to the few nationals that we were gonna run. The first race we ran for them was at Mid-Ohio, which we promptly won.

"Then for the '69 season, we determined that we would run both cars in A-Production and that we would run the major distance races. And that started a string of race victories that was talked about for years. We won, I think, 22 straight. We qualified on the pole in probably all of those races; in the distance races we qualified on the pole and won the GT class. In '69 we were on the pole at Daytona but we did not win. One car was retired because it blew a tire while I was driving it, and the other broke a fuel pump which caused a fire which flared up when the car got to the pits and retired it.

"This wildly successful season continued into 1970 when we won Daytona and Sebring in the GT class. And we won the other national races that we entered but we were on kind of a thin budget because, lo and behold, we built two Trans-Am cars. Because that's where we wanted to go. That was where the action was. It's awesome because on one Trans-Am grid all the factories were there, and we were considered major independents. It was Roy Woods and Milt Minter, myself and Jerry Thompson, Mo Carter, the Chaparral Camaros, Jim Hall and Ed Leslie at first, then Vic Elford. The Fords

were Parnelli Jones and George Folmer. The American Motors were Mark Donahue and Peter Revson. And the Dodge was Sam Posey and the Plymouth was Dan Gurney and Swede Savage, and I'm probably forgetting some of the others.

"The 1970 season was very exciting," DeLorenzo continued. "We won all of our Corvette races, qualified for the runoffs. We finally lost a Corvette race at the runoffs in '70. We lost of course to John Greenwood. He and Jerry Thompson were dicing for the lead. I was in third and felt like I was running faster than both of them. And I was trying

Pick a line, any line. At Daytona in 1969, the Owens-Corning Corvette leads an older Sting Ray and a reluctant E-Type Jag into one of the infield turns. Dave Friedman

After Owens-Corning pulled out of racing, Tony Delorenzo and Dick Thompson were still out there slugging. The cars were the same under the skin, but had new paint jobs with some slick pinstriping on the hoods and rear decks. At the first Daytona Continental of the 1970s, these cars were the class of the field. The Delorenzo-Lang number 6 Corvette finished tenth overall and first in the GT class. Dave Friedman

John Greenwood jumps out of his Corvette at Sebring in 1970, ready to hand it over to Alan Barker. As with all new racers, things rarely go well the first time out. But Greenwood would be back another day. He would win his class the next year, in 1971. Dave Friedman

to figure a way around them. At that point my motor quit. It was a loose fuse, which I somehow found and replaced. And then somewhat grimly, driving like the proverbial man possessed, I augered my way back up to third, but by that time the thirty minutes was up."

About the same time, Owens-Corning decided it had gained enough exposure through motor sports and announced that it would soon be withdrawing its sponsorship. Without a budget, the team broke up and vanished from the national scene. Tony DeLorenzo continued driving as a professional for years. He has recently returned to Corvette racing, only this time as a Vintage racer. When a private owner restored the Owens-Corning Corvette team cars and invited DeLorenzo to drive, he couldn't say no, and he won several vintage races.

Running with the Ponies

After World War II, the United States experienced a period of growth and prosperity unprecedented in history. As our industries boomed, a new generation was growing up, becoming teenagers, beginning to drive cars. The emergence of a vast youth-oriented market of automobile buyers, along with some tremendous marketing savvy, gave rise to a new class of automobile in the mid-sixties—the pony car.

The first and most charismatic of the pony cars was the original Mustang. The Mustang caused Ford dealerships to be swamped when it appeared in 1963, the same year as the debut of the Sting Ray. One man put a down payment on a Mustang,

The back end of that same pit stop shows a disciplined crew hard at work. That team spirit would make the difference just one year later. Note just how big that rear fender flare is. In a few years Greenwood would take the Corvette where no production-based race car had gone before—over 200 mph. Dave Friedman

At Daytona in 1970, Greenwood picks up more pointers. His cars were very fast on the high banks of Daytona but they had reliability problems. Dave Friedman

John Greenwood, one of the key figures in Corvette racing in the 1970s. Greenwood was an inspired maverick, a true American original, in short, a Corvette racer.

then slept in the car till his check cleared the bank the next day, lest the dealer sell it out from under his deposit.

General Motors responded to the Mustang with the Camaro and the Firebird, beginning a cycle of product competition which inevitably spilled over into racing.

It took the SCCA with its penchant for production-based racing to come up with a proper series for the ponys to run in. It was called the Trans-America, to emphasize the domestic nature of the machinery. From the late 1960s to present day, Trans-Am racing has seen some magnificent battles as America's two largest car makers duke it out in yet another arena.

Even floundering American Motors got involved in the Trans-Am, with their Javelins and AMXs being raced to victory by the brilliant Mark Donahue.

Many of the names associated with Corvette racing became involved in Trans-Am operations, mostly in Camaros. Roger Penske, Dick Guldstrand, George Wintersteen, Jim Hall, Owens-Corning and others added Trans-Am Camaros to their stables. As old Corvette buddies, they often traded drivers, tires, advice and lies in the pits. Penske was the most successful of this group, with Mark Donahue at his best. Reaching a first peak in the early 1970s, Trans-Am competition provided some of the most thrilling and memorable racing of its time.

As Trans-Am grew in popularity and became more heavily sponsored, more manufacturers wanted to use it as a showcase for their wares. The number of makes in the series grew in the 1970s, with imports such as the Nissan Z cars and Mazda RXs making a strong impression. It was only a matter of time till Corvette rolled up its sleeves and got into the brawl.

Perhaps the best-known Corvette name in Trans-Am racing is Greg Pickett. Pickett bought a tube-frame IMSA (International Motor Sports Association) Corvette from John Greenwood when the rules changed for the Trans-Am in 1976 and allowed such purpose-built cars. Pickett had the car modified to comply with the SCCA rule book and he went racing, very successfully. Pickett drove his Corvette to a Trans-Am championship in 1978.

In more recent times, the late 1980s, Bob Riley designed a tube-frame Corvette racer with a new independent rear suspension. Riley hoped that his design would break the dominance of the Fords in Trans-Am. This car was introduced to serious competition by Greg Pickett at Sears Point in Sonoma, California, near the end of the 1987 season. Although Pickett seemed bound to win that race, an overheating problem sidelined him before the finish.

Throughout the 1988 Trans-Am season, Pickett and Darrin Brassfield drove that car, but with little luck. Then the car was sold to Tommy Morrison, who ran it with Brassfield and occasionally Jack Baldwin driving in 1988 and 1989 in both Trans-Am and IMSA GTO classes as the Mobil 1 Corvette.

In the late 1980s and early 1990s, the Trans-Am became the stomping grounds of the Ford-powered race cars of Jack Rousch, whose Merkurs and Mustangs have been the class of the Trans-Am field for half a decade.

Greenwood Does Daytona

John Greenwood was one of the leading figures in Corvette racing during the wild and wacky

One of Greenwood's Stars and Stripes Corvettes looks very aggressive at the Watkins Glen six-hour in 1972. By this time, Greenwood was building the strongest big-block road-racing engines in the United States, but the strain of doing it all was beginning to mount. Dave Friedman

The Kemp-Pickett Corvette big-block runs ahead of a Ferrari Daytona at the Watkins Glen six-hour in 1972. By now the Corvettes were back on their form and the Cobras were also-rans. Dave Friedman

1970s. Greenwood began the decade with back-to-back championships in SCCA A-Production for 1970 and 1971 with a big-block Corvette which Greenwood tuned. Having absorbed years of speed secrets in the Detroit area where he grew up, Greenwood was in a unique position to get the most out of Chevy's special L88 competition 427 motors.

In 1974, Greenwood produced a Corvette that went further in the direction of a competition car that the 'Vette had been taken since the days of the Grand Sports. Greenwood had Protofab, a respected racing shop, build complete tube-frame racing cars with Corvette suspension parts, drivetrains and running gear. These chariots of fire were eventually raced at Daytona and Sebring and in International Motor Sports Association GT endurance races. One of them was sold to Greg Pickett and became a famous Trans-Am racer.

Greenwood is in many ways the perfect Corvette guy. He's got money, that's never been a big problem, yet there is something blue collar about him after all. He likes to get his hands dirty, get that blacker-than-night stuff under the finger-nails, where it remains for decades. He likes to build his own cars, and he likes Chevy motors. And, in the end, Greenwood is more than a little bit of a maverick. He is stimulated, inspired by the underdog position, although he often decries it.

In 1976 Greenwood and Dick Smothers of the Smothers Brothers won Sebring in a car Greenwood called the Spirit of Sebring '76. That same year, Greenwood, Smothers and others went to Le Mans but engine troubles kept them from placing in the race, after they had easily taken the pole position!

All of this was done on BF Goodrich street radials. An important sponsor for Greenwood, Goodrich required that he run his full-race cars on street tires, for the public relations gains. And when he won, there were gains. But there were also times when Greenwood's very fast Corvettes cooked their engines trying to keep up with cars on stickier rubber. Still, for street tires, the BFG radials made it through a lot of racing. They were, of course, shaved to racing depth of 3/16 in. tread.

This photo, taken in 1990, shows one of Greenwood's early 1970s cars, now completely and lovingly restored. Green-wood and Dick Smothers drove some memorable races in this patriotic Corvette. B.F. Goodrich

John Greenwood: Driver and Engineer Extraordinaire

It's no surprise that John Greenwood grew up in Detroit. From that tough and practical midwestern city, Greenwood absorbed a love of working with his hands. And from the very air of Motown itself, he inhaled the magic vapors that make a man build powerful racing engines.

Greenwood began as a street racer on Detroit's Woodward Avenue. In 1960, he promoted himself to a 1955 Pontiac and immediately began tinkering with it. He managed to find a Pontiac 421 NASCAR motor and put it in the Poncho. With this rig, he raced up and down Woodward Avenue, meeting people and learning a lot about cars by racing every night. Greenwood had some frightening experiences, like one night when his brakes went out and he couldn't stop for an intersection. About 1964, Greenwood changed over to Chevrolets and Corvettes. At the same time, he was beginning to do engine work for friends in his garage—mostly clutch jobs and racing modifications. He wanted a Corvette because he saw that the power-to-weight ratio would be on his side in drag racing. Buying a 1964 coupe, Greenwood immediately replaced the stock 327 with a 427 big-block, which he acquired under the table from friends at General Motors.

At that time in Detroit, if you had the money, all kinds of exotic factory engine parts could be found. In Greenwood's case, it was an early version of the Mark IV 427. He blueprinted the big-block and stuffed it into his '64 coupe.

Greenwood slowly learned what made high-performance engines tick. He got into carburetors and intake manifolds, modifying them as he learned more about flow and cylinder filling. He drilled out idle circuits and added or removed air horns to customize the power curves of his motors.

As the police began to hassle the street racers of Woodward Avenue, Greenwood took his wife up on a dare and entered a gymkhana. When he discovered road racing, Greenwood changed gears completely. The straight-line racer now wanted to turn corners as well. But when he went to driving school at the Waterford Hills track in Clarkston, Michigan, it was not what he expected. There was a lot more to road racing than putting your right foot down hard and flogging the steering wheel. Greenwood had to juggle a big ego with his desire to learn something new.

Greenwood found a 1968 Corvette and began a long process of dialing the car in. He got some advice and help from Gil Hufstader and from some Chevrolet engineers. Before Greenwood knew it, the '68 was a fast, good-handling car. At the end of 1969, Greenwood could boast that he was winning national races. In a sorry incident, another driver wiped out his Corvette and left him holding the bag.

With the help of Art Jerome, the car was soon rebuilt, and with it, Greenwood began running the long-distance races which he would soon master.

In 1970, Greenwood took the A-Production title away from the dominant Owens-Corning Corvettes. In 1971, he recaptured his A-Production championship, won the GT class at Sebring partnered by Dick Smothers, a four-hour race at Michigan International with Bob Johnson, the Donnybrooke Un-Cola 500 at Brainerd, Minnesota, with Dick Smothers, and the GT class at Watkins Glen with Johnson as his co-driver.

Like Mark Donahue, another great driver-engineer of the time, Greenwood was both a good racer and a very talented racing development technician. Greenwood would put the car together and then go out and race it. This gave him in-depth knowledge of how everything should be working.

Greg Syfert, a chief mechanic for the Owens-Corning team, said that Greenwood beat them at the national runoffs in 1970 on horsepower. "We knew what he was doing with his engine and we had to decide whether to go with something new and untested or to go with the old setup that we knew worked. We went with the old setup and lost," Syfert said.

Engines were key to Greenwood's many victories. When you had a single, capable individual who built an engine, developed it and raced it, a lot of communication errors just didn't happen. Other factors, like a solid 8000 rpm redline on his motors compared to 7000, used by most everyone else, counted too.

By the mid-seventies, Greenwood began to burn out. He was doing most of his own mechanical work, driving in all the races and managing the team as well. Add to this time spent on other business activities, sponsor demands and travel and there wasn't much left of a twenty-four-hour day for home life and sleep.

Greenwood began racing tired and his string of victories began to taper off. At this time, he went to the radical tube-frame concept which provided the platform for his last convincing wins in the latter 1970s. In 1974 Greenwood had Protofab construct several cars with tube frames and very interesting coil-over shock, twin A-arm rear suspensions.

This custom rear end was built for two reasons: first, because the cars mounted new ultrawide racing slicks, and second, because the twin A-arms offered better power handling and better adhesion on rough track surfaces. Greenwood also felt that there was too much squat in the Corvette's rear suspension for racing, and more importantly, too much positive toe change in corners, caused by the Corvette's swing-axle type of rear geometry.

While these Greenwood IMSA racers are called tube-frame cars, they still use the steel birdcage frame from the production Corvette, heavily reinforced, as a starting point, with the front and rear tube sections attaching to it.

By 1976, the tube-frame car had been developed into a formidable racing machine. In a comparison test for *Road & Track*, Greenwood's *Spirit of*

continued on next page

America which had recently won the 12 Hours of Sebring, was compared to a stock Corvette. The Greenwood car was a monster when placed next to the somewhat mild L82 1975 coupe.

The Greenwood car (see spec box) used an aluminum block ZL1 454 ci big-block V-8. The engine was bored out 0.060 in. for a total displacement of 467 ci. It had Carillo rods, a Chevy crank reworked by Moldex, General Kinetics camshaft, with timing chain and roller rockers from Ed Iskenderian. The motor used a dry sump with a Weaver four-stage pump. A custom radiator was fabricated, much thicker than the stock unit.

The aluminum ZL1 had a unique induction system, developed by Greenwood. A magnesium cross-ram manifold was the heart of this custom fuel injection, built around Lucas components. The manifold had a clever fuel cooler built into it at the bottom. A blueprinted Muncie M22 "rockcrusher" four-speed transmission took the power back to a 2.73:1 rear end.

The engine's power was rated at 700 bhp at 6800 rpm, and torque reached 620 lb-ft at 4000 rpm. Riding on 28 in. racing tires in back, the car was ready for 221 mph in race form, at 7000 rpm.

In comparison, the L82, 350 ci powering the 1976 street Corvette made 210 bhp at 5200 rpm, and 255 lb-ft of torque at 3600 rpm.

At the time, Greenwood seriously planned offering a street version of his racer, with the big engine, blistered and flared fenders, the arched hood and various aerodynamic devices sticking out hither and yon. Due to the complexity of certifying such a car for federal standards and the extreme liability of putting such power into a street car, the project never came off.

Not too suprisingly, the street L82 Corvette was faster than the race car from 0-30 mph, taking 3.4 seconds to reach this speed. The Greenwood Corvette took 4.0 seconds to make 30 mph, but that was with a good deal of feathering the throttle and dancing on the clutch. Reason: Race cars are not geared for standing starts. After 30 mph, the street Corvette was lost in the dust. The Greenwood racer exploded away and took just 9.8 seconds to reach 100 mph from zero, while the street car made the century in 23.6 seconds. And, where the production car topped out at 132 mph, the Greenwood IMSA racer kept pulling until it was running over 200 mph.

After his disappointment at Le Mans and other setbacks in 1976, Greenwood retired from racing and looked after his nonracing business interests such as his name brand of Corvette body parts and aero kits. Although John Greenwood will be busy in the intervening decade, we won't hear from him again as a Corvette racer until the Corvette Challenge begins at the end of the 1980s.

Mom Always Liked Your Downshifts Best

In 1971, John Greenwood called Dick Smothers and asked him to co-drive one of his Corvettes in some upcoming endurance races. At that time Smothers was a well-known national figure who had taken quickly to motor sports. His comedy-variety show with brother Tommy was a huge if controversial hit on network TV.

Smothers began racing as a lark but soon discovered that he had a natural talent for it. He was also very cautious, not wanting a severe accident to end his booming TV career. Greenwood said Smothers was the best co-driver he ever had.

Old Sting Rays don't die, they just get more radical. The past and the present of Corvette racing dice it up at Laguna Seca in 1977. By now, chin spoilers and other aerodynamic aids had made the older racing Sting Rays competitive again. Dave Friedman

At that same race in 1977 at Laguna Seca, Sam Posey puts his Datsun 280Z racer in front of a local big-block roadster. As Dick Smothers said, it's good that Posey is an announcer now. Dave Friedman

Smothers was defensive and he wasn't going to do something stupid. Greenwood liked that Smothers didn't crash the cars.

And if Smothers ran three to four seconds behind Greenwood, that was fine; they still won plenty of races that way, including the hard-fought Sebring of 1976. Greenwood said that Smothers would use his head and not get into trouble. These traits made him an excellent endurance driver. He was consistent, respectful of the power of his ride and cool-headed.

For endurance races, Greenwood would start and go like hell, then Smothers would take the car and keep up a steady pace, maybe losing a little ground. Then Greenwood would get in the car at the end and make a banzai charge for the lead and the win.

Smothers was not freeloading on Greenwood's reputation or grandstanding for publicity. From the mid 1960s to the mid 1970s, he was a serious racer.

Specifications, Production and Racing Corvettes, 1976

	Production	**Greenwood Racing**
Price	$7,605	$35,000
General specifications		
Weight (lb.)	3,610 (curb)	2,885 (race)
Weight distribution (%)	49:51	47:53
Track, front/rear (in.)	58.7/59.5	59.5/64.2
Length (in.)	185.2	187.0
Width (in.)	69.0	82.0
Height (in.)	48.0	47.0
Ground clearance (in.)	4.4	3.0
Usable trunk space (cu.ft.)	4.4	none
Fuel capacity (gal.)	17.0	32.0
Engine		
Bore x Stroke (mm)	101.6x88.4	109.5x101.6
Displacement (cc/ci)	5,737/350	7,654/467
Compression ratio	9:1	11.8:1
Bhp @ rpm (net)	210@5200	700@6800
Torque @ rpm (lb-ft)	255@3600	629@4000
Induction	One Rochester 4V	Greenwood magnesium cross ram
Fuel requirement	Unleaded 91 oct.	Premium 102 oct.
Drivetrain		
Gear ratios:		
4th	1.00	1.00
3rd	1.23	1.27
2nd	1.61	1.64
1st	2.43	2.20
Final-drive ratio	3.55:1	2.73:1
Chassis		
Brake system	11.75 in. vented discs front and rear, vacuum assisted	12.1 in. vented discs front and rear
Swept area (sq.in.)	498	497
Wheels	Cast alloy, 8x15 in.	Sterling; 11x15 in. front, 17x15 in. rear
Tires	Firestone Steel Radial 500, GR70-15	Goodyear Blue Streak; 24.5x10-15 front, 28.0x17-15 rear
Front suspension	Unequal-length A-arms, coil springs, tube shocks, antiroll bar	Unequal-length A-arms, coil springs, Koni adjustable tube shocks, antiroll bar
Rear suspension	Lower lateral arms, axle shafts as upper lateral arms, transverse leaf spring, tube shocks, antiroll bar	Unequal-length A-arms, coil springs, Koni adjustable tube shocks, antiroll bar

Source: *Road & Track.*

An example of the Greenwood bodystyle. To accommodate ultrawide racing slicks and improve aerodynamics, Greenwood came up with the full-race Corvette body. It was bought by many racers, and copied by others. This car is the Oyler-Murrati-Smit racer at Sebring in 1977. Dave Friedman

Looking like a kid, but serious and talented, Dick Smothers began racing as a hobby when his TV show was one of the most popular and irreverent in the United States. Teamed up with the mercurial John Greenwood, the steady and reliable Smothers made an ideal teammate.

"It was serendipity or something," Dick Smothers said. "We were right in the midst of 'The Smothers Brothers Comedy Hour' on CBS and I was asked to be Grand Marshall for the old, now-defunct Easter races in Santa Barbara. Nick Reynolds, the old Kingston Trio guy, was a racer out there and a bunch of other people. I had never even seen a race or been to a race in my life—wait, during the war, World War II, my grandpa took me to see some indoor midget races in LA. I think they were on boards, banked.

"But I was born liking cars; as a kid I knew every car, every make, everything about them. And I just sort of liked cars, but it never entered my mind to be a race driver.

"So about 1967, I went to the Easter thing, was Grand Marshall, and Max Balchowski had *Ol' Yeller* there; it was like an old jalopy—had all these Stromberg downdraft carburetors on it. If you didn't keep your foot all the way on the floor, it would spit gas back at you. It had machine guns on the hood, and oh, God, was it yellow!"

Smothers continued: "I got to do a pace lap in it. And then after the race, the winner of the race was Scooter Patrick in a 906 and I got to sit in it for his victory lap—and he scared the holy bejesus out of me. And I know he was only doing a cool-off lap. But I'd never been in a car where you shifted at 7000 rpm. And I thought, 'This is frightening.'

"But a short time after that, Hugh Powell asked me to sponsor his Group 7 car. When you're on television, everybody thinks you've got a zillion dollars, and I said, 'I don't want to put any money into it.' He said, 'No, just your name will help us get sponsorship.' So, I said, 'That sounds like fun.'

"So to get me into the Group 7 racing he asked me up to Willow Springs to watch them test. So I did and it was a Lola and they had the Jim Russell school for driving there at the racetrack. They put me in a Formula Ford and they put a little helmet on me and I went around real slow. So I did three laps at that school and bought Lou Sell's Formula B Brabham. When I do something, I just do it real quick."

Because amateur racing was not his style, Smothers went pro and created a race team which bought the first Dan Gurney Formula 5000 Eagle and, "Lou Sell won the championship for Smothers Brothers Racing. The fields were so small, they put us in the same fields. Now, these are 450 horse-

Graduating quickly from smaller Formula cars, Smothers bought himself a Chevron Formula B racer and had a couple of good seasons with it before joining Greenwood in his wins at Sebring and the assaults on Le Mans.

As the 1970s turned into the 1980s, Corvettes went Trans-Am racing. One of the leading Corvette Trans-Am drivers was Greg Pickett, seen here in a Morrison Trans-Am car at Road Atlanta. A complete tube-frame design by Bob Riley, this car was fast, but came at a time when lighter turbocharged four-cylinder cars were cleaning up. Morrison Motorsports

power cars, racing with Formula B, which had 175 horsepower. So you learn very quickly to watch your mirrors.

"I remember that at Lime Rock, I beat Sam Posey at his home track. He was driving a Caldwell Formula A, and Caldwell was a weird designer. If you recall, Sam drove a rigid-axle Group 7 car. No independent suspension whatsoever. Sam was not

You don't want to see Greg Pickett's eyes in your rearview mirror on a Trans-Am circuit. Chevrolet

Darrin Brassfield took over for Greg Pickett in the Mobil 1 Trans-Am Corvette in 1988. Although this car was fast and competitive, it could not run away from the turbocharged Ford Mustangs and Merkurs. Chevrolet

too smart but very brave. I'm glad that he's an announcer now, and not dead.

"So within about a year after I was driving *Ol' Yeller,* and had Scooter Patrick scaring me, I bought, from Fred Baker, a 906E Porsche. It was the last factory long-nose ever made. In fact it was a factory race car and Fred got it from them. It had never lost a distance race. So Fred and I drove at Sebring and we won our class.

"That was the week we taped the Smothers Brothers show with Dan Rowan, from Rowan and Martin, standing in for me. That was the show that got the Smothers Brothers fired from television. That's a day that will live in infamy; it was '69. We finished about sixth overall in this little two-liter car. And, boy I had the bug. I was really very strong in racing at that time."

But with his career changing rapidly, Smothers pulled back on his privately financed racing activities. From out of the blue John Greenwood called Smothers.

"He just approached me and asked if I wanted to drive some endurance races with him," Smothers said. "And I'd never been offered a ride where I didn't have to pay through the nose. So, that sounded great to me.

"Greenwood said, 'Hey man, I've got these huge engines and we'll just smoke 'em. We've only got one problem. B.F. Goodrich is our sponsor and we have to race on street tires.' Those were the first 60 series radials, and they'd shave the tread down. And we won the races. Kept on winning the races with these cars.

"I raced Sebring with him and we won our class there. I missed Daytona. I never did drive Daytona 24 Hours; I really regret that. And Greenwood was clocked at 196 mph on the banking at Daytona, with street tires. Goodyear was ready to sue Goodrich.

"We went to Brainerd and won a race up there and the Watkins Glen Six Hour. But then we started having some reliability problems. You know how you get, you want bigger and stronger engines. We had probably 455s or whatever they were. And with 700 horsepower, the engines started getting fragile."

Smothers was favorably impressed with the Greenwood Corvette as a race car. "It was a stable car. You felt safe as hell in it. Directional stability was terrific. Where it felt uncomfortable to me was when we were going those extreme speeds at Le Mans. It felt like it was dancing. The thing seemed to work, like flex. And not the chassis, the body. It would shimmer at that speed.

"On a normal track, like Brainerd or Sebring, it was like a rocket. It was just terrific. And Sebring is a rough track."

However, Smothers acknowledged that the Greenwood race car had some faults too: "The car jumped; it made noises. The chassis was made to go 200 mph. It wasn't like my formula car. Jeez, you could file your nails in there.

"It was a heavy car and it felt heavy in the tight turns. Very heavy, ponderous. The brakes were not a real problem. We never screwed up the brakes. I was always told, the same thing when I drove the NART Ferrari, that if there's a weak link in a big car like that it would be the clutch and transmission. And that turned out to be the case.

"It would pop out of first gear occasionally. And with that hard steering you'd try to take a hairpin turn in first gear and have it get into neutral each time was a drag. So, I'd hold it in gear and try to turn the wheel with one hand. I hope nobody took pictures of my racing line; it's not good.

"John is well into six feet; he may be 6 ft. 3 in. or 6 ft. 4 in. and I'm 5 ft. 9 in. So I carried a beautiful white pillow, with a beautiful lace pillowcase, to sit on. There was no formed seat, so every time John came out, we'd put the pillow behind me, strap me in and it was like peeking out of a cave."

A Good Record

By the end of the 1970s, Corvettes were once again on top in American auto sports. In the last two years of the decade their racing record is an admirable one:

1978: First Overall, SCCA Trans-Am Category II
SCCA A-Production Champion
SCCA B-Production Champion
SCCA B-Stock Solo II Champion
SCCA B-Prepared Solo II Champion
SCCA B-Stock Ladies Solo II Champion
IMSA All-American GT Champion
1979: First Overall, SCCA Trans-Am Category I
SCCA B-Production Champion
SCCA B-Stock Solo II Champion
SCCA B-Prepared Solo II Champion
SCCA B-Stock Ladies Solo II Champion
First Overall, Riverside Vintage Car Races
(Grand Sport number 003)

Downside of the "Me" Decade

Although the 1970s had been a good decade on the racetrack for Corvettes, the same was not true

Darrin Brassfield at speed in the Protofab-Morrison Mobil 1 Corvette. Brassfield specialized in throwing the *Corvette around tight city street courses, like this one at Long Beach, California.* Chevrolet

Based on the new, post 1984 bodystyle, this Trans-Am Corvette, sponsored by Electronic Data Services, the former Ross Perot company that is now a GM division, represents the latest technology in Corvette racing. Still, *it is struggling to hold off a charge by Robert Lapallainen, a Finnish driver in his black Ford turbo Rousch Mustang. Chevrolet*

for the street car. The oil embargoes of the early seventies had made for profound changes in Detroit, and had taken the big-block engines out of the Corvettes. As the 1970s drew to a close, the Corvette was limited to a 350 ci small-block engine and no fuel injection. This did not translate into a workable racing package, so Corvette victories in SCCA production racing began to taper off.

One of the most important events of the Corvette's life cycle occurred in the late 1970s, when Dave McLellan took over from Zora Arkus-Duntov as head of Corvette engineering. McLellan had been Zora's assistant for years and he had learned much from the old master. But McLellan was his own man and, much as things changed and stayed the same when Bill Mitchell took over from Harley Earl, they changed and stayed the same at Corvette engineering.

After many years of dedicated service and some of the most profound innovations in the racing and sports car world, Zora, the master, the gentle father of the Corvette was retiring. Like Shakespeare's old Prospero in the *Tempest*, Zora

was letting go of his magic, relinquishing his powers. But, Zora the man was still sharp and active. He would continue as a power in Chevrolet engineering for some time, and even in 1990 is happy to talk about his love-child, the Corvette. Yet, it was truly the end of an era.

Aided by Don Runkle and others in the new Corvette engineering group, Dave McLellan was overseeing the birth of a new Corvette that would be the best car Chevrolet ever produced; a world-class sports car that brought the best of Corvette tradition into the high-tech world of the 1980s and 1990s.

With a completely new digital fuel injection and electronic ignition, advanced digital instruments and exotic chassis components like the one-piece, single-leaf, fiberglass transverse rear spring, this new Corvette would be the most complete new car since the marque was born in 1953. Not only would the new Corvette be a solid step forward, it would soon explode as the terror of American racetracks in one of the most successful forms of racing in the 1980s— Showroom Stock.

Chapter 9

Offshore Efforts: Focus on Le Mans

As you're coming down toward the kink at 200-some miles an hour, you have to kick the car sideways, still on full power and the car drifts through that turn to the other side. You've just got to make a decision to do it, and you just kinda throw it in. It's interesting.

—John Greenwood, on Le Mans

It's dawn in the French Chateaux country of the Loire Valley. You're in a region of picturesque old mansions and lush dairy farms. The first rosy light of day is sprayed softly across the sky by diffusion from ground fog and fine drizzle.

Suddenly, out of the darkness, a dragon bursts upon you, roaring, his eyes gleaming yellow in the

In 1967 the Corvettes returned to Le Mans. Here Dick Guldstrand takes the big-block Sting Ray past the pits and timing stands at the 14 km long track. Unfortunately, *the car did not last through the night, the critical phase of the twenty-four-hour race. Dave Friedman*

117

fog. Fire shoots from his flanks as he passes, flying by you so fast that only his echoing bellow reminds you that he was here at all.

You are standing at the side of a French road, the N 158, in a northwestern province of France, about three hours drive from Paris. The road is called the Mulsanne and today it is part of the racetrack for the 24 hours of Le Mans. Now, at 6:00 a.m. we've been racing for 14 hours and there are ten more to go. Everyone you see looks exhausted, and they are.

At the spot you picked on the Mulsanne straight, a more or less ordinary piece of Gallic blacktop, cars were beginning to exceed 250 miles per hour, a speed which has recently been lowered by the shameful addition of two chicanes to the Mulsanne.

Since 1923, with a pause in 1936 and a ten-year gap from 1939 till 1949, Le Mans has been the scene of the most challenging motor sports event in all Europe, one which has powerful consequences around the world. For car makers and drivers, a win at the 24 Hours of Le Mans is a ticket to the big time, a place in history, a shot at fame and fortune. Win this race of races and you are an instant celebrity. In the whole world of motor sports only the Grand Prix at Monaco and the Indy 500 have the clout of Le Mans. For sports cars and their drivers, there is no higher ground.

It is necessary to take a shuttle bus back from that dark, damp and lonely outpost on the Mulsanne to the pit area, where many of the grandstands are. You don't want to walk because it is several miles. The track at Le Mans is so big, a golf course gets lost somewhere in the infield. And even

Briggs Cunningham was one of the greatest amateur sportsmen in the history of the USA. He also raced for and won the America's Cup in sailing, and brought American cars and drivers to the punishing 24 Hours of Le Mans. Road & Track

with thirty or more prototype racers running open exhausts in anger, when the cars move on from your section of the track, it becomes so quiet you can hear the dairy cows lowing.

The pit area is in many ways the focal point of the track. The start/finish line is there, along with the press buildings and the Bugatti Automotive Museum. Behind the grandstands, from Mason Blanche to a point past pit road, a double row of concessionaires in tents offer everything the racing fan could desire—from sausage and eggs breakfast to T-Shirts with a cartoon of the Queen of England driving a Jaguar XJR-9.

Croissants have been baked at the track over-night and platters of them are stacked at the front of the concession booths. They give off a heady smell and a whisp of steam. If you buy a hot chocolate to warm up from the damp, chill night, it's served in a glass soup bowl, also steaming. Made with the local, fresh milk, this chocolate is so good that you have to stop yourself from ordering a third one.

For those with stouter tastes, beer, wine and brandy are available around the clock. For those with insomnia a huge carnival has been rioting all night, with riders on the Ferris wheel screaming as the cars rocket by below them.

I Came, I Saw, I Corvette

To many American racers, a win at Le Mans represents the pinnacle of success in road racing. Not only is the contest twenty-four unending hours long, beating the Europeans at their own game is sweeter than a win at U.S. endurance races. While Ford had a very successful factory program at Le Mans in the sixties with the GT40s and Mk IVs, Chevrolet, as a manufacturer, has never been interested in the race. As an American car maker which does not export its products to Europe in volume, Chevrolet has concentrated on its home turf with NASCAR, SCCA and more recently IMSA.

Nevertheless, Corvette, with its heavy infusion of European blood via Zora Arkus-Duntov, has always had an infatuation with Le Mans, although it has never managed to win the prestigious twenty-four-hour contest.

Factory support notwithstanding, several private teams, including native Frenchmen, have raced Corvettes at Le Mans, often qualifying and running up front until they suffered from a variety of mechanical problems, many of them engine- or drivetrain-related. No Corvette has ever won Le Mans.

It seems that, while Chevy engines do fine for most racing, there are few or no engine builders who really know how to make them last for twenty-four hours under the high speeds and inclement weather conditions at Le Mans.

Arkus-Duntov was a young lad in Belgium and he doubtless heard legends of Le Mans, stories of the great Bentleys and Bugattis. As a young adult he had raced at Le Mans several times and loved the place. His pet Corvette racing projects often involved plans to send factory Corvettes to the French race, especially the Super Sport and the Grand Sports, but fate, budget and politics always intervened. He would never get to race one of his own Corvettes at Le Mans.

Briggs Brings 'Em

So it's probably fitting that Briggs Cunningham should be the first American privateer to take a team of Corvettes to France in 1961. Cunningham brought three Corvettes, painted in his distinctive colors: White bodies with a wide double blue stripe running from nose to tail down the center of the cars.

Cunningham was one of the more colorful men in the history of U.S. motor sports. Although he was a rich boy from a Cincinnati banking family, he was also a guardian angel to American auto racing and the prototype for many other young, wealthy men who would follow him to prominence in international motor sports, such as Peter Revson, Lance Reventlow and Sam Posey.

Briggs was the picture of the dashing playboy of his time. In his prime he was tanned, handsome and liked to dress well but casually. His interests included flying, golfing, yachting and eventually automobile racing. Toward the end of his life he founded one of the major collections of competition and classic cars in the world, which was housed in Southern California. After his death, much of that collection was sold to the Collier Museum in Florida.

In the late forties, Briggs joined the Sports Car Club of America, which had only a handful of members at that time. He loved the excitement of racing, the thrills. He had a special car built for himself, a hot rod. He took the chassis and body of a Mercedes SSK racer and had a Buick V-8 put into it! He drove this "BuMerc" at SCCA races in his home state of Connecticut and around New England, collecting a second place finish at Watkin's Glen in 1948.

For the 1950 running of Le Mans, Briggs had two cars with Cadillac power. One, with a special streamlined body, was appropriately nicknamed "Le Monstre" by the French. His other entry was a mostly-stock Coupe deVille. Both cars finished the race, the "Monstre" taking 10th place and the Coupe deVille right behind it in 11th.

Cunningham's 1961 Corvettes were equipped with 283 fuelies, RPO 685 chassis and suspension options, and had cut-down wind screens. They were driven by Dick Thompson, Walt Hansgen, John Fitch, Bob Grossman, Windridge and Cunningham himself.

"A very easy person to get along with," said John Fitch of Cunningham, "very undemanding, very considerate."

"Briggs Cunningham was a wonderful guy," echoed Thompson. "He created a wonderful atmosphere for everybody there. He would never try to pressure anybody to do better, just to go out and have fun. There was never any pressure with Briggs. He was a sportsman. This was sport, it wasn't business. And he treated it as such and wanted us to treat it as such.

"It was a little hard for us at times. Walt Hansgen was a very competitive guy and I think I was too. And sometimes we had a little problem with that attitude. But it did create a very relaxed atmosphere. Briggs just wanted you to have a good time and don't wreck the car."

But even with Cunningham's experience and deep pockets, the Corvettes he had shipped to Le Mans were about the same as the cars which raced at Sebring.

"The cars had very little changes from the normal SCCA race cars that you would see," Thompson said. "We again had brake problems there. That was really the only problems we had. The cars ran very well.

"Kinda shook up some of the French observers because it was a great big car on little skinny tires, so we did a lot of sideways driving and that upset them a little bit, but after they realized that that was the only way you could drive the thing, well, they accepted that and the cars went very well."

Despite careful preparation, the Corvettes were racked by their chronic problem: bad brakes. This not only contributed to the wear on the engines but stressed drivers as well. Hurtling around the French track at racing speeds with little or no brake left is the act of a very courageous

Bob Bondurant concentrates on hitting an apex at Le Mans in 1967. A small part failed on the car's engine and put the Corvette out of the race. Dave Friedman

man. When the rains and fog came in the early morning hours, it made the race even more difficult for the Cunningham team.

Thompson was amazed by Le Mans. "The whole thing was quite an experience. Particularly the first time there, at night in the fog and rain and whatnot. Because about half the time, you're out of sight of anybody! It's like going through the countryside at night in the rain as fast as you can go. You don't see anything. You may see a flagman about every fifth turn, and no spectators, no nothing. You're out there all by yourself.

"Then when you come past the pits, there are all kinds of lights on everything, and then all of a sudden you flash out of that and you're in the countryside again. The weather conditions of it, the time element, going the twenty-four hours. And usually they have that morning fog. Our shifts were an hour and a half to two hours of racing. You usually figure a tankful of gas, and that would generally take an hour and a half to two hours.

"Brakes took out my car only indirectly. The engine finally blew, but it had been over-revved by about a thousand rpm on the tell-tale tach. And not trying to go faster but it was the downshifts, trying to get it slowed down. And the motor finally gave up on us. And the car that finished had a head gasket go, undoubtedly from the same sort of thing. And the third car got caught in a thunderstorm with dry tires on it and got wrecked."

John Fitch said about his eighth-place Corvette, "We were losing coolant and there was a very imaginative technician from Chevrolet. Le Mans limits the periods when you can put coolant in the car, and the engine was overheating badly and we would have lost the engine had we carried any speed at all. So he got ice from the drink cooler and, since we couldn't put water in the radiator, packed the manifold between the banks of the engine with ice. And that cooled it down enough that we were able to finish the race."

A First in "GT" Class

Even with these problems, the Fitch/Grossman Corvette placed well—in the top ten: eighth—and was first in the GT class, much the same as it had fared at Sebring in 1957 with a less-experienced crew. "We were delighted to finish at all," Fitch said. "It rained during the race and I liked to drive in the rain because I could see well. Dick Thompson told me in 1987, in Monterey, that during one rain period I picked up seven places. I didn't know that!"

The race was won by Paul Frere and Oliver Gendebien in a 3.0 liter, V-12 Ferrari. Other Ferraris took second through seventh places. A Corvette was eighth, an Aston Martin ninth, and another Corvette, entered by Lucky Casner's Camoradi Racing Team was tenth. These two top-ten finishes for Corvette are, surprisingly, the best record for Corvette at Le Mans overall, and they came in the car's very first attempt.

Guldstrand and Bondurant in 1967

Another Corvette stalwart who made the long march to Le Mans and back was Dick Guldstrand. It seemed like there was magic in the air in 1967 as Corvettes once again put on their long-distance shoes. Could this be the year for a Le Mans win? For Guldstrand, the ride at Le Mans came as a natural part of his growing career as a driver.

"I'd had the privilege of working with Penske and the whole crew, George Wintersteen, and all running the Daytona car in '66," Guldstrand said. "And I'd had some other rides in stock cars and so

The same car, as restored for the Chevrolet weekend at Monterey Historic Races in 1987. While some things are different about the car, as the photos indicate, it is still wild, different and looks like it's ready to cruise outer space. Greg Von Dare

At Le Mans in 1976, the John Greenwood Corvette was a side show of its own. The French loved the car for its speed and radical shape. Road & Track

on and then the Indy ride which I ultimately crashed and it about killed me. And that was pretty much the end of my career with Mr. Penske.

"I was looking for something else to do. And I worked with Bondurant in that movie 'Grand Prix', and I was manager of Dana Chevrolet, and there was a lot of things going on. I got out of the hospital and we started work on a Group 7 car, a prototype, so it was going pretty good. And I thought wouldn't it be great if we could have a Stingray win all three, Daytona, Sebring *and* Le Mans. So that caught on at Dana and Peyton Cramer who owned the company, or was general manager decided that that was a great idea.

"So he went to Botany Clothes and got sponsorship, and here comes a brand new L88, '67, which we of course took all apart and made all the changes and went to Le Mans."

Those Crazy Californians

Guldstrand laughed, "And you should have seen those crazy Californians at Le Mans! First of all they weren't going to let us run the car. You know, it was too heavy, everything was wrong, we didn't have the right lights or numbers, and on and on. They were just giving us a fit.

"So we finally got through inspection. And we set the track record, which held for a long, long time. And led the race for twelve, fourteen hours, something like that. We dominated the GT category. And then to blow it up, you know? That was devastating.

"But that's motor racing, and it was some penny-ante part, a wrist pin, that did it. I wanted a better one, but Chevrolet wouldn't homologate it, they wanted the car to be completely stock. I knew it might be trouble, and you should always go with that [notion], but I didn't, so . . . To have come that far . . .

"But, when you beat the Mercedes, you beat the Jaguar and you beat the little Porsche; that old 'Vette, it was second to none, man! Nobody was getting in your way. Nobody. It was the best there was. We showed them the short way around those race tracks!"

Parlez-vous Greenwood?

After winning the twenty-four-hour race at Daytona in 1971, John Greenwood had shown that he knew how to make Corvettes last over the long haul of an endurance race. Always eager to expand his operations to the limit, Greenwood decided to tackle Le Mans in 1972. A fast qualifying time and a good showing in the early hours of the race came to nothing when both big-blocks exploded over night.

Undaunted, Greenwood returned in 1973. But with all his racing and other projects running simultaneously, Greenwood's preparation wasn't up to that of his first year. His team again qualified well, but the race saw Greenwood stop far short of the finish line.

When the opportunity came for Greenwood to go in 1976, he jumped at it. He would not only have a chance to race again at one of his favorite places, but he would represent America with a Corvette in the Bicentennial year.

"In '72 and '73," Greenwood remembered, "a guy who was working for us actually took care of everything for us over in France, Benoit Froget. He became one of the top people at Le Mans, at the race track, and today is the head man of Le Mans. He's also the head of some of the production racing series over there and he's working with IMSA right now, putting together a combined GTP and Group C rules.

"He was instrumental in our going in '76. But, we didn't really make a deal to go there until two weeks before the race. When we went the other years, we probably spent four months doing logistics and then two months preparing for it, at least. And the logistics of getting everything ready, the people and everything lined up ready to go over there is tremendous.

"He more than helped us. Set up everything but the car. He got us over there, the crew and everybody and all the equipment, and got us through customs and to the race track, and our places to stay and garages to work out of and the whole shot.

"The two cars that I would have taken, I had [taken] so far apart that there wouldn't have been any way of putting them together again in a two week period of time. So what I had to do was borrow one of my customer cars.

"Rick Mancuso, who owns Lake Forest Sports Cars in Chicago, has a Ferrari dealership and all that, loaned me the GTO car that he had at our shop that was his. And we went ahead and repainted it our colors and prepared it and took that car over there.

"The car ran real well. We actually had a brand new fuel cell come apart at the seams. It literally separated and wouldn't hold gas at all, so it put us out of the race. It didn't happen until the race, in the first few hours of the race. And we tried to find something else to put in place of it, but there wasn't anything that would fit in the space that we had. So we were out of it."

Smothers Gets Frenched

Dick Smothers went with Greenwood to Le Mans in 1976. Smothers had been one of Greenwood's best co-drivers. And now that a rush was on, Greenwood wanted Smothers because he knew that he could last. For Smothers, it was a great time.

One Corvette Lap of Le Mans
(with John Greenwood)

"With the Le Mans track and the Daytona track, there was a similar set-up as far as gearing and everything. The car would do 103 miles an hour in first gear. You can imagine that the car would lumber a bit coming out of the slow turns. Which, fortunately at Le Mans, there was only one of.

"Coming down the start/finish straightaway at Le Mans, they've got big grandstands on one side, the left side, the whole length of the straight, and on the whole right side is the pit lane and the pit lane has lounges over the full length of the pit lane.

"So you come out of a slow turn onto the start/finish straightaway and that is a first gear turn and you're going 30-40 miles an hour. You accelerate through first gear there, go into second gear, into third gear. Now you're coming up to a right hander in third gear and you're still passing the grandstands and everything. And then you start coming around a full throttle, right hand sweeper, in third gear, still accelerating. That's where they have that Dunlop bridge, that famous tire that you come under.

"So just before the bridge you kind of straighten the car out so that as you come under the bridge, the car gets airborne and you're going in a straight line when the car lands.

"Now you're coming down a hill and still accelerating. At the bottom of the hill there's a 90-degree left-hand turn. All the turns there, generally, except for maybe a couple coming back toward the start/finish straightaway, have a little bit of bank to 'em.

"We don't drive the cars like today's GTO cars or GTP cars or like a Porsche would where they actually picked the fastest arc that they can drive through the corner. With the Corvettes, what we actually used was a drifting line.

"You'd either get on your brakes and start the car coming sideways and go back on hard throttle while the car's drifting, or like at Daytona you'd just jerk the car sideways while you're still on full throttle and start a drift.

"The car liked a real late apex line, a real understeering line. It seemed like an understeering line, because once you started your drift there was no steering other than letting off the throttle or more throttle. You could turn the wheels back and forth and it wouldn't have made any difference. So you had to point the car the direction you wanted to come out the other side. Whatever angle you wanted it to come out the other side is what you put it at before you went into the turn.

"Now you're coming down this hill and then you start braking hard to go into this left hander and you bring it down into second gear. And before you get off the brakes you turn the steering just a little bit and bring the back end around sideways and go back onto hard throttle.

"Now this track has guardrail all the way around. What I would do with that car is start drifting and come in to the apex and come up over the white lines. There was probably a whole car width between the white line and the guardrail. And I would come right up to the guardrail drifting through and then as I came across the apex on the left side and just cleared the guardrail, then I would flip the car back the other way and actually turn so that you're drifting in the opposite direction now to go into a right-hander. So what you're doing is going through a couple of tight esses there.

"That right-hander had even a little more bank to it, so you just stayed right on full power while you were accelerating, and again go over the white lines toward the guardrail. And you come out straight the other way, heading toward the next right hand turn that goes onto the Mulsanne straighaway.

"So there you go from second gear into third gear and accelerate up through that right hander and back down into second gear and, I believe into first gear there."

The Infamous Mulsanne

"Start drifting, making your right-hand turn, and again come close to the guardrail on the inside then all the way to the guardrail on the outside. And you go through first gear quickly, now you're going downhill and then you go into second gear, into third gear, and you're still going downhill and it doesn't level off until you're in high gear. You really bring your speed up quickly because you're going downhill.

"Now the different times we ran there, with B.F. Goodrich in '72 and '73, and then when we ran with this GTO car, each of those years and in '76 we had the fastest car on the straightaway. So, even though we had to detune the engine to run on pump gas, and the street gas they had there wasn't very high octane. The car would probably go 215-220, somewhere in there. And the year we're talking about '86, we had that cross ram injection, so the car was pretty fast.

"Anyway, you get down to the bottom of that hill and I would say that within three-quarters of a mile you're probably up to full speed. And now you're going down the straightaway, the Mulsanne. When you drive this road in a street car at 60 mph, it seems perfectly flat, perfectly smooth. And then, when you get down to the kink at the end of the Mulsanne straightaway, you don't even hardly realize you're in a turn, it's so long. At speed the car has some pretty high-velocity altitude changes as it's going down the straightaway. And so the car is going up and down and you're passing people and there's little restaurants on either side of the guardrail, which is interesting.

"As you're coming down toward the kink at 200-some miles an hour, you have to kick the car sideways, still on full power and the car drifts through that turn to the other side. You've just got to make a decision to do it, and you just kinda throw it in. It's interesting.

"So you drift on through that and you come up to a hill, you're still accelerating, and you come up over the hill and you start braking as you go down the other side. It's going to be a first gear, right-hand turn, and right there is where the signaling pits are."

Back to the Start/Finish Line

"You go all the way down to first gear, make a right-hand turn and start accelerating again in front of the signal pits. And then you accelerate down a chute that's probably three-quarters of a mile long. You might even get into fourth for a moment. And then you start bringing it back down and you get into second gear and you go into a banked, sweeping right-hand turn and imme-diately into a banked, sweeping, left-hand turn. So you've got the esses right there.

"Then you come out of that turn and you go through two gears, probably back into third gear and then back down into second, down into first for a sharp right-hand turn. Even though it's more than 90 degrees, it's probably six lanes wide so you get to drift out and go through first gear, second gear, third gear and fourth gear, and then you start braking for a sweeping, second-gear right-hander and then left-hander.

"These turns are like off-camber. So those turns are the only ones on the track, even though they are two high-speed sweepers, the car doesn't just absolutely dig in. Then you come around for a tight right-hander onto a short chute and then you come up to a set of first-gear esses to come back on to the start/finish straightaway."

Dick Smothers, seen here with his mentor Lou Sell, was John Greenwood's co-driver at Le Mans in 1976. But again a simple problem, this time a ruptured fuel cell, put their car out of the race when it was one of the fastest cars on the track, hitting over 200 mph on the famous Mulsanne back straightaway.

"We took the cars over there and we stayed in the little town of Louer. Masten Gregory was staying there with the NART Ferrari team. A tiny little town with no stop lights. About 60 kilometers out of Le Mans. I'd never been to Europe in my life. We were there ten days early to acclimatize.

"So my girlfriend and I acclimatized in Paris for four or five days, went all over the place and ended up in this wonderful little town and went to the track a lot. And tested and tested. And the cars just seemed fantastic.

"And there are people sitting outside at this tiny restaurant. They're on the left as you hit the first dogleg in the Mulsanne. And people are just sitting there drinking their booze. And a little tiny metal barrier, I didn't know then, but they were just stuck in the dirt. You hit them and it's a catapult.

"What John didn't do and I wished he had, and it's real easy to look backwards, to take out the qualifying engines and for at least one car have a reliable engine. We started the race with my engine that had a miss, and we lost reliability. I tried to take it real easy and I almost spun out on the second turn. In fact, I almost spun out on the pace lap. That puckered me up a little bit.

"Once the race started it was so much fun. I would pass cars. I would *wave* at cars. We passed every production Ferrari. You know they were going to nail us with those Daytonas. They were not even close!

"This was a stock-bodied, stock-engined car, extensively modified of course, but this was not a tube-frame racing car. To push that thing through the air at over 200 mph, it was a pretty healthy engine. But the only way to overcome the penalty of our street tires was to have ungodly speed and make it up that way. That was the first race I was ever frightened in my life.

"I never really did settle in at Le Mans. It was a beautiful race track to drive. But you're passing these little production cars at maybe 60 miles an hour difference. You really have to watch that car; hope that he's doing what you think he's doing and be ready for any, any thing. When you're going that fast, 180 and up, even if he twitches and touches you you're into those trees. You just guessed wrong. Jo Bonnier got killed in that race."

The Big Oiseau—Corvette/Eagle

Paul Canary is a Corvette racer who worked his way up through SCCA club racing, national runoffs and into IMSA GT classes. He drove a distinctive yellow Corvette in endurance races in the eighties. In 1990, Canary, Jim Bruckner, Jay Drake, engine builder Joe Schubek, driver Dennis Kazmerowski, and Corvette stalwart John Greenwood went to Le Mans with a racer that is at least in some small part a Corvette.

They took one of the Corvette GTP cars (see Chapter 11), which was originally a Lola chassis, and fitted it with a magnificent 10-liter Eagle engine, designed and built by Schubek. This DOHC, four-valve-per-cylinder, 621-ci monster bellowed like a tyrannosaurus and made over 1,000 normally-aspirated hp.

However, like many other Corvettes at Le Mans, the engine and drivetrain of the Eagle didn't survive more than a half dozen laps of practice on the week preceding the twenty-four-hour classic in June of 1990. The Eagle Performance Racing Team planned to return in 1991 if funding was found.

Chapter 10

Straight-Line Speed at Bonneville, the Dry Lakes and the Drags

Usually when you spin at Bonneville, everything happens so fast that you don't have time to be scared; you might afterwards. But at the time you just hold on and, what's the old saying, clean out your shorts.

—Bruce Geisler, Long Course Racer

We just run straight racing gas, no alcohol or propoline oxide, just racing gas. We don't take any free horsepower, all the speed we've gained, we've

earned. With the white car we're looking to go about 230 mph with a small block. If we don't make it, it don't matter—we'll just come back the next year and try harder.

—Alan "Bucky" Goddard,
Bonneville Corvette Mechanic

With their high power-to-weight ratio, streamlined shape and wealth of speed parts, Corvettes seem like a natural for drag racing and setting top

The classic American face-off, Cobra against Corvette. Tony Stoer prepares to take a small-block Cobra against a '59 solid-axle at the Henderson Drags. Don't know who won, but the solid-axle Corvette was no slouch on the drag strip. Dave Friedman

Out on the salt, this B-Grand Touring Corvette is staged at the starting line. Corvettes have a proud history on the Bonneville salt flats, but when the Sting Ray came along with its independent rear suspension, it was not as stable *at top speeds as the older solid-axle 'Vettes. The driver had to stay between the two wide black lines to validate a speed record run.* Dave Friedman

speed records on the dry lakes of southern California and the desolate Bonneville Salt Flats.

Yet, surprisingly, Corvettes are not known as world-beating cars at the drag strip or the "salt." Yes, they are fast, and they do win races. But cubic inches is the story in straight-line racing, not good handling and sophisticated suspensions. If you are racing on the quarter mile, you want a whopping-big Chrysler/Keith Black Hemi. Even a Rat motor is not the same.

O.K., that's oversimplifying. There is class racing on the quarter mile, bracket racing and so on. But as for cubic inches being the main thing, not good handling, that's still true.

While Corvettes were reshaping American road racing, they had a lesser impact on the very private world of the long-course racers at Bonneville and the California dry lakes and the riotous circus of pro dragsters. Yet, the folks who stop their cars with parachutes have always had a soft spot for Chevy's pride and joy.

Solid Axle, Solid Performer

Few Corvette racers have competed with the passion and determination of Bruce Geisler, a long-course racer. And few have had more fun. Within the friendly and supportive atmosphere of the top speed kings, Bruce Geisler and his Corvettes felt right at home.

Geisler began drag racing in 1951 and, "drag raced all up and down Southern California until

about 1956, when I went to the dry lakes and fell in love with the dry lakes. In fact, what happened was, I had the SR-1 Corvette. I bought it about November of '57 and I bought it from a fellow in Sioux Falls, South Dakota, and I paid $4,000 for it.

"See, it came with Halibrand knock-off mag wheels, the Cerametallix brake linings, the steering column was shortened, and all kinds of little stuff. And we never did know what was in the engine, we never tore it down. Mainly it was just blueprinted, because it ran awfully hard. And they came with a three-speed transmission, it didn't have a four-speed then. And the farmers in South Dakota kept asking him if he couldn't afford hubcaps, when he had these magnesium wheels on. So he got disgusted and that's how I got into the picture."

According to Geisler, General Motors made six of the SR-1 Corvettes. The cars were taken off the production line, sent to the racing division and stripped down to the frame and given a complete rebuild. Three of these cars were raced. Geisler bought one of the three spares.

"It's a '56," he recalled. "Everytime I mention SR-1, people think it was a '57. This was a '56, 265-cubic inch, dual four barrels, three-speed transmission, and it came with a 3.70 rear-end ratio. And it used an aftermarket type Positraction. The '56 looks just like a standard Corvette except it had these big air scoops on the side to cool the rear brakes, and it had air scoops in the front to cool the front brakes.

The Weston-Leggitt Corvette prepares for a speed run in 1965. This car is running a dual-carb setup on what must be a cross-ram manifold. The headlamps are located in the front grille, because the normal flip-over units have been glassed over. The four header pipes exit behind the front tire. Dave Friedman

"Originally I ran A-Sports Car, or whatever they called it back then. And then when the '57s came out I couldn't compete against them, even if I came out of the gate faster, they got me at the other end. Then in late '57, they created the B class and I was back in the winner's circle again.

"The SR-1 was a fantastic car, and it's a shame that when I had it, I didn't road race it at all. I had this road race car that I was drag racing. It's a shame I didn't realize what I had. My speeds were going down, so I rebuilt the engine to bring speed back up and then in 1958 I bought a brand new, in-the-crate '57 fuel-injected engine, complete. And I put it in the SR-1 and then my speeds went up to about a hundred and five, a hundred and six, seven. So it really improved it. And I moved back to South Dakota with it and eventually sold it.

"We're talking of speeds of about 120, 130 miles an hour, and with the hard top off, it would drop off about three, four miles an hour. All I had was just a windshield. But it would make a difference, that windshield would really slow you down. And then the difference between hard top and the soft top would be another mile, mile and a half top speed.

"I ran that car completely stock, the way it came from the factory. I did change gears. For drag racing I put in a 4.56. And scattershield. I tried running a velvet-touch clutch disc and that didn't work very well. The stock tach wasn't that great, so we put a Sun tach in with higher rpms.

"And I've talked to many Corvette people and at high speeds, none of them handle. Littlejohn had the same problem, and so did Bob Kehoe. They put a 9" Ford in the rear end of their late-model Corvette, to get rid of the independent suspension. Those things were really bad. With Kehoe you're talking about a 240 mile an hour Corvette, so it helps anyway."

Moroso Rides Into Business Success on a Corvette

Dick Moroso heads one of the most active and successful companies in the automotive aftermarket. A large line of speed and racing parts bear his name, and many of them originated as pieces Moroso made for himself of necessity and a small budget in the early years. He began drag racing in 1958, in Atlanta, Georgia, with a 1955 Chevy Bel Air two door hardtop.

"I drove into a used car lot one night," Moroso said, "to look at this real neat '57 fuel-injected Corvette. I was a kid in college, at Georgia Tech. I didn't have any money. I'll be damned if that guy didn't talk me into buying that car that night. He gave me a great deal. That was my first Corvette race car.

Bruce Geisler pushes his solid axle Corvette against the wind at Bonneville. Notice how light the front end is becoming. Bruce Geisler Collection

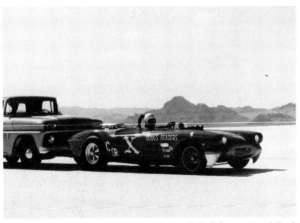

Called the X after the X-15, this modified Corvette of Jack Lufkin's was the fastest Corvette in the world for years. Seen in this trim the car ran 213 mph on the Salt Flats. Jack Lufkin Collection

"I took a real nice '57 fuelie Corvette and screwed it all up. This was before the days of the Christmas tree, y'know, and unless you had the fastest car, period, you didn't have a chance.

"The biggest class in Georgia was 'cheatin' four-barrel.' I dominated the thing with my Corvette, so they decided that there'd be no Corvettes allowed in cheatin' four-barrel.

"I did a lot of street racing back then. I had a 377 cubic inch stroker motor. The thing wouldn't start on 12 volts so I had another little battery hidden under the top because you could only have one battery in a modified production car.

"I had this little switch from J.C. Whitney, and I would push the button and get 24 volts to crank it. I didn't know what I was doing then and I must have had about 17:1 compression. I'd go down and buy aircraft gas at the airport, cause the thing would ping in 'neutral,' you know?

"The year I was most successful was 1966. I ran in the 11-pound class, C-Modified and D-Modified sports. I held the record in C-production."

When Moroso went to Englishtown dragstrip in 1966, he suddenly discovered a new class, B-Modified. Moroso "put a tremendous hole shot," on his competitor and beat the record by .12 of a second. But, the officials threw him out because you had to run within a .10 to be legal.

"I won the class at Indy and I got to the final in street eliminator and broke a clutch. I'll never

Lufkin stands confidently next to the X before a record run. Because he was a master engine builder with years of experience at Bonneville, Lufkin drove his home built Corvette faster than any other man of his generation. Jack Lufkin Collection

forget. It was a Weber clutch and it had little eyebolts and they used to break when you put big springs in 'em.

"The next year I became partners with Jerry Stahl. And in '68 I moved back to Connecticut and started Moroso Performance and I didn't have much time to race.

"Back then we didn't know any better but we put an I-beam between the front suspension and the frame which raised the front end way up, and you had tons of ground clearance. We didn't have a dyno or anything, but it definitely picked the thing up. I used to run Dover Dragstrip and win just about every week. So people would see something like that and say, 'gee could you build me one of those?'

"So we started building oil pans, a kid named Jimmy Palmer and me. His father owned a sheet metal shop where we'd go to work at night. Then we designed a hood scoop, a takeoff on something I saw Grumpy Jenkins build, a rear-opening scoop, but I made it real wide at the base by the windshield and funnelled it down hoping to force more air in there. A lot of people wanted those too, and that's kinda how I got into the parts business.

"I had an exotic suspension I built myself on my '61. I had a single bar and I had a flimsy single leaf spring and some airlifts. It was just to get the car launched straight. My trick was to put the thing on the floor and slide my foot off the clutch. And I had a suspension that would work with that style. I would shift at about 7500 rpm, but I'd come off the line a lot higher than that.

"We didn't have any dynos, so I have no idea what kind of horsepower it was making. I'd guess somewhere in the 425-450 range. Now they'd probably be making more like 600! I held the record at a 12.12-second run in C-Modified. And I could run 11.90s at about 113 mph. After that I just got too involved in the business and didn't have the time or the desire to go racing."

Moroso is known today for his line of speed parts, which are used by street racers, drag racers and the top-of-the-heap Busch Grand National and Winston Cup circle track racers. Moroso also heads a competitive Winston Cup race team himself and spends time commuting between his race shop in Georgia and his home in the Florida Keys.

The Boys of Bonneville

Jack Lufkin is a tall, good-natured guy who can, in the space of a morning, tell you about building a jet car, and take you for a ride in his near-perfect, original, unrestored Model T station hack, a car that starts up with a cheeky rattle after a few seconds of cranking.

Lufkin is one of the most respected men on the salt. He may not be the fastest man ever at Bonneville but he's one of the most experienced and one of the most fiercely competitive, despite his friendly nature. Lufkin has owned, prepared and driven some of the fastest Corvettes to ever grace that

There's no voodoo magic in one of Lufkin's engines, just a thorough knowledge of the craft of engine building and tuning, and a tremendous attention to detail. As far as the eye can see, this is a typical performance Corvette engine with the Hilborn injectors and Vertex magneto. Jack Lufkin Collection

Lufkin used a tube space frame for his world record Corvette, the X. The solid axle is preferred at Bonneville, but the front suspension is Lufkin's own work. Having learned about front suspension from Indy-master Frank Kurtis, Lufkin always put his own brand of front end on his speed record cars. Jack Lufkin Collection

outpost of desolation, the Bonneville Salt Flats, outside Wendover, Utah.

"The Corvette that I made my mark with was a '62 Corvette," said Lufkin as he reminisced in the office of Ak Miller's shop. Lufkin is a longtime employee of Miller's. They have shared many trips to Bonneville and between them have owned a fistful of class speed records for everything from flathead Ford roadsters to jet-powered Land Speed Record attempts.

"This car was the first gasoline-powered, normally-aspirated car to go 200 miles an hour," Lufkin smiled, showing me his Corvette. "That's the one I got in the 200 MPH Club with. It had 302 cubic inches, Hilborn injectors, straight pipes, a Vertex magneto. We were in a center spread photo in *Hot Rod* magazine in 1963 with that car. It was a beauty; it was a pretty car. It had a 'takeoff' of a stock body, a lightweight fiberglass body. And there were three of them made. This one, Dave MacDonald used to race one. He had the original one, and I had the second one and there was one more.

"I built my car out of a stock Corvette chassis and it finally went 213 miles an hour at Bonneville. After we had established a record at 193, I started drag racing it as well as running it at Bonneville. In '63 it went 176, which was a new record. And later, it kept going faster and faster and in '64 was when I got in the 200 club. At 204.248. That was my entry speed into the 200 MPH Club.

"And it was stable at those speeds. It had a Corvette chassis, and the rear end and everything was all Corvette, but I had a torsion-bar front end on it that I built up. Before Frank Kurtis died, he and I became good friends, and it had a Kurtis front end.

"It went 131 at the drag strip. We held a national record with it at the drags. It held two national class records at the drags. It also set a record at the half-mile drags, at the quarter mile, and at Bonneville, so we called it a 'triple threat 'Vette'. [Ed] Iskenderian advertised the car because it had one of his cams."

Finally the day came when Lufkin would make his bid to enter the elite 200 MPH Club, as small and expert a group of racers as you will find anywhere, anytime. But Lufkin was not going to have an easy shot at his record. The salt gremlins were working overtime on him that year.

"The next morning was my run for 200 miles an hour. We went down to pick up the car and I was driving the tow truck, driving the car back on a long cable and the guy that was in the car got salt in his eye and when I stopped, he didn't. He ran right into the back of the tow truck and smashed the front of my car all up.

"It ruined the car. The whole front was destroyed and I thought, there's no way I can get this damn thing fixed by tomorrow. Mrs. Smith, who owns the Stateline Hotel, heard about my dilemma and she said, 'Jack, if you want to bring it inside, you can work downstairs in the Stateline.'

"So I went in there and I put little plates and drilled holes and bolted everything together, all the pieces as best I could. Worked all night on it, and masking-taped it all back up and made it safe to go

Mickey Thompson accelerates one of his Z06 Corvettes up to top speed at the salt flats. Thompson was an old hand at the salt, with some of his cars competing for the ultimate prize, the Land Speed Record. At about the time this picture was taken in 1964, MT, as his friends called him, was experimenting with super-wide tires which would change the face of racing for all times. Dave Friedman

The Scace-Hirsch Corvette was for a time the fastest Corvette Sting Ray on the salt. It was sponsored by a Chicago businessman and driven by a corner garage mechanic. That's the charm of Bonneville, the little guys can still play. Dave Friedman

high speeds. The next morning I had it pretty well done and went into the hotel and took a shower.

"That day I got into the 200 MPH Club, and needless to say, I was pretty happy. At that time it was the first car that ever went 200 miles an hour on gas, and I had Bill Scace's wheels and tires on the car when I got in. He had the proper gear ratio."

Scace Shakes the Salt

Mr. Bill Scace was a well-known figure on the Bonneville Salt Flats in the sixties. A businessman from Chicago, Scace was bullish on the idea of ultra-fast Corvettes. And he had his share.

Scace brought a Mercedes-Benz 300SL to the Salt Flats in 1955. In those days, they had only two classes for sports cars, over and under 1,500 cc. He enjoyed running the big Silver Arrow but didn't get what he wanted from it. Then he ran an SL Roadster, but Lufkin, "kept beating me with his Corvette. He had a '57 Corvette that was in the same class.

"We set several records in different classes. We had a '59 Corvette that didn't get anywhere and a '60 Corvette. Then we had a '62 Corvette in 1962, and that was a 315 [cubic] inch. It ran 164.69. And the Jaguar convertible, the XKE, [ran] 147.966. And then we supercharged the Corvette in '63. The first time out we set a record of 169. And then the record runs were cancelled by rain.

"The '64 Corvette was a destroked job, [it ran] 155.52, although we did a lot of better qualifying. Then in '66 we had a 427 and we qualified but didn't set a record. Then in '67 we took it out and got a 192.879 record. Jack Lufkin got in and drove it on a qualifying run and he got 196.39. And then I got into the 200 MPH Club and I kinda lost interest because that was the only thing to shoot for.

"Bob Hirsch was a kid at the corner gas station. He was quite a mechanic and I had some money. He was the brains and I was the cash."

Hirsh did most of the mechanical work on Scace's Bonneville Corvettes, along with his brother-in-law. Then when they went on the salt, Hirsh did the driving, although Scace took an occasional run himself, to be a part of the excitement. Interestingly, when Scace got into the 200 MPH Club, he did it in Lufkin's streamliner. When Lufkin's Corvette went over 200 mph, he did it with a ring gear and tires belonging to Scace. In the narrow world of the long-course racers, what goes around does come around.

Harry Kissel's Corvettes

Alan "Bucky" Goddard is the chief mechanic for two Bonneville Corvettes owned and raced by Harry Kissel. A self-admitted car nut all his life, Bucky claims to have rebuilt a Jeep for President Ronald Reagan when he was but twelve years old.

This formidable blown small-block coupe was the handiwork of master engine tuner Bob Johenks, who prepared the Washburn Chevrolet Corvettes driven by Bob Bondurant. Note the tidy headlamp treatment and the crust of salt on the front tires. The thin stripe of salt shows that the front tires were not making much contact at speed, when most of the car's weight would have shifted to the rear. Dave Friedman

At a party for the Southern California Timing Association (SCTA) and Corvette Club at his beachfront resort, Paradise Cove, Kissell had his two Bonneville Corvettes on display, along with several other Bonneville cars. With hot dogs cooking on the barbecue just a few feet away, Bucky Goddard talked about the tech end of Harry Kissel's Bonneville Corvettes.

"There's a few people that have run Corvettes over the years but right now, actively running, there's us and Mel Bolson, who has got, I think, a '78 Corvette which is basically stock," Goddard said. "Then at Bonneville there is the Wheel Center Corvette which is a '67 convertible like this one here but with a big-block in it. Those were the only ones that ran in 1990."

Bucky was standing next to a maroon '67 roadster with extensive modifications to its engine, body and structure. He turned around and looked at the car. "We bought it three years ago to see if we liked this kind of racing. The first year, without doing anything other than tuning changes and tire changes, we went faster than the guy that we bought it from, and every year, we've just progressed a little further up the ladder. And we're faster now with a small-block in it now than he was with the big-block. He went 190 with the big-block and we went 192 with the small-block, naturally aspirated. It's a 355 cubic inch small-block.

"We've changed a lot of things on it now, repainted it. I fabricated the hood scoop, we grafted a Pontiac Firebird front end on it because it had so much lift on the front end. And we're continuously changing.

Why are these men smiling? Because they are living a dream. Jack Lufkin (right) needed a certain final gear and a set of tires to take his Corvette over 200 mph at Bonneville in 1968. Bill Scace (left) loaned them to Lufkin. To repay the favor, Lufkin let Scace race his streamliner. Scace joined the elite 200 mph club that day with a 221 mph speed, and he was sixty-eight years old. Both men are Bonneville legends, and Lufkin still runs on the salt today. Jack Lufkin

"The motor is running a Carillo rod that's stronger than stock. It's running a high-top TRW 12.5:1 piston, and there's a Snyder roller cam out of San Diego, and we're running a Doug Nash five-speed behind it, with a Tilton ultralight clutch assembly and a stock Chevy crank and oilpan. It's got Hilborn injection on it. The fastest time with this motor at Bonneville has been 192 and at El Mirage dry lakes, 180. We've never had this motor on a dyno so we don't know what kind of horse-power it's making. Everything's been tuned by ear.

"The rear suspension is a Speedway quick-change. I made all the brackets and stuff to put that in there. The front suspension is basically stock. It's got some smaller springs in it to get it down on the ground for aerodynamic purposes. The headers on it are Hooker sidepipe headers. It's got MSD ignition in it. Rear-only brakes and a chute. We run different gear ratios for different tracks. Anywhere from a 2.70 gear ratio up to a 3.75.

"We hope to eventually set a record with it in C-Modified Sport [class]. The record there is 199-point something, but we have got to go 200 to set a record, so we've got another 20 mph to pick up. The motor that we're going to put in next year will have the aluminum heads. It's put out 625 horsepower on the dyno. And we're guessing that this motor that's in here is putting out 500 horse.

"We run several different-style tires," Bucky continued, pointing to the tires on the maroon roadster. "Michelins for the dry lakes, then we've got Talladega Raceway tires that we run at Bonneville and Goodyear front runners that we run on the back for Bonneville. The reason for the different tires is that it's harder to get hooked up with the ground at El Mirage than at Bonneville.

"There is no money in it except what you put in. If you set a record, you get a trophy at the end of the year and your name in the books, that's it.

"You don't necessarily have to run against the record. You can just run against your best time, which some guys have to do, because some of the records are so far out of hand that you can't even touch them."

Kissel's other Corvette is a brutal-looking, white 1980 Sting Ray that was a record holder when run by its former owner, Juris Mindenburg. The white Corvette is close to stock but has the purposeful stance of a race car. The full roll cage and parachute on the rear let you know that speed is a priority.

"That white car was quite a challenge on its own," Bucky Goddard said, taking the hood off the car. "I started on a Thursday morning. That white car had no transmission, no rear end, no fire system, no engine and no brakes. I worked Thursday, Friday, Saturday, all night Saturday and was at the 'Lakes' at 7:00 a.m. Sunday morning to run it. Even the motor was a short-block when I started on Thursday.

"When we bought this white car, it had been the record holder at Bonneville at 239 miles an hour in A-GT class. That was with a naturally-aspirated big-block, I don't know what cubic inches.

"The white car is basically stock in the front end, it's an '80. First off, the class is GT class. Which means it got to be a two-seater, production sports car and you cannot modify the interior. The interior has got to be completely intact. The car still has its AM/FM radio, which still works. You can add the roll cage and you can change the bucket seat to a smaller seat for room. The only modification you can do is that minor chrome trim can be removed. But, on a Corvette there is no minor chrome trim.

"And then the rear end can be changed from the independent suspension, because they're not very stable at high speeds. This one has been changed to a '66 Pontiac rear end. The spare tire carrier is where we carry our ballast. We use the stock fuel tank for cooling. We carry 22 gallons of water in the fuel tank. And we run an alternate fuel tank for the motor at the front of the car. In case something was to go wrong, you don't want that much fuel on board.

"We've got a 357 cubic inch small block in it, a bowtie, high-nickel block with 13:1 J&E pistons, Crower rods, Crower rockers, Crower stud girdles,

a Chevy Bowtie intake with an 850 cfm Holley, an Alterdyne cam. The motor has not really seen its potential because we've had problems with the heads melting between the center two ports. This year, we've had it out three or four times and burned it down twice.

"We just run straight racing gas, no alcohol or propoline oxide, just racing gas. We don't take any free horsepower, all the speed we've gained, we've earned. With the white car we're looking to go about 230 mph with a small-block. If we don't make it, it don't matter; we'll just come back the next year and try harder."

Harry Kissle's two Corvette Bonneville racers bask in the afternoon sun on a day off at the beach. Both are powered by naturally aspirated small blocks. As crew chief Bucky Goddard says, they like "honest" horsepower. Greg Von Dare

Crew Chief Bucky Goddard points out the push bar on the rear of the Corvette roadster. On the back of the car it says, "If it don't have a 'chute', it ain't a race car." Greg Von Dare

Corvette Pro Stocking

Jim Oddy is one of those guys who you've just got to envy. He's a champion drag racer, a successful car builder and tuner, and the owner of his own racing garage. Oddy's racing career began at the end of the fifties when he joined a car club. This group had a field trip to a drag strip one weekend, and Oddy was thrilled by what he saw. Since then, he's been a straight-line guy, and he has done pretty well at it. Today, Oddy races through the Southeast and Northeast with the IHRA circuit.

The engine bay of Harry Kissle's Corvette roadster was clean, despite a recent run at the dry lakes. This 355 ci small-block engine was producing 625 hp, with more to come. Greg Von Dare

Harry Kissle's other Bonneville Corvette, a 1980 coupe. It is remarkably stock, including the interior. Greg Von Dare

"I went home and started building a '36 Chevy that I had found. And in 1960, we got to the drag strip. That '36 Chevy had a straight-six engine in it and it ran in E-Gas. Times were in the 14s and the thing just wouldn't break a hundred miles an hour.

"A year or two later we put a 327 V-8 in that. It had six carburetors on it and a four-speed and 5.57 rear gear, and it was still a daily-driven street car. I went down to Erie, Pennsylvania, to Watsburg Dragway and uncapped the headers and took the tools out of the trunk and set a C-Gas record with the car at 12.22, 112 mph. Then we put the collectors back on, capped 'er up and drove back home. That's what we refer to as the 'good old days.'

"We had a few drag cars after that: an Anglia, that we won the Indy national drags in 1965. Then we built a 1948 Austin that was in the current, late '60s, A-Gas, supercharged killer car, that we match-raced around the country with K.S. Pittman and Stone, Woods and Cooke, and Ohio George Montgomery.

"Then I sort of retired from racing and concentrated on the business from about 1976 to 1989, when we got involved with this Corvette. The rules said that it had to be a production-style car with the driver sitting on the left, but it was 'run what you brung' kind of racing. At the same time, we had been working on a high-horsepower, big-block Chevrolet motor in our dyno room. We got the motor up over 1,600 horsepower, so it looked like a real good test bed for the motor.

"So we went back in the chassis shop here and started building a car. We got it out in 1989 and probably by the tenth pass with the car, it had become the quickest 'door slammer' in drag racing history, with a 6.69 pass at 206 mph. It was just a natural.

The interior of Kissle's white Corvette coupe remains very close to stock. Additions include a roll cage, fire bottles, NASCAR memory tach and other instruments and hefty, five point racing belts for driver. Greg Von Dare

"I had read some article somewhere that a Corvette almost in production form with a pretty hefty motor, the car had run 263 mile an hour at Bonneville, so we know that there's a body that should be easy to get to go 200. And it was. I think the second or third pass with the car we hit 202 mile an hour. The very first race we attended, we were runner-up, and we might have won it but we broke a clutch in the finals. Then the next meet we won, and the next, and the next one we ran that 6.69, which is still the quickest run ever for a 'door slammer.'

"We built the motor, the car, everything in-house. And the body is close to stock: the 104-inch wheelbase, we didn't chop the roof, it's the total Corvette aerodynamic package in a fiberglass-replica body. And we use a four-speed Lenko, planetary style gearbox. We have a coil-over-strut front suspension on the front, and on the rear we have a coil-over-shock with a four-link bar system.

"What really interested us was that 'run what you brung' idea, the no-class, no-rules. Everything is so restricted today. In almost every form of racing there's so much restriction. So, this really got our attention. There were so many things we wanted to try in our motor shop and our chassis shop that you can't hand to a customer and ask him to go try them.

"We just built an extremely strong car. That was our main goal. You just plan on the car making a 200 mph tumble. You're building it on the jig and with every tube you put in you think, how would this survive at 200 mph, upside down? Our chassis is probably the strongest and heaviest one out there. But it's extremely safe and rigid and the car works very well."

The fastest "door slammer" in drag racing. Jim Oddy's Corvette Pro Stocker was so fast the rule makers loaded it with lead. And it still shut down the competition. Here driver Freddie Hahn heats up the slicks with a smooth, smokey burnout. BME Photography

Oddy uses a Chevrolet steel, production big-block. He does a lot of cylinder head work and a lot of supercharger work. Then he camps out in front of his dyno, spending hour after hour dialing the engine in. He has a special high-volume fuel pump and ten huge injectors. He claims it's an ongoing search for the perfect fuel curve.

Oddy prefers a GMC Jimmy-style super-charger, he likes the BDS 1471 blower that he has modified. He has made a lot of changes in the rotor style, blower opening and clearances as an ongoing R&D project. He's looking for the maximum seal and the minimum friction.

"The heart of a supercharged motor is the blower and fuel system, period. We generally run the motor to 8000 rpm and the blower is driven 40 percent over engine speed. So, we're in the 11000 rpm range."

Hahn at the Wheel

The "fastest door slammer" in drag racing is still a big driving chore. Jim Oddy doesn't do his own driving any more, but allows a friend to play with his 200-mph toy. Freddie Hahn is the driver of record for Oddy's extremely quick Corvette. Hahn got interested in drag racing at the end of the sixties, when he was in high school.

"The guy that I used to work for had a '66 Plymouth Belvedere that they used to run in Super Stock D-Automatic, that was a Hemi car," said Hahn. His own first drag race car was a 1968 Dodge Coronet, with a 440 wedge engine. It ran mid-10s to 11s. Then he went to a C-Gas 1972 Dodge Demon that ran low 9s and 140-145 mph.

Continuing to race Hemi-powered cars, Hahn worked on perfecting his driving style. He grew accustomed to the tremendous torque of the Chrysler motors, and to the explosive launches they produced. Hahn met Jim Oddy in 1974 or 1975, when Oddy did some work for him on the rear end of Hahn's Plymouth Duster. They've been good friends ever since. They have been working together for about 15 years, Hahn reckons.

"The car that we presently have is a four-link car. In 1990, when Pro-Modified started, they

Hooked up and honking; a 526 ci blown alcohol motor powers this Corvette Pro Stock extravaganza to 202 mph speeds and times under six seconds. This Corvette drag-ster is one of the most successful cars in the recent history of the sport. BME Photography

changed the rules quite a bit and we had to put suspension on all four corners of the car and shorten the wheelbase and move the motor forward—they limited us to a 10-percent engine setback. Our 1989 Corvette actually is the fastest car in the world with doors on it.

"It's an alcohol supercharged car with a big motor in it. That car had a 572 cubic inch motor in it. For 1990, they limited us to a 526-inch motor. So they ended up taking quite a few cubes away from us. It had aluminum Dart heads on it. The ignition was a Vertex deal or Mallory deal."

Driving such a car is an exercise in discipline. Everything has to be perfect the first time through. And perfect it better be with races lasting a tick over six seconds.

"At the flash of the yellow [from the Christmas tree], you immediately do what we call swapping feet. You would depress the accelerator to the floor release the clutch. Then the car sets you back pretty well. You have to make your one-two shift almost before your eyes get back from the tree to the track again. The one-two shift comes that fast.

"You're in second gear and everything's going good and straight. You make your shift into third gear and hopefully by that time, everything starts to settle back down. When you make your third-to-fourth gear shift, by that time everything should be pretty 'kosher,' and you're actually reaching for the parachute almost at the same time you press that button. Then your mind is more on stopping the car than it is on going. It happens pretty fast. This car normally runs as straight as a string. We seem to be able to get this car down the track better than most other people on a given day. I think we've only aborted one pass in this car in two years."

Chapter 11

GTP Cars of the Eighties

When I first drove it, it had no problem with throttle lag; it was the most responsive turbo engine I'd ever driven. It was incredible. It had a bunch of power low down, very good throttle pickup, and was unbelievably smooth. That V-6 was incredibly smooth. I think it's the smoothest engine I've ever driven. It was quite uncanny, considering the horsepower it was making.

—David Hobbs, on the Corvette GTP

We ran our first race at Elkhart Lake, and we were fast but we didn't finish—a turbo broke. It went on from there and we continued to do development and we won our first race with the car at Road Atlanta, and then also that year, we won West Palm. We sat on an enormous number of poles. The car was extremely fast. But between you and me and the gatepost, the car was a shitbox.

—Ryan Falconer, engine builder

Hustling toward an apex at Road Atlanta in 1986, the Corvette shows a little oversteer, as the driver rotates the car to prepare the chassis for the awesome onset of boost.

IMSA stands for International Motor Sports Association. The international part of the name has to be taken *cum grano salis* (with a grain of salt) since the organization really operates only in the United States and Canada. However, the racing promoted by this relatively new sanctioning body is truly international in its quality and participants.

Concentrating on sports cars, IMSA dominates the high end of professional sports car racing in North America. Their annual GT series of races offers top-level competition at tracks and street circuits all over the country and at one or more venues in Canada.

IMSA assumed control of endurance racing at Daytona and Sebring, Watkins Glen, Road America, Riverside and other well-known road-racing venues from the SCCA and USRRC (United States Road Racing Championship). It provided classes for the import cars like Porsche, Jaguar, Mazda, Nissan and Toyota to fill.

John Greenwood, when he raced his radical Corvettes at Sebring and Daytona, was usually running in IMSA GT, or Grand Touring, class. Corvettes have a strong history with IMSA, yet that relationship would peak in the latter 1980s with the competition career of the remarkable 1,000 plus hp, turbocharged, V-6 Corvette GT prototype racer.

In 1980 IMSA created a new category as its top draw. Grand Touring Prototypes, or GTP, cars replaced GTA with an even more exotic formula. Patterned after Europe's Group C endurance racing prototypes, the GTP cars would be very fast and poised on the leading edge of technology. With their turbocharged engines, some GTP cars were capable of qualifying horsepower in the low four figures and top speeds over 250 mph. These were serious puppies.

Double Your Prototype Pleasure

Two Corvette GTP teams raced through the streets of America in the late 1980s. One was a large-scale, semi-factory effort led by Rick Hendrick Motorsports using a high-tech V-6 turbo engine. The other was a well-engineered but under-

The Corvette family resemblance shows best in a front quarter view. This shape was retained through the racing life of the car—with a number of small additions and refinements. Chevrolet

139

financed attempt by Peerless Racing to mount a serious GTP effort with a very recognizable Corvette body, and V-8 power.

The Peerless car showed superior handling to the factory machine in the only race they shared, but the Hendrick cars, in their turbo form, with 1,200 hp on demand, were simply the fastest vehicles on the IMSA trail through 1988. Thanks to an engine by Ryan Falconer, an Indy-winning motor man, the Corvette GTP had all the power in the world, it just didn't know what to do with it.

Although most people think of Rick Hendrick as a NASCAR team owner, and a very successful one, he was the man who made the GTP effort a reality. Chevrolet realized that if Hendrick was interested in GTP, the cars would be well managed and driven.

Hendrick himself had raced before he became a wildly successful automobile dealer and businessman. He entered the GTP program to explore a new kind of motor sport and to gain experience with the V-6, which was rumored to be the next NASCAR motor in the mid 1980s.

Ken Howes, team manager for the Hendrick Corvette GTP squadron, had been managing a March-Porsche with Kreepy-Krauly sponsorship. At the end of 1985, it was widely known inside IMSA that Chevrolet would be joining the series, but no teams or staff had been announced.

Showtime! The Hendrick team pit crew flies into action at Charlotte in 1986. Tires are changed, windshield washed and the all-important driver change takes place. Note the air hose in the fender behind the front left wheel; it pumps up the onboard jacks, raising the car off the ground for pit service.

Howes says that in the spring of 1985, out of the blue, a phone call from John Pierce invited him to join the Rick Hendrick operation as team manager.

"The car was actually designed and built as far back as the winter of 1983-1984," Howes said. "Nothing came of the project at the time, although some testing was done in 1984, mainly with Ryan Falconer who had built the engines. When I first saw the car in 1985, it was up in Detroit and under covers. And I gather it had been there for some time.

"Initially, the car was very fast but unreliable. Race records would show that it was on the pole position many times over the years. But we only won two races out of all the cars we entered in three years of racing. There were a lot of lessons to be learned."

Howes also kept track of all the drivers who tried their hand, and feet, at the Corvette GTP racer. "Vern Schuppan was another driver at the time, in early 1985. As the years went by, Elliott Forbes Robinson was a driver for some time. At Mid-Ohio in 1987, Michael and John Andretti drove one of the Corvette GTP cars. Bobby Rahal drove one of our cars, late in 1988. He drove, in fact, at Portland, Columbus and Del Mar. Arie Lyuendyke drove one of the cars at West Palm Beach in 1988," Howes added.

Although he is not a technician, Howes thought the Lotus active suspension had potential for the Corvette GTP. "It needed development," Howes explained, "because it really was a system taken from a Formula 1 car. There were many problems which only became apparent after the first race at Columbus and then, just as quickly as it arrived, it went away.

"Chevrolet decided that it was going to be extremely expensive to keep the car running. It needed massive support in terms of technicians, engineers and equipment. And the finance wasn't available or didn't make sense, so that was the end of that."

John Pierce, Corvette's Inside Man

John Pierce of Chevrolet's race shop was the engineer in charge of chassis, running gear and wind-tunnel testing for the Corvette GTP effort.

Pierce recalled: "It started back in 1982 when we were helping the Interscope people, that was Ted Fields and he had Danny Ongais driving, and they had Lolas they were racing in the IMSA series. We wanted to promote the V-6. So back in 1982, Interscope team put a Chevy V-6 into one of their cars. It showed a lot of potential. It was a real rocketship, but unfortunately it was sort of fragile. So, it didn't finish any races, but it certainly showed the potential.

"That was a 3.0 or 3.5 liter engine, a 90 deg. V-6. We had a twin turbo in 1982, and then in 1983, again with Interscope, rules changed, and it went to a single turbo. Seeing what the potential of that combination was, we at Chevrolet wanted to have some Chevrolet product identity. And the Lola T-600 didn't look like anything we built. So, our design staff conceived the idea of doing our own sort of look-alike Corvette and calling the car a Corvette. So they modeled what finally evolved into the Corvette GTP, and it had some identity, family heritage. If you had some imagination you could see there was Corvette there in the background.

"We had debuted a full-sized car at the Detroit Grand Prix in June of 1983. It wasn't really a running car but it was a full-sized rolling car. Because it generated a lot of interest, we thought we'd pursue it. So, we commissioned Lola Cars to actually build a race car based around our V-6 engine, which they did.

"That was first run in March of 1984, in England," Pierce continued, "and the program never really got on firm footing because there was never a team created or proper sponsorship. It sat dormant for almost a year, until the Hendrick Motorsports people got involved, and GM's Good-wrench as well.

"So, the race debut of the Corvette GTP was in August of 1985 at Elkhart Lake. That was when the program really got under way. It peaked out in 1986, I think, and then it was a plateau, and downhill from there. There were a lot of poles, and two victories, West Palm and Road Atlanta. But we were asking an awful lot out of a V-6 engine, so it did the best it could but I think we were overstressing it.

"They had aluminum honeycomb monocoque chassis and, certainly, Lola never tooled up for high-volume production. We went from a 600 horsepower level to an 800 horsepower level. Hewland had to come up with a bigger gearbox, bigger brakes, everything was stressed to the limit. We tried quite a few different shock absorbers. We had Konis, Bilsteins and we ended up with Penske shocks, almost identical to the Indy car pieces. Each chassis was one-of-a-kind, different from the next one. They kept evolving."

Suspension was very traditional: pushrod suspension on the front, and on the rear, an Indy car type. There was nothing revolutionary about the car. The front suspension was hung off a subframe, and the rear suspension attached to the gearbox. The body was carbon fiber and Kevlar panels.

Designs for the GTP car were drawn up by Randy Wittine of Styling Section and then the engineers had to make it aerodynamic. Pierce and his assistants had a powerful challenge: preserve a low coefficient of drag, and high downforce without losing the distinctive Corvette nose of the GTP car.

"We at Chevrolet had never worked on a ground-effects car," Pierce said, "so we spent a lot of time in our wind tunnel developing the vehicle dynamics. We were always plagued with engine cooling problems, with the intercooler and the side air intakes; that really limited the amount of air we could get through the car. It was an ongoing battle to keep the water temperature and the intercooler temperature in a desirable range anyway.

In these sketches by GM designer Randy Wittine, the basic form of the Corvette GTP car took shape. Although the finished product was noticeably different, the profile and paint of the Corvette GTP were largely settled in these renderings. Chevrolet

Teething pains. In this early profile, the GTP racer has most of its elements in place: a Corvette-like nose, the large side intakes for radiator cooling, BBS wheels and the pylon-mounted rear wing. Chevrolet

With its front clip removed, the GTP gives us a look at its front suspension geometry. The beefy front subframe locates the upper A-arms and provides a mounting point for pushrod rocker arms and the small antiroll bar. Shock absorbers are located in the center front compartment, just in front of the windshield wiper pivot. Chevrolet

"We worked a lot with various cooler manufacturers like Harrison Radiator and other suppliers. With the turbocharging, of course, the packaging for the intercooler demands just a big volume of air and that doesn't leave a lot for engine water and oil cooling.

"And if you look at a picture of the car with the side air intakes, you can see that we're limited in the amount of airflow to the coolers. We finally put the oil cooler in the nose because we couldn't get it to work on the side. So that was one of the big limitations of the car—cooling. It was always borderline.

"The Corvette GTP was probably, the basic shape and the graphics, the most exotic-looking car in the series. The others all looked alike. But almost everybody would comment on the appearance . . . and you'd see this thing coming around the track and it looked like it was going at the speed of light. It was an exciting car."

Ryan Falconer, Engine Wizard

Like a fictional scientist who gave life to a frighteningly powerful creature and later regretted it, engine builder Ryan Falconer was the man behind the fleetness of the Corvette GTP. In some ways, he is responsible for the whole thing, since he

Step into my office. From this seat, the driver of the Corvette GTP controlled a maximum of 1200 hp. One of the major complaints about the car was its dated aluminum monocoque box construction. The GTP never had a chance to run with a state-of-the-art carbon fiber chassis. Note the right-hand shift lever, the right-hand drive, and the electronics black boxes close to the driver, where it's as cool as it gets inside a race car. Chevrolet

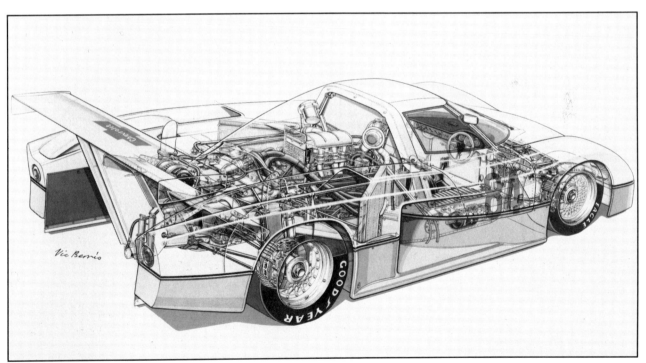

A potent, turbocharged V-6 surrounded by the best car Lola of England could make—that was the formula for the Corvette GTP. Following modern racing design, the engine became part of the frame of the car, with the rear suspension hung off the transaxle. In this phantom drawing, the engine placement is clear, as are the rear suspension components. Two periscopes ran from the back hubs up through holes in the body to carry cooling air to the rear brakes. Chevrolet

Ryan Falconer took this Chevy V-6 and turbocharged it but good. With its unique "mushroom" plenum, the magnificent little motor made as much as 1200 hp for qualifying runs. Note the wide-diameter injector stacks at the top of the engine and the tidy oil pump at the bottom. Chevrolet

built the screaming 1,200 hp Chevrolet V-6 that launched a race car.

Falconer, one of America's best racing engine builders, a former Indy 500 winner, has been at the leading edge of motor sports since 1961. At that time he went to work for the Granatellis, Andy and his brothers. They had recently bought the Novi. Falconer worked there in the machine shop and got to know Gene Marstenak. Marstenak was the master craftsman who had built the Novis since their inception.

Falconer became good friends with Marstenak and did a lot of work for him. Marstenak was a much older man, in his sixties at that time, and the younger Falconer became a willing apprentice and student.

Eventually, Falconer took over building the Novi engines, up until he quit in 1964. Then he went to work for Carroll Shelby, when Shelby was going to build four-cam Ford engines. And although he went to Shelby's, they were just working on the 289s, the Cobras. He never handled four-cam engines at that time. So, Falconer was a little disgruntled over that, although he enjoyed working for Shelby.

Although it was a mighty racing engine, the short-stroke V-6 retained pushrods throughout its career. Fuel-injector nozzles were placed in curves of intake runners, not right at ports. Exhaust tuning was not critical due to the turbocharger. Chevrolet

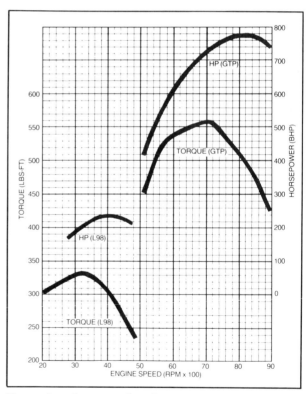

If you thought a regular Corvette engine was strong, compare it to the GTP motor. The IMSA engine actually produced more horsepower than this chart indicates, but Chevrolet didn't want to scare the competition. The sharp torque peak of the GTP car indicates a 7000 rpm shift point in the lower gears. Chevrolet

According to Falconer, "At that time, I started building engines on the side. Shelby only wanted to go so far, I wanted to go further. We were actually doing quite well; I was building engines for John Mecom. So finally Carroll called me and said, 'I don't think it's a good idea that you're working for me and building engines on the side.' And I said, 'I think I'll leave.' So I started my own business and that was in 1966. I started out fairly slow but then I was immediately contracted by George Bignotti and John Mecom to go to Indianapolis for two months to build a dyno cell and to do development on the new Ford four-cam engine. And then we ended up winning the race. So, in 1966 I built the engine that won the Indy 500, so that was a personal plus for me."

Falconer met Eric Broadly of Lola at the Speedway, and Broadly said, "If you'll build Chevrolets, I've got a deal for you." So Falconer started building Chevrolet engines for the Lola GT cars which would be going to Le Mans that year. That launched Falconer into work on Chevy racing motors.

Beautiful fabrication work is evident in this shot of the GTP's engine bay. The V-6 was mounted north-south, with the turbo and wastegate directly behind the engine. The rear-mounted alternator, the twin fuel inlets in front of the engine, and the rear suspension upper A-arms are all visible here. Chevrolet

Chevy V-6 at Indy?

In 1980, Vince Piggins, who was in charge of product promotion at that time, approached Falconer and said, "Do you suppose we can race a V-6 at Indianapolis?"

Falconer replied, "Why not; what are the parameters?" Piggins said, "Well, we need 600 horsepower, and we're allowed this much boost and the engine can only be so big." They had a block and some pieces to work with. In a few weeks, Chevrolet sent the pieces to Falconer, who developed the engine in about three months.

"We had to make everything," Falconer said. "And the first run on the dyno was 625 horse. So, we were in. But it was a very low-budget deal. Vince Piggins was known as 'high-pockets', he had deep pockets, but he never pulled any money out. So, very cheaply we had one engine and, like a long block."

They made a deal with Lindsay Hopkins for an entry to the Indy 500, Johnny Parsons to drive. Unbelievably, the car was very fast. They ran, "right at 190 mph, which would have put us inside the second row or outside the first row. The time was third or fourth quick. Which was unbelievable straight out of the box.

"Then what happened," Falconer said quietly, "was that Johnny Parsons came up to me and demanded $15,000 or he wasn't going to qualify the car. And I said where in the hell am I going to get that kind of money. And he said, well, get it from Chevrolet! And I told him he could go to hell.

"So they put Hurley Haywood in the car. Hurley's a nice guy, but we immediately dropped down into the low 180s. And we qualified mid-field

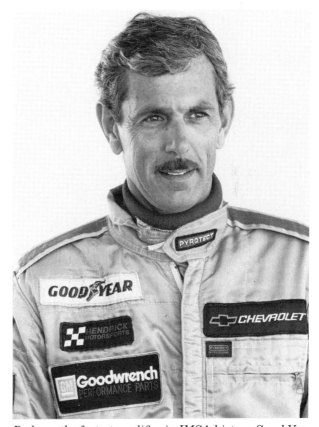

Perhaps the fastest qualifier in IMSA history, Sarel Van Der Merwe was the number one driver for the Corvette GTP car. His courage and skill put the Corvette on the pole many times, and scored two outright wins. Merwe is a South African rally champion, a gentleman off track and a fierce competitor on. Chevrolet

somewhere. And, after all the pit fiascoes, the engine basically finished the race. Which was a miracle, because we still only had one engine."

But Chevrolet was not enthusiastic about their V-6 and the project was allowed to slip onto the back burner, the very back burner. At the time, Falconer was building road engines for Danny Ongais, for his endurance cars. He was intrigued by the idea of putting the powerful V-6 in Ongais's IMSA racer and mentioned it to Chevrolet.

Falconer continued: "And they said well, go ahead. There ain't no money involved but go ahead. So I took the parts that I had and converted it over and I made a deal with Ongais. And I converted the Porsche injection to go on it. Basically it was the same size engine, a 3.4 liter, 209 cubic inch. And I put all the Porsche hardware on it. And we put it in his T-600 Lola and tested it a few times.

"We took it to Daytona," Falconer said, "for the finale and we missed the pole because of a screw-up somehow. We had a tire problem. But the Kremer brothers brought their super killer Porsches over. The race started, Danny went to the front, we blew a right front tire entering turn one, I forget how many laps later. So he had to go that whole four miles around. He got back to the pits. We had a hell of a time getting the tire off, changed the tire and Danny went back out, like in fifteenth spot. In another fifteen laps, he was in the lead. The car was awesome."

After some persuading, Vince Piggins agreed that Chevrolet would ante up and build more engines. They would be the same as the first prototype—cast-iron blocks, aluminum heads, a 90 deg. V-6. But once again Falconer had only one engine and a partial engine.

"At that time, once we showed the potential, that's when Vince started conjuring up the deal. We started talking about having Lola build us a car, a GTP car, just as a Corvette, because that's how he wanted to sell it to Stemple and the brass," said Falconer.

First Testing at Goodwood

Falconer recalled the V-6's testing at Goodwood, England: "When the car was completed in

One of the first drivers assigned to the Corvette was Elliot Forbes-Robinson. EFR, as he's called, was fast in the Corvette but left the team to drive the Nissan 300ZXT GTP for Electramotive, a move he later regretted. Although he is not normally associated with the Corvette GTP program, EFR helped develop the car into a contender against the Porsches and other IMSA top dogs. Chevrolet

Jack Baldwin was David Hobbs' partner in the Peerless Corvette. An old Chevy hand, Baldwin is most often seen in a Trans-Am Camaro. Chevrolet

1984, I flew to England along with John Pierce, who was the liaison between Lola and Chevrolet. John and I went over and it was the first test of the car. We went to Goodwood and Jonathan Palmer drove the car and the car was very quick. And that was in our very early stages of the engine development. We were only pumping out 650 horsepower at the time. Very low boost.

"But the car was fast, showed potential. It had heating problems because Eric Broadly—you know they develop cars to run in pissy, rainy cold weather in England, then they bring them to the United States and if the sun shines, they overheat."

But an argument between Danny Ongais and Chevrolet suddenly drained the life out of the GTP project. Chevrolet parked the Lola car and it sat for nearly a year, untouched. Falconer asked if he could work on the car, Chevrolet said yes.

Falconer brought the car to his shop. He called in Jim Chapman and together they reworked the exhaust system and rebuilt the shrouds and other pieces.

"Now we could go more than a lap around the racetrack without burning the rear hood off. When we first tested it, you had to take the rear deck off as soon as it came into the pits or you'd burn it down.

"So, we cured all those problems and I got a couple of test drivers that I knew like Mario Andretti, Al Unser, Junior, as favors to me, because our friendship goes back a lot of years. So they tested the car for me at Laguna Seca and we got it to where it was competitive.

Fast and sometimes impulsive, Doc Bundy is a versatile driver who has matured into a reliable and capable competitor. He later drove for Lotus in the Bridgestone Supercar Series. Dave Friedman

The "other" Corvette GTP racer. Owned by Peerless Racing, this identical chassis and body used a V-8 engine for power. It had softer suspension and better handling *than the Hendrick Corvette, but a lack of funds limited it to a few appearances. It was driven by Britisher David Hobbs and Trans-Am specialist Jack Baldwin.* Chevrolet

147

"Along about this time Rick Hendrick enters the picture. And Rick being the mega-dealer and all that, he came to see me and they put the GTP deal together where we're gonna go campaign the car and it's gonna be run."

"We ran our first race at Elkhart Lake, and we were fast but we didn't finish—a turbo broke. It went on from there and we continued to do development and we won our first race with the car at Road Atlanta, and then also that year, we won West Palm. We sat on an enormous number of poles. The car was extremely fast. But between you and me and the gatepost, the car was a shitbox."

Can't Get a Handle on It

Falconer continued: "It did not handle. It would not put its power down. The car started out at 650 horsepower and when I was through with it, it was 1,200. Sarel Van Der Merwe loved the car because it had so much power. So what he would do is drive at 200 mph. I think at Watkins Glen we still hold the record on the back straight. But it didn't put its power down well. It was terrible.

"And they blamed it on the engine being too severe or it doesn't come on, got too much lag or whatever, and in the end, after they put the V-8s in

'em, they finally realized they couldn't even drive 'em with the V-8s. Which is totally easy to modulate power.

"One thing I wanted to accomplish—I wanted to be the first one to win a GTP race with that Chevrolet or a V-6 and I did that."

Corvette GTP Technology

The Corvette GTP car as raced by Hendrick Motorsports was a direct descendant of the Lola T-600, one of the earliest and most successful of the GTP cars in the early 1980s. The T-600 was a breakthrough design for Eric Broadly, whose Lola Cars had been going through some rough times in the later 1970s. Broadly gambled that the new GTP car would be more than a match for the aging and highly compromised slope-nose Porsche 935s.

The T-600 was a mid-engine coupe, very low and streamlined, with little ground clearance due to its two ground-effect tunnels running under the body to generate downforce, keeping the car glued to the track. Major air inlets for cooling and for the engine were two huge NACA ducts amidships, on the flat sides of the body. At the back, a large wing rose from the rear deck.

During a break-in practice at Elkhart Lake, Wisconsin, Van Der Merwe confers with the pit crew about how he will leave the pit lane in the race. Note the extra front *spoiler on the nose of the car. Front-end lift was a problem that had to be addressed at the faster tracks. Chevrolet*

Because the T-600 was so dominant, Chevrolet thought seriously about a GTP car of its own, both as a testbed for exotic technologies and for the substantial publicity value. The project was sold to management as a Corvette GTP racer, and suddenly, Broadly was commissioned to modify the T-600 design, and to adapt it for all new Corvette bodywork which would come from the GM styling studios.

There Jerry Palmer and Randy Wittine designed a body which, in its front half remarkably resembles a production Corvette but was from the doors back pure racer and all business.

Lotus-Built Active Suspension

In the mid 1980s General Motors was becoming a big client of Lotus Engineering of Hethel, England. GM used Lotus as a top-level consultant for some of their most prestigious projects, mostly in chassis engineering, handling and other performance-related areas. At that time, Lotus was bankrupting its Grand Prix team with a piece of technology that was not ready for world-class racing—active suspension.

The idea of active suspension is simple. Instead of "dumb" springs and antiroll bars which do nothing but react to inputs such as bumps and body roll, active suspension uses "smart" components to sense road surface and chassis dynamics and actively flex the suspension to compensate. Active suspension should eliminate body roll on cornering, squat on acceleration, dive on braking and should keep the tires firmly planted on the road no matter how it bobs up and down or how bad it is, while transferring none of its noise or movement to the driver and passengers inside the car.

It's a great idea, but the Lotus system involved marrying the very latest in computer technology with a complex and heavy system of hydraulic pumps, hoses and rams, which was needed for the actuators that replaced shock absorbers and springs. In practice, the nineteenth-century hydraulic technology was a bad mate for computers and electronics, the technology of the twentieth century.

The hydraulics were simply too slow and too heavy to make the whole system workable on a Formula 1 car, where each ounce is critical. The pump that powered the active suspension itself was a hastily converted unit from a Beachwood aircraft, and the system was run by a computer that was not state of the art, even then.

Lotus bet the farm on perfecting active suspension. They hoped that, like their innovations with downforce a decade earlier, active suspension would give them an unfair advantage for a season or more, and perhaps a championship. Although Ayrton Senna won two Grand Prix for Lotus with

Is this the second most successful man in American motorsports after Roger Penske? Maybe. Rick Hendrick is a phenomenon. Businessman, car dealer, former racer and the owner of a leading NASCAR team, Hendrick was the only man Chevrolet would trust with their precious GTP car. Hendrick built a fine team around the car and campaigned it with success from 1986 to 1989.

"active" cars, Detroit and Monaco, on street circuits, where Senna is unsurpassed as a driver. Lotus ultimately lost the bet, lost their prestige and have now all but vanished from Formula 1 racing, a venue where they once were counted with the mighty like Enzo Ferrari, Bruce McLaren and Jack Brabham.

It was thought, with some justice, that the bigger, heavier, roomier GTP Corvette might be the perfect place to continue development for the system, since it was just too bulky for the pencil-slim Grand Prix cars.

After much secrecy, the active suspension Corvette GTP was tested and found to be very quick. The problems with the active suspension were no different than on the Grand Prix car, but they were less noticeable on the GTP.

Ryan Falconer was pulling back from the GTP program at that time, but he was impressed by the active car.

"It was awesomely fast with the active suspension," Falconer recounted. "The active car ran at Columbus, Ohio, and there was a screw-up with the

In practice for Sears Point in 1986, Doc Bundy tries to set the car up for maximum bite. One recurring theme of the Corvette GTP was how to get its massive power to the *ground effectively. Note the twin-hole fuel inlet behind Bundy's head.*

hydraulic pump, and come to find out that the guys from Lotus knew that the pump was not reliable and they had a fix for it, but they never said anything. A million-dollar car down the tubes. The car was prepared to race again but they never, ever raced it again, they just shit-canned it. Which was pitiful. So then they went on with the standard V-8 car."

Drivers Speak

Most racing fans know that David Hobbs had a successful career as a racing driver before he donned the blue blazer of a TV commentator for ESPN, a cable sports news network. Before that saturnine face and sandpaper-dry wit flavored racing telecasts, Hobbs raced for nearly three decades altogether, driving every kind of car from a

Formula Junior to Can-Am heavies to the Corvette GTP car.

"It was really the factory people that contacted me first," Hobbs said. "It was a combination of factory and Lola, really. Because, at that time the car was very much a Lola. And I had driven Lolas, either for privateers or the factory since 1963, when I first drove a quasi-factory Formula Junior. So, I've known Eric Broadly for twenty-five years.

"And of course just at that time, I was on Chevrolet's smiling list because I had just won the Trans-Am for them in 1983 in a Budweiser Camaro. And I suppose I was just the sort of name that popped to the top when people started talking about testing the GTP car.

"The first time I drove, of course, was Road Atlanta. It was a very different Lola to anything I had ever driven before. My initial impression was very favorable. I was super-impressed when I drove it at Atlanta. And I could see that the car had massive potential—apart from the fact that it had massive horsepower. That was the Falconer engine. And it drove very nicely.

"I seem to remember that very first test, we had some overheating problems. It got pretty hot. This was, pretty basically, the car that had been around then for two years. It had never done anything but sporadic testing. Jonathan Palmer had tested it and Stefan Johansson had driven it at places like Silverstone.

"Our first race with it was Elkhart Lake, an IMSA race. It ran pretty well," Hobbs continued. "We had some little handling problems, throttle response problems. That was the initial thing. When I first drove it, it had no problem with throttle lag; it was the most responsive turbo engine I'd ever driven. It was incredible. It had a bunch of power low down, very good throttle pickup, and was unbelievably smooth. That V-6 was incredibly smooth. I think it's the smoothest engine I've ever driven. It was quite uncanny. Especially with the horsepower it was turning out.

"The gearbox started to be the weak link in the chain for that car—because of the horsepower. We were up in Watkins Glen testing in September, and the car didn't like the bumps there. It's not very good over the bumps, and I had a horrendous spin coming out onto the back straight, when the car literally jumped off the road, flipped round in the air and, luckily, only just nudged the guardrail at about 140 miles an hour. I remember when we went back the following week for the race, in qualifying I did about 204 down the back straight at Watkins Glen, which is by far the fastest anybody had ever been there. And we still hadn't got its performance over the bumps sorted out. So I was coming on there nothing like as quick as I could have done. The car had tremendous performance.

"And then, of course, I drove that other GTP Corvette for Peerless. Their whole philosophy was different. They had a chassis engineer who worked for Chevrolet and was there on a part-time basis with Brad Francis who was the team manager.

"We went testing at Mid-Ohio with Al Holbert. And we were faster than Holbert, and that was when he was at the height of his prowess with that 962. We were quicker that day and the team was as excited as hell. I had been complaining about some slightly steppy handling. I said it just could be something like the differential. And when we got it back to the shop it was broken.

"So with a broken diff, I was lapping Mid-Ohio about 1:20, which, for '85 was a pretty good time. Right under the lap record."

Hobbs went on: "Then we took it off to the street race in Columbus. And I drove with Jack Baldwin and we came fourth. In fact, Jack was passed by Mauro Baldi on the last lap of the race,

At Palm Beach in 1988, the Corvette was running one of its best races ever, when a fire broke out in the monocoque from leaked fuel. While an astonished Doc Bundy watched in horror, the car flared into a blazing pyre and was totally destroyed in moments.

During a long pit stop at Mid-Ohio, Doc Bundy is about to replace Sarel Van Der Merwe. The car has already seen a *rough race. Note the rub marks on the nose and the chipped fiberglass at the left fenderwell.*

and we lost second or third position. So we had a pretty good debut. And people like Martin Brundle were very complimentary. He said, 'Christ, first time out, that's going pretty well, isn't it?'

"But their philosophy was very different from the Hendrick guys. They were very stiffly sprung, very European in their outlook. Where the guy from Chevy was very much for compliance, he wanted the suspension to really work and certainly at Columbus on the street circuit, whatever we did seemed to work pretty well. It didn't work as well at Tampa or Del Mar. It had good potential but never was fulfilled.

"The disappointing thing was, in Columbus we raced head to head with the Hendrick effort. And about lap five I passed Sarel Van Der Merwe in the Hendrick car right in front of the pits and just drove away. The car was performing much better than their stiff suspension. They ran the tires off

their car in no time and our tire temperatures stayed very good; we ran pretty strongly throughout the race. We were only running about a second off the Jaguar pace."

The Doc Hasn't Got the Cure

When David Hobbs left to join the BMW team, Chevrolet needed a new driver with excellent credentials. It just so happened that Doc Bundy, a driver for the Ford Probe GTP car, was at the end of his contract, and Ford was having second thoughts about their GT racing program.

The Probe, a four-cylinder turbo racer developed by Zakspeed in Germany, was a very fast car which had a reputation for leading races and then breaking. Ford was then shifting its emphasis to the Jack Rousch Mustangs in Trans-Am and away from GTP. So, Doc Bundy was trying to get an answer about his contract from Ford, and they couldn't make up their minds.

At that time, Bundy met with Rick Hendrick and agreed to join the Chevy team. If the Probe had been fast, the Corvette GTP was even faster.

"The car was incredibly fast," Bundy recalled. "The only problem was I didn't give them much empathy, much leeway because the car was an old design and it really needed updating and really needed a new design. It wasn't an evil car; it was pretty tough until we went to a new shock absorber and that suddenly gave the car a suspension. Until that point, you swore it had no suspension at all. And we couldn't use anywhere near the power that was available to us. Once we made that move with the shock absorbers and got the car to feel like something, that's when we started utilizing some of the power that was available to us, and that's when the car really came into its own. It really got good.

"Again, it had weaknesses, it had certain things it couldn't do. It was basically an understeering car and we'd have to compromise it to deal with that understeer. And we'd end up making it an oversteering car. It was without a doubt the fastest car on the straightaway and we didn't want to give that up.

"We did win a couple of races. Races that were a surprise to me that we did win. But a lot of it had to do with the excellent crew we had. They were hardworking, very talented and they were slick on the pit stops. We usually made time on the pit stops. And in all honesty, it was the best team that I'd driven for, up to that point in my career.

"We came close with the active suspension car, with the Lotus-designed suspension for the Lola, and it was just such an incredibly expensive operation that I think that broke the camel's back. So much was spent on that project and we didn't have good success. And the stuff itself was excellent. It wasn't anybody's fault, it was just very expensive. It was a mind-blower. It would do amazing things, but it was very difficult to set up."

For Doc Bundy, the peak of frustration came at the West Palm Beach race in 1988. There, he had to abandon his car when a fuel fire broke out. Then he had to stand helplessly by while the car was allowed to burn to the ground, its Kevlar and carbon fiber bodywork rapidly flaring into an inferno. Corner workers and safety marshals all dropped the ball, none of them grabbing a fire extinguisher and dousing the burning Corvette. Bundy was furious.

"The best chassis that we ever had was the one we lost in the fire at West Palm. That was its third race and it just kept getting better. We were real encouraged.

"The problem that caused the fire was that the fuel system was pressurizing. It expanded the fuel tank back into the alternator pulley and the bolt on the pulley just drilled a hole through the fuel tank.

So, fuel got into the engine bay, because the whole bottom of the car is sealed off because of the underwing. Finally the turbo ignited the fuel."

One GTP Lap at Elkhart Lake

Doc Bundy narrates one lap at Road America, in Elkhart Lake, Wisconsin, from behind the wheel of a Corvette GTP:

"The car, when it was going up the start/finish straight, when it ran with the V-6 turbo, just had tremendous power. Elkhart Lake, or Road America, is made up of three very long straightaways. So that car just loved it, it could get its legs and just run.

"Going down the start/finish straightaway I think we would get very close to 200 miles an hour. Probably in the 190s. And then the turn at the end was pretty good for the car. The downhill was not quite as good but still OK. And then we go down that straightaway behind the pits which ends up in a downhill at the very end of it where braking is so very key. Again, we were so fast down that straight.

"Then we came to a slow corner, and there some of the weaknesses of the car would show up. It would understeer in that slow corner and come off the corner, not quite as good as some of the other cars.

"Then we go up the hill and under the bridge and through another left and a quick right. And the left would be a high second or third gear corner. The problem with Elkhart is that you need two seconds, two different second gears, and two different third gears, and probably two different fourth gears. It is a very difficult track to gear properly. You're always compromised in at least one or two of the corners.

"But the car was still good. Then there was a quick right-hander. One of the problems the car had is that it didn't like left-right transitions, coming off one kind of turn and right back into another one. You had to feather and wait for the car to do the transition. I think part of that was the flexibility of the chassis and the suspension geometry. We had to have a fair amount of roll in it to get the grip we needed.

"You come off of that little right, almost like a kink, and downhill again and into another second gear corner that the car would understeer through. Then you shift up and then go through the carousel. The car was not too bad in the carousel itself. We would control the car with throttle. And even though we ran a fair amount of wing, we still wouldn't lose the car's strong point, its high speed.

"Then you would come up on the high-speed kink. Again, because of the flexibility in the chassis, we weren't able to do that kink flat out. We could get close, but there always was just a feather or a touch of the brake. A 'piece of mind' touch. And down the back straightaway.

"Even though the back straightaway wasn't straight, that was probably the fastest part of the track. I'm almost certain we got a tad over 200 there. Then we'd have a pretty slow corner at the end of it. And then a right-hander, second gear and shift up to third and then bend under the bridge, a left-hander that kinda would go away at the exit, like an off-camber exit. You used every inch of road, plus, there. Bend back around to the right, which is the last corner on the circuit, which I think was a third gear corner and again it would be a bit of an understeer problem. You'd put the car through the corner and then back on an uphill to the start/ finish straightaway."

The End of the GTP Dream

In the fast-paced and murderously expensive world of GTP racing, only those with the strongest motivation can survive. By the end of 1988, the Corvette GTP car was part of the past. No longer would Sarel Van Der Merwe tear off one of those breathless qualifying laps, when the Corvette GTP seemed like the fastest thing in the history of motor sports. No more would Corvettes race at the level of the best Porsche, BMW and Jaguar teams in the world.

The GTP era of the mid 1980s ignited another generation of Corvette racing fans. It produced some of the fastest and most exciting racing of the eighties. And it is directly responsible for the success of the electronic engine management system which is on the current crop of Indy-winning Ilmor Chevrolet engines.

While the Grand Touring Prototype Corvettes never reached their potential on the track, they were the most exotic and exciting Corvettes since the days of the Grand Sports, twenty-five years earlier. As the 1990s begin, another Corvette GTP racer is in development. It will likely be less exotic than the previous car, but more reliable as well.

Let's remember the Corvette GTP car this way: low, sleek, beautiful and so fast it made your eyeballs ache.

Chapter 12

Corvettes Dominate Showroom Stock Racing

During the 1980s, when mercurial Roger Smith was chairman of General Motors, the huge corporation sought to make itself more modern and efficient internally.

The existing structure of GM, which saw cars such as Cadillac decline due to design and quality problems, had reduced the old divisions to marketing organizations. The consumer was increasingly

It was a whole new ball game. The 1984 Corvette redefined American performance and put the world on notice that the United States could build a sports car on production lines that few in the world could match. With a 350 ci small-block making 350 hp, a backbone frame to *supplement the Corvette steel birdcage and advanced rear suspension, this new Corvette was prettier and faster than anything since the big-blocks of the late 1960s.* Morrison Motorsports

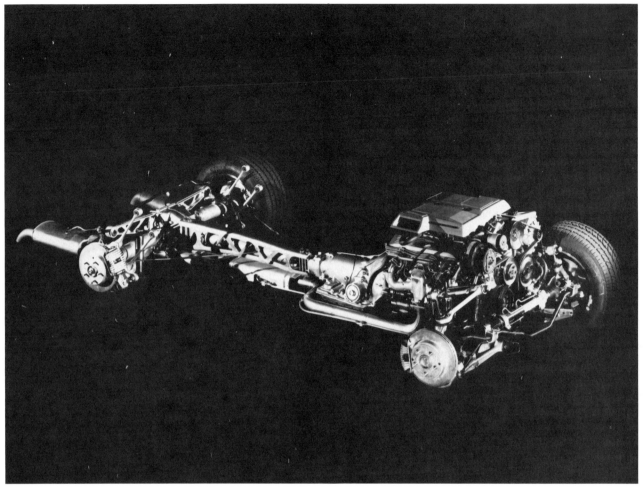

The chassis of the new Corvette, the 1984+ model. Corvettes of the nineties still use this elegant and highly successful structure. The engine is as it appeared in 1984. Chevrolet

Front suspension for the new Corvette consisted of forged aluminum, unequal length upper and lower A-arms. Note the substantial anti-dive offset in the angle of the top A-arms. This is an excellent piece of modern engineering. Road & Track

left out of the loop. The Japanese had turned up the volume to an almost unbearable level. Too many GM models looked and felt identical, people said. Automotive writers called it badge engineering. Something had to happen.

The new order saw GM divided into two mega divisions: CPC, for Chevrolet-Pontiac-Canada, and BOC, for Buick-Oldsmobile-Cadillac. Each of these super-divisions shared engineering, design and manufacturing resources.

In short order the classic divisions of GM, Buick and Cadillac bottomed out and then began long but powerful recoveries. The other divisions such as Chevrolet went through chaos, but bounced back.

The Corvette engineering group within CPC was formed with Dave McLellan at its head. The group would be in charge of all engineering for the Corvette in the future, separately from the mainstream CPC staff. An arrangement, in reality, almost identical to what Zora Arkus-Duntov had when he was Corvette engineering honcho.

A New Car for a New Time

When Dave McLellan inherited Zora Arkus-Duntov's job as head of engineering for the Corvette group in 1976, he also inherited Zora's plans for a mid-engine Corvette, supposedly the next-generation car. McLellan respected Zora tremendously, but his instincts told him that the Corvette should stick with a front-engine layout, at least for the present. The highly evolved Mako Shark style body and the frame-chassis, which dated to the original Sting Ray, were both ready for a major update.

While mid-engine cars do have a performance advantage in high-speed cornering, they are inhospitable and offer limited visibility and storage space. McLellan strongly believed that American sports car buyers didn't want the cramped cabins of European super cars such as the Lamborghini Countach or Ferrari Testarossa.

For years, Arkus-Duntov had lobbied for a true mid-engine Corvette. This, he felt, was the way for a sports car to go in the future. It would also have kept Corvette among the world's super cars, as exotic as anything from Europe. Along the way, there had been flirtations with gas-turbine-powered Corvettes and Wankel rotary-engine Corvettes. But, no matter what the motor, Arkus-Duntov wanted a mid-engine car, in the fashion of Ferrari and Lamborghini.

Executives at Chevrolet resisted Zora. They didn't want to commit to a car so radically different. They thought the risk was too great in terms of cost and of alienating former Corvette buyers. With memories of the Corvair still fresh in their corporate minds, they dragged their feet through the 1970s until Arkus-Duntov was ready to retire.

So, McLellan's proposal for a front-mid-engined type chassis for the new Corvette, and a powertrain based on the existing 350 ci small-block engine, met with enthusiastic approval. This new vehicle would be unmistakably a Corvette, yet it would use high-tech solutions and race-car type components for both chassis and drivetrain. Suddenly, the term world-class was being used about the new Corvette and no one was laughing. It was, oh happy day, true.

Based on familiar and reliable engineering, the Corvette of the 1980s and early 1990s was as much of an improvement over the previous car as the first Sting Ray had been over its solid-axle predecessor.

Dave McLellan told me, "You're not designing a race car when you design a Corvette, but you certainly want to keep those high-performance tasks in mind. And putting the car on a racetrack is some kind of ultimate expression of what the car was purposed for.

"Just in order to have the car well balanced and capable you wind up worrying about center of gravity, suspension attributes, brake capabilities, weight distribution. There's a synergysm between doing a high-performance street car and a race car."

The new Corvette was revolutionary as well as evolutionary. Its most profound change came in the use of a "backbone" style chassis. Unlike the ladder or perimeter chassis, this backbone uses a short, stiff central section linking the front and rear suspension carriers. The result looks like a capital I.

In the Corvette's application of Colin Chapman's backbone system, simplicity is the key. First, a C-section girder runs back from the transmission to the differential, alongside the driveshaft. A front subframe mounts the engine and locates the front suspension. The steel birdcage from the Sting Ray was retained, but lightened, simplified and lowered. Many suspension components were made from forged aluminum, saving weight overall.

With its torquey, fuel-injected motor, fully independent suspension and low, wide profile, the Corvette was more of a race car in street trim than ever in its history.

And that was just the 1984 model. In short order, Dave McLellan and his engineering group began showering the Corvette with an abundance of high-performance goodies. For example: Tuned Port, electronic fuel injection with Hemholtz ram-tuned induction runners; bigger brake discs; 17 in. wheels; a six-speed manual transmission made in Germany by ZF; zero scrub-radius front-wheel geometry; three-position, cockpit-adjustable shock absorbers, or Bilstein gas shocks; and tire pressure sensors that will let you know if you have a deflating tire long before it goes flat.

In the 1980s, ABS brakes allowed Showroom Stock Corvettes to go at racing speeds in the rain when other fine cars such as the Porsche 944 Turbos were spinning all over the track. Aggressive factory development with leading Corvette racing teams in the 1980s quickened the pace of the new Corvette's adolescence. Morrison Motorsports, Bakeracing, Rippie Racing, Powell Motorsports and other teams who raced Corvettes against each other every weekend were used by the factory to obtain information on durability and performance for drivetrain, chassis, tires—all the critical racing components.

This program, combined with the fierce competition shown by a new generation of Corvette racers in the 1980s, made for some of the best and most exciting racing since the golden days of the early 1960s. Even though Corvettes were able to beat every car that challenged them in SCCA's Showroom Stock series, they still had to race each other. That's where the fun started—along with the backbreaking work.

RPO Z51

Even though production Corvettes in the post 1984 generation had stiff suspensions, Chevrolet offered an all-out competition package with its own RPO number, much as they had for the 1956 Corvettes at Sebring. For the new Corvette, this package of high-performance goodies was immortalized as RPO Z51.

The Z51 option was a racing-inspired package which turned the Corvette into a stiffly sprung coupe showing darned little body roll through corners and offering shock absorbers that were one tick this side of solid metal. For the very reasonable price of $51 you got stiffer monoleaf transverse springs, more aggressive shock absorbers, denser suspension bushings and a larger diameter antiroll bar for the car's front end, up to 25 mm from the stock 20 mm. Quick steering was also included in the deal. A custom rack-and-pinion gearset increased the production steering of 15.5:1 to a sharp and instant 13:1.

Driving a Z51 Corvette was a sweaty-palm experience. The car had so much lateral grip, it was scary. A Z51 coupe could be tossed around like a female Tango dancer, flung into corners with advanced abandon, then gathered up neatly, with ease really, and blasted into the next piece of unbent road. It was a gas to drive such a car in the mountains, but hard to live with one. The Z51 package was rock hard, on top of the early 'Vette's already stiff suspension. Anything other than flat road made for a spine-pounding ride. It could be tolerated for a while, but even tar strips on highways, over a long drive or commute, became sharp kicks in the butt.

Still, Z51 was the perfect thing for the racetrack. Corvettes raced by Kim Baker and Tommy Morrison in Showroom Stock served as development vehicles for the entire Corvette line, but they especially improved their own racing package as they went.

In 1985 a change was made to both the production base suspension and the Z51 RPO. Responding to repeated criticism that the car's ride was too harsh on the street, Corvette engineers eased up on spring and shock absorber rates. They also learned that, in racing situations, more suspension travel made the cars track around bumpy corners better and didn't hurt them on fast, smooth corners.

At the rear end, this new Corvette chassis featured an updated IRS with many of the improvements made by Dick Guldstrand now added to the stock suspension. You can just see the arching, plastic monoleaf spring behind the differential. Each of those rubber bushings leads to a body mounting point. Road & Track

Origins of Showroom Stock

It's dark now, and chaos would be a nice name for what's going on out there. The road in front of you is shiny with rain, and spilt oil makes the water slick with deadly, iridescent rainbows. You know that your race car has no brakes but there's forty-five minutes remaining in your shift before the next poor slob takes over. You take corners by downshifting very early and letting engine compression slow you to a workable speed. If you need brakes in an emergency, it's adios amigo, and goodbye race car.

When a guy in a Corvette passes you like you've got concrete tires, and you see him reach over and change stations on the radio as he rockets by, you decide that the fun is over. This isn't why you came to "the Ledges."

Outside the small, quiet town of Parkman, Ohio, there is a narrow and bumpy little racetrack known as Nelson Ledges. Scene of club and amateur racing for many years, sleepy little Nelson Ledges had a major impact on Corvette racing, in an offhand sort of way.

John McGill has been manager of the Nelson Ledges racing facility for twenty years and he says that in that time it "hasn't changed a bit." For ten years, starting in 1970, the track played host to a twenty-four-hour motorcycle race. "It started on a very low key," McGill said, "and then it got to be a pretty big happening.

"We just got to talking with some of the guys around the track one day whether the cars were tougher than the bikes; because the bikes could go twenty-four hours of racing and they were pretty much Showroom Stock bikes, and would cars do it? And a group of us said, maybe it would work. So we talked to everyone we knew and printed up a bunch of 'intent to enter' forms and passed them out to everybody that came through there that year. And that's how it got started.

"The first year had pretty much Volkswagen Rabbits, your little Chrysler cars, Pintos, stuff like that," McGill continued. "There were about nineteen entries the first year, 1979. I think a Saab won the first race. It was a big hit and got a lot of interest up. A lot of people started to ask about it.

"You see, our track's located fairly close to Detroit. We're just a hundred miles from Detroit and a lot of automotive people race at the track.

"So, the following year some of the engineers from Ford, Chrysler, who was getting their stuff together at the time, had been racing there and they got teams together of their friends and got cars from the manufacturers, and that got everybody started.

Body-Chassis	Major specifications 1984 Corvette	1954 Corvette
Frame	Unitized steel and aluminum central cage	Ladder-type, boxed steel, with central X-brace
Body	Fiberglass, two-door, two-seat fastback coupe or roadster	Fiberglass, two-door, two-seat roadster with cloth top
Front suspension	Independent, unequal-length A-arms, transverse monoleaf composite material spring, hydraulic shocks, antiroll bar	Independent, upper and lower A-arms, coil springs, hydraulic shocks, antiroll bar
Rear suspension	Independent, upper and lower trailing arms, lateral links, tie-rods, transverse monoleaf composite spring, hydraulic shocks, antiroll bar	Live axle, semi-elliptic multi-leaf springs, hydraulic shocks
Wheels	Unidirectional, cast alloy, 8.5x16 in. front, 9.5x16 in. rear	Stamped steel, 15 in.
Tires	Goodyear Eagle VR50, P255/50VR-16	6.70x15 in. white sidewalls
Steering	Power rack-and-pinion	Saginaw worm and sector
Turns (lock to lock)	2.0	3.7
Turning circle (ft.)	40.0	37.0
Brakes	Power, four-wheel ventilated discs, 11.5 in. diameter	Four-wheel drums, 11 in. diameter
Dimensions		
Wheelbase (in.)	96.2	102.0
Length (in.)	176.5	167.0
Height (in.)	46.7	51.3
Width (in.)	71.0	72.2
Track front, rear (in.)	59.6, 60.4	57.0, 59.0
Ground clearance (in.)	5.0	6.0
Curb weight (lb.)	3,200	2,850
Engine and drivetrain		
Type	Cast iron, watercooled, 90 deg., V-8	Cast iron, watercooled, inline six
Main bearings	5	4
BorexStroke (in.)	4.00x3.48	3.56x3.95
Displacement (ci)	350	235
Compression ratio	9:1	8:1
Induction	Twin, throttle-body fuel injection	Three Carter sidedraft carburetors
Horsepower@rpm	205@4300	150@4200
Torque (lb–ft)@rpm	290@2800	223@2400
Transmission	Four-speed automatic	Three-speed manual
Rear-end gear	3.31:1	3.55:1

Dave McLellan, left, successor to Zora Arkus-Duntov, decided that his new Corvette would retain front engine-rear drive layout. McLellan's expertise guided the Corvette into world-class territory for the first time ever. Here McLellan talks about Corvette performance while Canadian promoter and racer John Powell looks on. Powell would soon create the Corvette Challenge. Chevrolet

"That's when Guldstrand and his bunch came out from California with their Camaros; that was when the new Camaros came out. And at the same time, we did some juggling with our rules and we made the race open to what we called 'prototypes', which could be a 944 Turbo and stuff like that.

"Of course, everybody thought the 944 Turbo would eat everything up, and it did but it wouldn't last. They hadn't tested it as much as they thought they did. The original 944 had Volkswagen front suspensions and they would break. So then this got to be a battle with the Camaros and then it was just a step when the Corvettes came in. And then the Escort thing came in, and it just grew; it just exploded in its third year. Everybody wanted a piece of it."

As McGill said, everyone expected the beautifully made Porsche Turbos to take overall victories in the SSGT (Showroom Stock Grand Touring) category. What few were prepared for was the remarkable string of decisive victories won by

Corvettes from Morrison Motorsports were some of the fastest and best prepared in the Showroom Stock series. First sponsored by Playboy *magazine and then by Escort radar detectors, the Showroom Stock series turned into a* romp *for Corvettes, which won fourteen out of fourteen races, until they were banned from the series. Morrison Motorsports*

Corvettes during the entire history of the original Showroom Stock series. Corvettes accomplished the mission impossible of winning every race in four years, a stunning nineteen victories in nineteen races.

The Porsche 944 Turbos were very fast cars and they had tremendous bloodlines in their heavy-duty Porsche engineering, as well as being fine cars in the feel of their shift linkages, steering racks and big disc brakes. But, the Corvettes soon had ABS brakes and were able to go at absurd speeds in the wet, a feat the Porsches were not capable of until years later, toward the end of the 1980s. But by then the Corvettes, ever-moving targets, had improved still more.

These races were won by a mixture of different Corvettes, drivers and teams, including the big guns of Bakeracing, Morrison Motorsports, Rippie Racing and Powell Motorsports from Canada.

Many of these talented and dynamic teams are headed by individuals who are or have been racing drivers themselves, and all three of these men share a dedication to Corvettes which goes beyond the merely practical.

While a rising generation of new Corvette champions came of age in Showroom Stock racing, the sport itself owes much to one of the original Corvette crusaders, Dick Guldstrand.

Guldstrand Rides Again

Dick Guldstrand never stopped being a Corvette racer in his heart, but his on-track career took him far beyond the red Corvette roadster with the upside-down roller skate on the roll bar. Guldstrand drove Corvettes at Le Mans, drove for Roger Penske, nearly bought the farm in a terrifying crash at the Indy 500 in 1966, and went on to race the thundering behemoths of the Can-Am series.

Guldstrand moved his own racing operations into a garage right next to the Traco shop in Culver City, California, a place suspiciously close to GM's Hughes Aerospace labs.

Guldstrand also brought a very competitive Camaro team to the Trans-Am in the 1970s and began spending more time in the shop than behind the wheel. Together with Bob Riley, Goldie perfected his own distinctive five-bar rear suspension for the later model Corvette. Along with a number of other Corvette and Camaro suspension parts, Guldstrand has supplied his five-bar rear suspension to scores of Corvette racers and owners who want competition grade handling from their street machines.

The Guldstrand rear suspension adds positive toe control and replaces the Corvette lateral links with beefier members and less flexible bushings. Something very similar to this layout became the factory standard on the new era Corvettes which debuted in 1984.

"The reason we started Showroom Stock racing again back in the early '80s," Guldstrand said recently, "was because there was complete lack of that. And I knew that with the new cars coming up there was going to be a venue that a lot of people would like to get into. SCCA no longer had a production category, they were all silhouette cars. IMSA had no interest in that sort of thing. Nobody did.

The famous number 4 Corvette of Bakeracing, driven by Kim Baker and all the usual suspects such as: Tommy and Bobby Archer, John Dinkel, Juan Manuel Fangio III, Jim Mineeker, R. K. Smith and others. Bakeracing won the Escort Showroom Stock series in 1986 and 1987. They helped Chevrolet develop the Corvette by breaking parts as fast as possible. Chevrolet

The win that made a team. In 1985, Bakeracing won a crucial victory at Mid-Ohio and took home a special $50,000 contingency prize from Goodyear. This money allowed Kim Baker to expand his racing organization and to make it more competitive. Here the crew gets their traditional victory ride.

"So I got together a bunch of people at the Nelson Ledges thing and said, what if we started a whole series? IMSA first agreed to sanction the thing and we sat down and wrote some rules. Then they backed out on me—and I had this whole series set up. So I went to the SCCA, who picked it up. In fact, I even promoted my own races, to get it going.

"There could be great racing with the new cars coming out. The new Mustangs and Camaros and Corvettes and Firebirds. And so it was, it was great stuff. Why not make some categories for front-engine front-drive and front-engine rear-drive cars? That worked extremely well, it went together in a hurry. And you can see what it's doing today. That was supposed to continue, but what happened was that the Corvette got so good nobody would run against it."

Stock Cars That Are or Aren't

If the name Showroom Stock doesn't already paint a clear picture for you of what these cars were supposed to be like, we'll look at the genre more closely. Certainly the idea is a simple one. Push a car out of a dealer's showroom, put numbers on it and go racing. OK, there you are. But, of course it's not quite that simple.

Some modifications were allowed on all the Showroom Stock cars, for safety purposes, such as a roll cage, racing brake pads, and the removal of the stock, catalytic converter exhaust systems, which tended to melt down over the course of twenty-four-hour endurance races.

Other modifications included substituting heavy-duty shock absorbers, the addition of two-way radios and the use of any other original equipment parts. As we have seen, since decades ago, Chevrolet was willing to stretch the definition of original equipment to just this side of Gasoline Alley.

But despite some allegations of cheating, the *Playboy* Series, as it was first known due to sponsorship money from the popular men's magazine, and later the Escort Series, after the well-known radar detectors, were largely grand and exciting venues for low-budget racing. In addition there were some worthwhile benefits—exposure to the media and high-dollar contingency prizes, such as the $50,000 Kim Baker collected from Goodyear for winning a race on its tires.

Morrison Motorsports, Brains and Brawn

Tommy Morrison may look and sound like a relaxed good ol' boy from the back hills of Kentucky, which he is, but he's also a qualified professional racer, a clear-eyed businessman and the head of Morrison Motorsports, one of the most successful Corvette racing stables in the United States.

As Bobby Archer climbs out of the number 4 Corvette, after another win, the checkered flags are passed out to crew and friends alike. The Corvette domination of this series puzzled Ford and Mazda, and it made Porsche very, very angry.

Driver Tommy Morrison headed up Morrison Motorsports, the other big gun in Showroom Stock Corvettes.

Morrison began racing at home, taking his own Corvettes into the twisting Kentucky hill country and mastering the cars on those kinky back roads. He claims that he never carried a trunkful of moonshine, just drove like he was. In 1982, Morrison went professional racing for the first time with some friends at Daytona, in a Mazda GTU car. The Mazda just happened to be available at the time Morrison wanted a race car, so he bought it on a "what-the-hell basis." The Mazda had been raced by what seems like every driver on the IMSA circuit at one time or another. Named *Wilma*, the Mazda was a good training car for Morrison and his buddies, some of whom would come to work at his race shop in the following years.

When Morrison began racing a fast Corvette at Daytona, he attracted the attention of the Corvette group, who were looking for a team to run in the newly born *Playboy* Challenge, later known as Showroom Stock and still later called the Escort GT Endurance series.

The connection between General Motors and Morrison became even more solid when Morrison's cars established a winning record in the *Playboy* series. In 1985, Chevrolet agreed with Morrison that his team would do development and testing for the Corvette. As a result of this connection, produc-

tion Corvettes benefited. Although, Morrison was not the only Corvette team with such a program; many had them.

Racing experience showed that certain Corvette parts were fine for the street but a little too fragile for the demands of endurance racing. Front wheel bearings, radiators and front brakes were soon beefed-up, and those changes were reflected in the production cars.

"IMSA, in those days, the late '70s, early '80s, was really a family type organization," Morrison drawled. "You had to spend a lot of money but an independent could go do Daytona and Sebring and a couple of those races without totally going broke, y'know. The first time I did Daytona, believe it or not, it was a choice of doing Daytona or buying a '78 Ferrari Boxer.

"We came in third I think. And the following year, there was a Corvette that was racing at the same track as our Mazda, and it was one of the newer body styles. We had worked out our contracts at Mobil to do endurance racing, IMSA was going to be doing a series. But then IMSA canceled the series and we had to go endurance racing, because that was the contract. It didn't matter if it was GTO, or what have you.

"Anyway, we were going to be at Riverside with the Mazda, so Jim Cook brings Dick Guldstrand

The competition. Everyone thought, going in, that the Porsche 944 Turbo would make mincemeat of the poor American Corvettes. Instead, Corvette won every single *race, Porsche won nothing, and the factory in Stuttgart began secretly buying Corvettes to dissect.*

A Corvette racer to be. Kathryn "Kat" Teasdale is shown poised to drive the famous number 4 Bakeracing Corvette in races under the successor series to Showroom Stock, *the World Challenge. Teasdale is a Canadian Champion with an international competition license.*

The only changes allowed in Showroom Stock were the installation of a roll cage, removing catalytic converters, heavy-duty shocks and racing wheels. This Morrison Corvette was regularly driven by Don Knowles, John *Heinricy, Bobby Carradine and other experienced Corvette hot shoes. Morrison also contributed heavily to the development of the Corvette in the 1980s. Chevrolet*

out there and introduces him to us, to talk about doing some Showroom Stock racing. So that was the beginning of the Guldstrand-Morrison-Cook project. And that was the beginning of our Showroom Stock stuff. That was like 1983. Guldstrand-Morrison-Cook was based out of California, but Morrison Motorsports is in Albany, Georgia. Back then it was called Team Morrison Motorsports. We didn't do Morrison-Cook until 1985."

After his varied wins, Morrison thought he would give Trans-Am a try. It turned out to be a tough go.

"We did Trans-Am in '88 with Brassfield," Morrison said. "You remember the Protofab-Morrison cars of '87? They had Protofab-Morrison on the nose? Chevrolet introduced the guy from Protofab and myself and we put together a program with Mobil 1 and ran Pickett and Riggins that year starting at Road Atlanta. That was the first time those Protofab Corvettes were introduced.

"Protofab handled the original build and design, it was a Bob Riley designed car. Then I came into the program to furnish funding and organization. Those were GTO cars for IMSA.

"Then in '88, Darrin Brassfield and us got together and did a car that was for Trans-Am. We had a lot of teething problems in the beginning of the year. Then we built a car later in the year, another Protofab chassis. Greg Pickett ran first in the car at the Meadowlands, then Baldwin at Mid-Ohio and then Tommy Riggins for the rest of the year. And that was a companion car to the first one in the year Audi did so well in the Trans-Am. The best finish we had all year long was a one-two at Mosport, where Darrin came in first and Riggins came in second. Baldwin came in second at Mid-Ohio and then at St. Pete's, the cars were working and working real well and they were fast. The Corvette that Riggins was in was the fastest rear-wheel-drive car, to the Audi."

Warren Hall is an old friend of Tommy Morrison's. When Morrison went racing, Hall was right there to lend a hand. A chemical engineer with Proctor & Gamble himself, Hall is an old dirt track and pavement racer who says he did a "terrible amount of street racing.

"Tommy first saw the Corvette at Sebring," Hall recalled. "We had leased the Mazda to some folks out of Washington and the opportunity came up for us to take a ride in this Corvette with an option to buy. It was very ill-handling and essentially fell apart during the Sebring race. The spring mounts, shock towers and all that good stuff just started coming unraveled.

"But the potential was real good. What we had to do to make it right was to go in and redesign the suspension pickup points, reinforce the spring towers, move the input points around. We had to stiffen up the chassis, 'cause it would flex, just

Although he doesn't race as much today, in the mid 1980s, Bobby Carradine was torn between his movie acting career and his love of motor sports. Carradine was one of the most promising Corvette drivers of the decade and had the respect of many full-time pros.

about like a rubber band. But that project got on a sidetrack as the GM involvement took place.

"We were reasonably successful with that and I think in '85, '86 we took the national championship, with the Showroom Stock Corvettes, when they were much more stock than they are now. One of the things that tickled me in postrace tech back then was that they checked if the power windows worked. Nowadays the endurance, I believe they call it World Challenge now, are stock chassis, but they are very quickly turning into race cars. Gutted interiors, racing seats, almost unlimited chassis, ride height and shock absorber combinations.

"What I relate it to is the old 'Prepared' classes in SCCA. Prepared cars had the rollover protection and you could play with the engines a little bit and play with the suspension."

The Baker Man

Morrison's major competition in Showroom Stock, and another eventual champion was Kim Baker and his Bakeracing team. Baker was a Corvette man who harkened back to the old days. He owned his own cars, worked on them, especially

Another Morrison Motorsports car at Riverside Raceway, just before that historic track closed its doors to profes- sional racing and became a housing development. Chevrolet

in building and tuning the engine, and he's a darned fine race driver himself, often hired by other Corvette racing teams for his smooth, fast and consistent style.

Baker started racing when he was five years old, in a quarter-midget around the western Massachusetts area. Then he raced go-karts for a while, eventually making the transition into sports cars. That was in 1970. He overlapped sports car racing and autocrossing for a while. In 1976, he won the SCCA National Championship in autocrossing with a Formula Super Vee, A-Modified class, setting fast time of the day.

Baker raced Fiats at a 24 Hours of Nelson Ledges in 1982 and 1983. It was his introduction to endurance racing, yet he won his class both times he entered. Through Baker's many contacts, *Road & Track* editor John Dinkel drove for him, and so did the magazine's resident Grand Prix *pilote*, Innes Ireland.

"Zora Duntov and I did a project for Yugo," Baker said. "We built two special high-performance Yugos that would be capable of setting a world endurance record in their class, under 1500 cc.

John Heinricy, A Hot Shoe

One of Tommy Morrison's best drivers was a slight, bearded figure with intense eyes and a warm smile. John Heinricy, an engineer for CPC, has spent much of his career in charge of testing and validation for the Corvette.

When Heinricy went racing in Showroom Stock in 1984 in a Chevy Citation, he discovered a natural talent for motor sports. In the 1980s, Heinricy raced mostly for Tommy Morrison, and helped Morrison to two championships. He has won seven twenty-four-hour endurance races, three of them in the highly competitive Firehawk series from IMSA. Obviously, he's a first-rate hot shoe.

Because of his engineering credentials, Heinricy provides excellent feedback on any car he's driving. When it comes time to dial in a Corvette before a race, few other drivers can do so with the skill and accuracy of John Heinricy. A participant in the ZR-1 speed record run and the newly begun Escort World Challenge, a reborn version of Showroom Stock, Heinricy has a full card of racing in front of him. He couldn't be happier.

166

"Then we took the cars down to Talladega [Alabama] for the actual record attempt. We set our pit structure up, sent our crew down there, built this big shelter and we had a tanker truck full of fuel. And then we got this phone call; they called it off the night before we were going to start. Several weeks later we learned that that was the day Yugo went bankrupt."

Then, for the 1984 season, Baker decided to race SSGT, the top class of Showroom Stock, and the Corvettes domain. At first he couldn't decide whether to get a 300 ZX Turbo or a Corvette. At that time he had never owned or raced a Corvette. But there was a delay in getting a 1984 Corvette with manual transmission, Baker's didn't arrive until July, and he had to rush a roll cage into it and go racing to get enough points to qualify for the runoffs. Which he did. In 1984, Kim Baker was National Champion in his Corvette.

"It was a tough race," Baker said. "The '84 Corvettes were actually down on power that year, compared to the 300 ZX Turbo. The Corvette was a little better on braking. So when that was over in 1984, they announced that there would be an endurance series that Corvettes would be eligible for in 1985.

"So, we went out and picked up an '85 Corvette to race in that series. It took us four races to get that kind of racing down pat. I had all different drivers that year. John Dinkel was one, Bob McConnell drove some races, Paul Tosi, myself, the Archer brothers. I was making driver and strategy adjustments all year.

"By the fifth race, which was Lime Rock, we had it down pat, and we won that one pretty easily. It was one of the highlights of our Corvette racing years, because that was when Goodyear paid $50,000 contingency per race. It was a three-hour and forty-five-minute race; Steve Lewis was co-driving with me. We started from the pole and more or less led the whole race."

Baker did pretty much the same thing at the next race, a twenty-four-hour bruiser at Mid-Ohio. He won that race and got another $50,000 from Goodyear. The two $50,000 purses made Bakeracing a much stronger team for the 1986 season. So strong, they took four out of six races—Road Atlanta, Mosport 24 Hour, Mid-Ohio 24 Hour and Portland—and again won the Showroom Stock Championship in SSGT. "It was about as good a year as you could have," Baker said, modestly.

"In '87 we decided we'd do the same thing again. And that was run the Escort Series. That year was pretty close to the same type of year we had in '86. We won about two-thirds of the races, I think there were seven races and we won four. In 1988, we didn't do any races," Baker recalled.

Chevrolet asked Baker not to race in 1988 so some of the newer teams, racing Corvettes, would

This version of the Corvette small block was the engine that powered every one of the Showroom Stock Corvettes to victory. Porsche bought a pair of Corvettes and took them apart to see why they were so fast. Ron Centra

have a remote chance for a victory. Baker agreed. There were also stories about secret engine computer chips and other factory-supplied go-fast parts which the others couldn't hope to match, and which violated the concept of a "stock" car.

At this point it should be noted that the Showroom Stock racecars, Corvettes included, were allowed to use heavy-duty shock absorbers and factory high-performance items, if they existed, very much like the old SCCA Production classes where Corvettes scored their early victories.

As Baker tells it, "How you build a fast race car is, you have a set of rules to go by and you take it as far to the edge of those rules as you can without going by. Those were not Showroom Stock cars; '85, '86, '87 were more like prototype racing. They didn't say you had to be stock. But there were specific discrepancies from stock. You couldn't just go do anything you wanted.

"There's obviously a different computer chip every year, and even through the year as you develop the car, the computer chip doesn't make a car faster, it's only to adjust for other things you've done. Every year, the prototype nature of the series was that you would have future model-year parts on your car. And that's where Chevrolet would get their accelerated development of parts—very efficiently and fairly inexpensively. In a twenty-four-hour race you can put 100,000 miles of wear on certain parts.

"We always used Goodyear S-compound in that series. So did most of the teams, with the exception of Rippie, which was using General and Morrison was using Goodrich. It made for good racing to have three tire companies competing to develop tires and paying contingency sponsorships. So it made for a very strong series.

"And there were prototype exhaust systems 'speced' out for the cars, larger diameter and better than anything I'd seen up to that point. They were mandrel bent, perfectly. And we used them until we ran out, then we duplicated them."

Baker went on: "In 1985, you could only balance and blueprint. In 1986 we had the prototype heads, which were just an early model aluminum head before they were actually on the cars. Then in '87 we had a different prototype head which was like the '88 head. And that gave Chevy the testing they needed, because there was some teething problem on those aluminum heads. All the Corvette racers had the same stuff. Chevy gave everybody a limited number of parts at the start of the season and it was your job not to use 'em up too fast. And they had to be returned, each part tagged with a note to the powertrain manager on how long it was in the car, how many miles, any problems,

any comments. So they got a tremendous amount of input for free."

Corvettes Can't Play Anymore

After a brilliant career in Showroom Stock racing, after having vanquished Germany's best in the 944 Turbo, after having won seventeen of seventeen races, Corvettes were cast out of the series like something unclean. The other manufacturers had made such a stink about the Corvettes that the SCCA had to act to preserve its series and its credibility. Corvettes were banned starting at the end of 1987.

But from this defeat came a wonderful victory, an all-Corvette racing series—the Corvette Challenge. Beginning in 1988, the Million Dollar Corvette Challenge would pit the best Corvette drivers in the country against each other to see who was king of the Corvette hot shoes. The racing was spectacular, of course.

From north of the border came John Powell and his striking Corvettes. Powell is a well-known figure in Canadian motor sports and the man who created the Corvette Challenge. Note the clever discs on the outside of *the racing wheels. These helped draw cooling air through the brake discs and kept the binders at top efficiency, especially at tracks with fast straights, tight corners and hot temperatures. Chevrolet*

Chapter 13

The Corvette Challenge Series, 1988-1989

In the Corvette Challenge there was plenty of casual bitching and moaning. Nothing new there, racers complain like Roman Legionnaires, endlessly. But within the griping were some genuine and well-founded concerns. While physical modifications could be flagged during tech inspection, subtle and significant changes to the car's engine control computer could produce more power with no visible clue.

—Scott Allman, Corvette engineer

In 1988 and again in 1989, a remarkable series of races exploded across the United States. In those races, a group of adventurous, competitive and savvy young men and women got together to win a million dollars doing something that most of us would be happy to do for free: drive in an all-Corvette, Corvette-*only* racing format.

In fact, one substantial reason why the Corvette is such a knockout street performer in the early 1990s is because this racing series acceler-

One of the exciting aspects of the Corvette Challenge was the close racing. Some cars qualified within hundredths of a second of each other, and they stayed nailed together *for the whole race. Here John Brandt in the Fredrick's Chevrolet-Thunder Racing Corvette number 27 stays just inches ahead of the number 4 car.* Chevrolet

169

Fifty identical Corvettes, said the Chevrolet press release. And Chevrolet engineers worked hard to make them identical. The idea was to put bright young drivers and old pros into Corvettes with equal engines and let the best racer win. For Corvette lovers, it was nirvana. Chevrolet

ated the Corvette's development to warp speed. Many components were modified, beefed-up or replaced with better parts as a result of the intensive feedback and enormous stress of sprint racing. With as many as forty identical L98 Corvette coupes racing at the same time, a huge number of testing and development miles accumulated quickly.

Known as the Million Dollar Corvette Challenge, this two-year program collected a remarkable group of drivers, some of them experienced, some unashamedly beginners. While some well-known folks such as John Greenwood, Johnny Rutherford, Juan Fangio III, Bobby Carradine and Olympic athlete Bruce Jenner were involved, other drivers in the Corvette Challenge were new to motor sports, drawn to this endeavor by the raw excitement of the Corvette, the million-dollar bounty and the dream of racing on a reasonable budget.

In 1989 the series ran ten races; in 1989 there were twelve, usually as the support event for a major racing format such as CART (Championship Automobile Racing Team) or IMSA GT. The events lasted an hour. They were very popular, according to the participants, and featured some remarkable and exciting wheel-to-wheel racing.

The series also combined road courses and oval tracks for the utmost test of driving skill.

There was even a drag race held in Minnesota at Brainerd International Raceway in 1988! It was won by Corvette engineer Jim Mineeker, something of a dark horse, and perhaps a Corvette hustler. Yet, the drag race provided a new challenge to all the drivers, and showed the relaxed sense of fun which the Challenge personified.

With no serious injuries and modest overall speeds, the Corvette Challenge was a safe way to experience the thrills of racing. For Corvette buffs, it was hog heaven.

Television came to be a big part of the Corvette Challenge. Cable TV's ESPN inked a package deal to televise every one of the races, the second year. In doing so, it provided some of its best and most technically advanced broadcasts to date.

ESPN's coverage of the Corvette Challenge included a remarkable on-screen readout that was generated by information from the race car's own real-time telemetry system. Race fans could watch the car's rpm, braking, and monitor various systems as the car flew around the track. The system and its use in broadcast TV were spectacular, although it did reduce the size of the in-car image by about one-fifth.

Although the Corvette Challenge lasted only two years, it gave another emerging generation of Corvette racing stars the all-important chance to shine in front of the TV cameras. It also gave those of us watching at home a front-row seat for some rip-snorting racing and a few superb, heartstopping close calls and close finishes.

Powell Challenges Chevrolet

Canadian motor sports fans and racers, perhaps because they have a shorter season in which to enjoy their favorite roads and racetracks, show a passion for competition matched only by their European ancestors. One Canadian who has distinguished himself by his association with Corvette racing throughout the 1980s is John Powell.

Surprisingly, it was Toronto race promoter Powell who conceived the idea for an all-Corvette racing series, modeled on Powell's Canadian, all-Camaro Player's Cup. Convinced that he had a great idea, Powell stormed the ramparts at Chevrolet. Instead of showing him the door, they listened.

This is how Powell remembered it:

"As late as September or early October of 1987 at the last Escort endurance race, SCCA announced that they were going to ban the Corvette from competition in 1988—because it had won nineteen out of nineteen races. And Doug Robinson, who was then the development manager for the Corvette, had a mandate from the platform to make sure that the people using Chevrolet Corvettes were assisted in doing the right thing and not tripping over themselves. He fairly said, 'That's a real blow.'"

At this point Powell had a brainstorm. He could organize a racing series similar to his all-Camaro Player's Cup, only using Corvettes. Since he was at a racetrack already, he hunted up Doug Robinson, the Corvette development manager, and mentioned the idea to him. Robinson thought it was a winner and encouraged Powell to contact others at Chevrolet. While he was at the track, Powell also spoke with the Goodyear representative, who was bullish on the idea of an all-Corvette series.

Powell continued: "So with Goodyear encouraging me, with Chevrolet encouraging me, I then looked around and talked to a couple of potential sponsors, Exxon being one of them. And I was confident I could get them in so I went to Ralph Kramer, the director of Chevrolet PR, and said, 'Ralph you helped me with the Player's series in Canada, I've got this hell of a deal, we want to have a place for Corvettes to race,' and he said, 'Well, I'll see what enthusiasm there is, take the temperature.'"

Next Powell had a meeting with Robert Berger, then general manager of Chevrolet. In response to all of Powell's enthusiasm, Berger simply replied, "Well we might as well do this, nothing else is working." And so was born the Corvette Challenge. Berger gave Powell a letter saying that Chevrolet approved of an all-Corvette racing series, but was not going to spend any money on it.

"I sat down with myself," Powell recalled, "and said, 'What's going to work here? Well, it's got to have TV and that's a bit tough. It has to have a prize fund, the races all have to be able to make money, it's got to be suitably prestigious.

"'It's got to have a million dollars in prize money, so it'll become the Million Dollar Corvette Challenge. Because nobody's ever offered money like that before and I think I can get a million dollars. And then I can charge people a very high entry fee, which was $15,000 or $20,000, to get into the series. And they won't mind paying fifteen grand if they figure they're going to earn back a couple hundred thousand in prize money.'"

Then, during the winter of 1987-1988, Powell was hired by Chevrolet to run a dealer training program using the Corvette. Utilizing this as a forum, Powell talked to a number of dealers, who said they would encourage and support his idea for the Corvette Challenge. Many of them did. Dealers

Tommy Sapp of Protofab engineering, an outside vendor that helped convert the Corvette Challenge cars from production-line machines to raceworthy competitors, is shown painting a special dye on the 5.7 liter Tuned Port Injection engines, at Flint, Michigan. This dye would show if the sealed engines had been tampered with, meaning modified for more horsepower. Chevrolet

Smiles from the winners at the first Corvette Challenge at Dallas on April 30, 1988. Although Mark Dismore (center) won this race, the team of Bobby Carradine (left) and Stu Hayner (right) looked to be the early force in the 1988 Corvette Challenge. Then Carradine had massive electrical problems and other bad luck that put him back in the points battle. Chevrolet

benefited from the Corvette Challenge by selling the original competition cars, new cars for 1988 and 1989, by sponsoring cars and drivers and by using the local races to stage promotions and advertising.

Sadly, Powell did not find the easy sell to sponsors that he anticipated. Indeed, there was much interest in the Corvette Challenge, but damned little hard cash. This shortage of funds would eventually be the undoing of the series. At the beginning, Powell's excitement may have kept him from realizing the depth of financial support he needed.

"In July I realized that I was going to be half a million dollars short on my budget," he said, "because not all the sponsorship had come in. Goodyear had fronted up, Exxon had fronted up, a couple of other people hadn't come in.

"And so I went to Mike Goodman, who was the sales and marketing manager for Chevrolet, my cap in hand, and I said, 'Notwithstanding my letter from Bob Berger saying do it so long as it doesn't cost any money, this obviously has some value for you, can you help?' And Mike Goodman looked at me and said, 'I'm not sure that I can, but I'll look at it.' Mike Goodman personally bailed it out by getting involved.

"In 1988, when I signed in July for that support, which was basically Chevrolet agreeing to sponsor the series," Powell continued, "they gave me an option for 1989 to proceed to a set budget, partly because they were convinced that they could get a sponsor just by snapping their fingers.

Danny Palmer in the number 65 Performance Unlimited Corvette is momentarily ahead of the thundering pack. Note that the outside edge of Palmer's right front tire is lifting off the pavement. Perhaps there's too much negative camber in his setup. Chevrolet

Corvette Challenge, year two. Stu Hayner leads the pack at Road Atlanta, in the number 1 EDS-N.B. Ventures Corvette. Other driving chores kept Hayner from repeat-ing his championship of the first year of the series, but he always gave a good performance behind the wheel. Mark Weber

"They failed, but they kept to their contract. They were honorable people and the 1989 program happened. The 1990 program looked like it was going to happen until the middle of September when Corvette sales improved in 1989, for the first time in a number of years. In September of 1989, Mike Goodman said, in effect, we've given it a shot for a couple of years, it's been great, but we can't afford it. And then," Powell concluded, "SCCA announced that the other manufacturers were ready to get their noses bloodied again. And they are prepared to take you on, Corvette. So we'll have you back. So, now there was no need to have a Corvette Challenge anyway."

The SCCA Side

Patc (pronounced Pat–see) Henry was the SCCA liaison to race promoter John Powell and to Chevrolet. She is a racing professional with the SCCA and found the Corvette Challenge one of her nicest assignments. The basic agreement that organized the series was worked out between the SCCA, Powell and Chevrolet.

"Three of us formed a triangle," Henry said. "SCCA did the sanctioning and basically arranged for the 'show' from green flag to checkered flag, including the final technical inspection of all the cars.

"It was John Powell himself who approached SCCA to be the sanctioning body for 'his' Corvette Challenge. He had Chevrolet's backing, totally. And he had put the program together. He then approached SCCA as the sanctioning body and within less than six months we had ourselves a program.

"I hired a lot of field staff, as we refer to them. We hired timing and scoring, people that were obviously SCCA members. We had our own timing and scoring staff. We had our own technical staff. We had our own registration staff. And we had our own chief steward (K. C. van Niman), who was the rule-guideline authority. For the two years of the Corvette Challenge, we had the same staff people both years."

Patc Henry appreciated the organization which Powell brought to the Corvette Challenge.

"John had 99 percent of the tough work together, which is providing a sponsor and providing a basis for it. Powell had a pretty good idea of where Chevrolet wanted to hold the races. We assisted him in getting the venues he wanted. But it was not a tough job at all. Most tracks were very anxious to provide a time slot for us."

Yet, one aspect of the series couldn't be handled through high-level negotiations. They needed a gaggle of bright and talented young drivers to make the thing work.

173

"One of the challenges was to make sure that we had 'quality' drivers. The drivers met a pretty high standard," Henry said emphatically. "And sometimes we had to say, 'I'm sorry but you're not quite ready for the series. You're not what we're looking for.' One of the toughest things I had to do was tell a driver that he wasn't qualified for this particular event. The number one criteria was prior experience. And a sportsman-like attitude, that was very important.

"One of the more exciting races was the Toronto race, where Mr. Lockhart, who is a native son of Toronto, was asked by our chief steward to kind of give a pre-race talk about what to do and not do on this particular street course—and promptly went out first lap and rolled the car!

"He was just a tiny bit embarrassed. He took a car that had previously had very bad luck, did not finish very high in the standings—basically the only things you could do were to set the ride-height and suspension settings that were allowed—and went out and won the race in that car. So I would say that was proof of the pudding."

One of the most impressive aspects of the Challenge was the high level of enthusiasm from the competitors—and the healthy turnout for every race. Even the pro, Patc Henry, was impressed.

"Our average grid was in the high thirties," she said. "We did not sell more than fifty cars, and on most of the street courses, you can't start more than twenty cars per mile. In Dallas, we had two more cars qualify than could start the race. We were normally oversubscribed, or just on the bubble."

The Technical Side

Beyond all the flashing colors and close racing on the track, Chevrolet realized that the heart of the Corvette Challenge was keeping true to the promise that all the cars would be equal. While this sounds simple for identical production cars, the reality is quite different. Two cars that have been assembled alongside each other may have engines which differ by 30 hp when they leave the factory. This is accepted as standard production tolerances.

One of the men behind the outstanding technical effort Chevrolet mounted for the Corvette Challenge was Jim Mineeker. As a powertrain engineer, Mineeker had some special headaches with the Challenge. Usually the problem in racing is making as much horsepower as an engine will bear. In the Corvette Challenge, the most serious technical hurdle was keeping fifty engines at the same power level all season long.

"I though the engines were as fairly matched as you could do it," said Mineeker. "We had an incredible team on site, one of the premier engine

Oval track racing was one of the novel features of the Corvette Challenge. Here, Stu Hayner leads Tommy Riggins at the Phoenix oval. Chevrolet

Take a big, heavy car like a Corvette and put it in a tight, confined racetrack, like most temporary city street circuits and you have the prescription for wild action. This number 8 Corvette has already seen a minor shunt; note *how the front clip is angled downward. Remarkably, the Corvettes continued racing even after major damage.* Chevrolet

calibrators, a software man, in Mike Dupree, looking over his shoulder at each one of the races. And he would periodically move the calibration PROMs [Programmable Read Only Memory chips] around. So, he was a watchful eye. And in year two, he took even a more active role in making sure that all the engines were really, really close. In year one they were reasonably close, in year two they were very close.

"Mike could adjust the power by moving spark and fuel around in the ECM [Engine Control Module, a microchip microprocessor]. So he went over 'em again on the dyno and put matched sets together. So a certain computer went with an engine. They were closer than 5 horsepower between engines in year two."

The problems of making engines that were highly matched in the hurly-burly of a mass-production environment posed special problems. The Corvette engineers were thorough and innovative in their responses to these problems.

"So, we couldn't raise compression ratio, fool around with pistons or camshafts or anything like that," Mineeker recalled. "The parts were street legal, but just very finely detailed. And care [was] taken to make sure that the clearances were absolutely what they should have been. And that processing was proper, from the same batch.

"We went to our sub-suppliers and said, 'You know, we're gonna build 300 engines; I want those components as closely matched as you can possibly make them.' Not necessarily to a race tolerance, because we were trying to equalize, not extract the ultimate horsepower.

"We sealed the engines with, not an ultimate deterrent, but an honest deterrent, if you would. We put some fluorescent paint on selected fasteners, that you have to put a black light on, and specially mixed it so that the color would be hard to match.

"All the sealing was done by yours truly and one of the manufacturing engineers up at Flint. I personally went around and dabbed the paint on those engines. It took probably an hour or so.

"We built 150 engines," Mineeker continued, "the thought being that we would take two engines per car to get through the year, and we'd want to do a routine freshening sometime in the year, and then one per car for a spare. And then if we overbuilt, we'd just put them in production cars. So, that's what we did. And we really didn't need that many. We had very few problems with the engines during the year."

Liberty, Equality, Fraternity

But for the Corvette Challenge, those engines which had been so carefully equalized at the Flint, Michigan, plant also had to be kept that way.

In assuring the many competitors in the Challenge that their cars were indeed equal, Corvette engineers made use of the sophisticated self-diagnostic capabilities of the Corvette. Through a

With their Dymag wheels, large numbers and striking paint, most of the Corvette Challenge cars were pretty to look at as well as exciting in the fray. Here Freddy Baker hustles his machine around the Phoenix oval. Chevrolet

Shawn Hendricks, another star of the Challenge, hustles his Valley Chevrolet-Rippie Racing Corvette around the oval at Phoenix. Running the stock Corvette wheels, this car seems more like a street machine than those with the dramatic Dymag wheels. Chevrolet

special plug in the engine compartment, the Corvette's ECM, engine control module, can download all its recorded and onboard data into a service bay computer, which analyzes this data for problems.

In the Corvette Challenge, this data link was ingeniously used to monitor the engine computers, to detect and prevent tampering with the chips for more horsepower—hot-rod hacking!

Presently with Advanced Vehicle Engineering Group of CPC engineering, Doug Robinson is the project manager creating the architecture for the next generation Corvette.

At the time the Corvette Challenge started, Robinson was Corvette development manager, heading the engineering group which was responsible for tuning and testing and validating the cars for each model year. But he soon had a new, part-time job as well.

"Part of the agreement with the SCCA was that I would be the technical administrator at the Corvette Challenge races as a part of SCCA field

My cup's bigger than your cup, says an excited Willy Lewis after his win at Phoenix in 1989. Points leader Bill Cooper (left) came in second, and Indy car veteran Johnny Rutherford was third. Rutherford brought his professionalism and wonderful sense of humor to the series; he was well liked by the younger drivers. Chevrolet

Wild man Lou Gigliotti in the number 2 Corvette runs through a chicane at Dallas, inches ahead of Randy Ruhlman. Note the full grandstands in the background.

The Corvette Challenge, unlike many support races, was a popular favorite at every stop. Mark Weber

Tommy Kendall, little more than a teenager, seems like a born racer. He's fast, versatile and possessed of a mature, winning attitude. After making his mark in the Corvette Challenge, Kendall went on to drive for Chevrolet in the Trans-Am, where he is a fierce competitor.

staff," Robinson said. "And they wanted to do that because the cars were prepared to be identical cars, and they felt that Corvette engineering knew the most about the cars, and had the best capability of keeping them equal.

"So for the two years the races ran, and that's 1988 and 1989, I was present at the races not as a General Motors man but as SCCA field staff in charge of the technical inspections.

"We had a tech area that was a tractor-trailer that John Powell owned; we'd set up an awning off the trailer and we had a lot of electronic equipment that was provided to us by EDS, which is Electronic Data Systems, the subsidiary of GM. The same kind of equipment they call 'CAMS' terminals, that you plug into the diagnostic connector of the car and a computer goes through and runs a series of tests that gives you a printout with the status of all the things it checks."

Robinson and another GM engineer, Mike Dupree, "supertuned" that system. They checked all the cars in, sometime during practice stages of the event they ran them across the machine again, then they gave them a final look-see after qualifying. Usually, they would check all of the competitors after a race as well.

At every event, they downloaded the data from the onboard computers at least three times. They also weighed the cars. One thing they didn't have to worry about was for strange and exotic fuel mixtures finding their way into Corvette Challenge fuel tanks.

Exxon was one of the sponsors of the series. They supplied a fuel tanker and mixed up a batch of fuel at the beginning of each season. The whole

Al Lamb pilots his Texas American Race Teams-Alpine Corvette around the back ess turns at Road Atlanta. The unpainted Dymag wheel on Lamb's left rear testifies to a

quick pit stop somewhere in the race. Pit stops usually meant disaster in the Corvette Challenge, since the races were run at sprint pace.

racing field took its fuel from the same source. Exxon also sent an engineer to each race to take fuel samples and deal with problems.

"All the engines were sealed with a paint that shows up under fluorescent light, and also with some wire-type, lead seals," Robinson continued. "So we would check the integrity of the seals.

"We also recorded things in the computer like the highest rpm the engine saw. They had rev limiters at about 5500 rpm, so that you couldn't just put your foot on the floor and rev the engine up and damage it."

Robinson's purpose at the races was also to get information that would make the Corvette a better car. He and the other Corvette engineers assigned to the Challenge collected tons of data, some of it working its way back to the production line in Bowling Green, Kentucky. "Whenever possible we tried to feed back to factory and into the original design," said engineer Robinson, "and were able to do that so things like synchronizer tweaking, and the clutch spring, benefited all the Corvettes that have been built with six-speeds since the '89 Challenge series. So we changed the production parts to meet that higher requirement."

Being racers, the Corvette Challenge drivers and crew chiefs also had a racer's agenda: to win. With this agenda comes the search for the unfair advantage. Against those instincts, Robinson and the Corvette engineers kept a watchful eye on everyone in the series. Even the grey areas deserved scrutiny.

"The kinds of things that we ran into," Robinson said, "were people trying to put a longer bolt in to get more adjustment in a rear spring or something like that. And whenever somebody would try something inventive, as the technical administrator, if I felt it was outside the intent of the rules and the original spec of the car, I would just go to them and tell 'em to put an OE [original equipment] part in the car.

"We let people use the full range of adjustment," Robinson said, casually. "In some cases where there was a rubber bushing we might let them use a harder rubber bushing if they found one, or we might let them put a solid washer in to replace a rubber bushing, if they felt that helped them get the car to handle better. In most cases the guys were pretty well able to tune the corner weights of the car to get it to handle pretty well. You've got quite a bit of camber adjustment, both front and rear in the Corvette. So they could put negative camber in to make the tires work well.

"We gave them a suspension setting to start with that would get them pretty close based on some of the more experienced people. We'd post that on the bulletin board, and everybody would come and look at it. And it all worked out pretty well. I really can't say that what you would typ-ically call cheating was going on. It brought out the best of everybody."

Robinson, as an engineer, couldn't help noticing that some drivers did better than others. The secret was in smoothness and in having a sixth sense about when the car was taking a beating.

"In '88 Juan Fangio III raced in the series. When he first started, he didn't do very well and we told him that he was overdriving the car and that if he would back off a little bit, he would do better. He tried it and he came back to us and he said he couldn't believe how much faster he went when he tried to go slow."

Sapp Flows with Corvettes

Sportsfab does prototype work on production cars and Showroom Stock type cars, some show cars, chassis and structure type work. They built the Geo Storm Celebrity cars in 1991. Tommy Sapp, president, had done Corvette development work when he was with Tommy Morrison. "I think I started with him in the fall of '85, really. I did his IMSA GTO cars. I built chassis and crew chiefed and looked after the cars. I really ran the shop more than anything else. Kept everybody goin'. And I was with him until the fall of '87," said Sapp. Then Sapp worked with Protofab, which was close by. He built roll cages and suspension parts.

Sapp continued: "I probably first heard about the Corvette Challenge from [Chevy engineer] Doug Robinson. And it was 'would I be interested,' sorta vaguely kinda deal. Then I was brought more into the loop as the process evolved.

"We installed seats, roll cages, fire bottles, modified the transmissions—they were all blue-

Stu Hayner takes a chicane at Dallas. Note that his car is just a little more balanced than Lou Gigliotti's in the same corner; that's what made Hayner a champ. Chevrolet

printed, and put an electronic harness in 'em. We put air ducts on 'em. The cars' engines were installed in Flint. The engines were built there and sealed and put in the cars. The places we dabbed that paint were like the fuel pressure regulator, throttle position sensor, the injectors themselves, timing cover bolts, oil pan bolts, intake manifold bolts, distributor bolts; there were a lot of them.

"Then people hired me to help them set up the cars. I worked with the Archer brothers, MPS Racing—that's Shawn Hendricks and P. D. Cunningham. I helped various teams at different times. If I was at the track, I'd help most anybody.

"The weakest link was brain fade with the driver, mostly," Sapp said with a chuckle. "Sometimes a preparation error, but when you had a car off the track, it was mostly driver error. The cars were pretty durable, and still are. They came with a set of Dymags and they had the option of running Dymags or production wheels—and stock tire sizes. Goodyear Eagle performance tires were shaved, and that was the race rubber.

"It was usually close racing, tight racing; if you keep cars bunched-up it's more interesting than if they are running around. And people like Corvettes."

Scott Allman, a chassis development engineer in charge of Corvette ride and handling, was on the Corvette Challenge technical team along with Doug Robinson. Allman remembers that there were few successful attempts to fool them.

"In the Corvette Challenge there was plenty of casual bitching and moaning. Nothing new there, racers complain like Roman Legionnaires, endlessly. But within the griping were some genuine and well-founded concerns. While physical modifications could be flagged during tech inspection, subtle and significant changes to the car's engine control computer could produce more power with no visible clue.

"Such changes in the data on a Programmable Read Only Memory [PROM] chip would be invisible to the naked eye, but not to another computer. To safeguard against re-programming of the ECU in the Challenge Corvettes, Chevrolet assigned several of its engineers to supervise a validation schedule that regularly tested and analyzed the Corvette Challenge engines and their associated electronics.

"What we did for each of the model years was to put together a car that would be representative of what we would sell and any changes we were going to make in terms of suspension pieces and that sort of thing. For instance, in '88 it was all fixed-valve Z51 shocks; in '89 we went to the FX3 and some changes were made in shock valving and the FX3 controller.

"All of those things we put together in a vehicle that we ran at every racetrack, except for the street courses, prior to actually going to the race," explained Allman. "So if you see a zero car or a double-zero car, those were our test cars."

Corvette Challenge Race Report

In the first season, hopes were high up and down the starting grids. Almost everyone thought they had a chance at the prize. Actually some of the drivers had a much better shot than others.

The first grid for the Corvette Challenge included: Bill Cooper, Mark Dismore, Andy Pilgrim, Juan Manuel Fangio III, Doc Bundy, Bruce Jenner, Scott Lagasse, Jeff Andretti, Johnny Rutherford, Boris Said III, Desiree Wilson, Brad Murphy and Jack Boxtrom.

The initial story was about changing fortunes. Those who were not doing well at the beginning of the season made substantial improvements, and some who started out with high hopes and pole positions, like Bobby Carradine, faded from sight as the season progressed.

In Carradine's case it was a hard-luck story. At the beginning of the season, he was fast and consistent. But by the middle of the year he was

Smart and articulate, Stu Hayner was the first Corvette Challenge champion in 1988, thanks in part to his partnership with actor Bobby Carradine. Hayner returned to race in 1989 but some bad luck and a horrendous crash in Dallas put a repeat championship out of his reach. Chevrolet

near the back of the points chase. His car, one of two partly sponsored by Tom Bell Chevrolet, had serious mechanical and electrical problems race after race. At Riverside he exploded a transmission in practice and joined the Challenge race dead last. In succeeding races, he had terminal difficulties with the car's coil and other wiring.

Bobby Carradine is not just an actor who dabbles in racing. He is a serious Corvette shoe who has driven many times for Morrison Motorsports in their Showroom Stock years. Carradine has shared race cars with such Corvette specialists as John Heinricy, Don Knowles, Stu Hayner and Tommy Morrison. After some impressive drives among these leading Corvette people, Carradine looked forward to the Corvette Challenge as a series where he stood a good chance of winning the top prize. He made an effort to organize his schedule around the Challenge races.

But by mid-season at Brainerd, Shawn Hendricks was in the points lead and Carradine's teammate Stu Hayner was second, showing that he was very fast and consistent in a Corvette. By the seventh race, at Mid-Ohio, Juan Fangio was in the points lead, with Hayner still holding on to second.

Hayner was glad to do so well, but he regretted Carradine's problems. They were partners in the team as well as co-drivers. As Hayner put it:

"I had heard about the Corvette Challenge and I started putting my pennies together and figuring out what I could do. I met Bobby Carradine through Morrison-Cook and I said to him, 'What do you think about the Corvette Challenge?' I told him how much it was going to cost for the year, and he about died when I told him, but he said, 'OK, Stu, I'll do it.' And we got up two cars and a truck and trailer and went racing."

Then, just like in the movies, a complication arose. Hayner recalled:

"And at the same time, Morrison called me back and said, 'Gee, Stu, we'd really like you to run the Escort races with us.' And I said, 'I'll try to make every race, but there are a lot of conflicting dates.'

"To make a long story short, I started the Corvette Challenge. And then the Escort season started. Tommy Morrison said that he couldn't put me in the number one car, and I told him it was OK with me. And as long as he was happy with that, I thought we would do well. We ended up winning; I'm not sure, but I think it was six out of eight races where we qualified on pole and won. So, I ended up winning that championship in '88.

"And, at the same time, we were doing the Corvette Challenge. I was the money and the team owner and the team manager and the driver and part-time mechanic, full-time truck driver and I had just started a new family. I had a lot of full-time jobs. Anyway, we ended up winning the Corvette Challenge also. So, I won two championships in '88."

It appeared that Bobby Carradine's car had a too-powerful (25 watts) radio for communicating with the pits, and the RF signal created by this radio was scrambling the brains of the car's engine control computer. Investigation proved that the engine computer had some questionable wiring. This revelation made the Corvette engineers a bit red in the face, but they toughed it out. Meanwhile, Shawn Hendricks, Andy Pilgrim, the Archer brothers and Stu Hayner were leading the pack in points scored.

Toward the end of the first season, Juan Fangio got into the swing of Corvette racing and made a charge for the points lead. Remarkable stories began circulating in the paddock, like the one about how Andy Pilgrim's pickup truck broke down, and he hitched up his Corvette Challenge car to the trailer, towed the pickup to the race at Brainerd, then qualified fastest and won the checker!

Lou Gigliotti got the nickname of "The Wild Man" after he led a multi-car pile-up at the beginning of the Mosport race in Ontario, Canada. Gigliotti claimed he was pushed, but others had trouble believing it.

At the last race of the season, in St. Petersburg, Florida, the whole field was trying to take the lead and win it. Mark Wolocatiuk won the pole at 75.796 mph and led the field into another exciting Challenge brawl. Wolocatiuk stormed into the lead on the third lap and held it till the checker. Jim Vassar took second, a position he had guarded since lap four, and Shawn Hendricks nipped into third on the last lap.

For the first year of the Corvette Challenge, final driver standings were:
1. Stu Hayner
2. Juan Fangio III
3. Tommy Archer
4. Andy Pilgrim
5. Mark Wolocatiuk
6. Shawn Hendricks
7. Mark Dismore
8. Peter Cunningham
9. Jim Vassar
10. Bill Cooper

At the end of the first season, the top three drivers had won a total of $358,550. Of that, Hayner grabbed $142,800, Fangio pocketed $115,300 and Tommy Archer won $100,450. The Million Dollar Corvette Challenge was off and running, with the first year a tremendous hit.

Second Season Race Report

As 1989, the second and, as it happened, final year of the Corvette Challenge began, enthusiasm

Corvettes everywhere! If you take a good look at the track surface to the left center in this picture, you'll see the marks of ABS braking on the pavement. ABS gave Corvettes an advantage when racing against other cars like Porsches, and kept the less-experienced drivers off the walls in the all-Corvette Challenge. Chevrolet

was high. Almost all of the competitors were back for another go-round, although some of the better known names like Stu Hayner and Juan Fangio had moved upscale: Fangio to GTP and Hayner (he thought) to Trans-Am.

This time there would be twelve races instead of ten. And the Corvettes for the Challenge were newly equipped with the sensational FX3 system offering three-position selectable ride control. Drivers could not only set their cars up better for each race, they could also change handling characteristics within each lap, if necessary. It looked to be another remarkable year, and it was.

The season began at Phoenix International, a short oval track, where the CART cars were the main attraction. There Willy Lewis posted the largest margin of victory in the entire series over Bill Cooper in second place, at 8.680 seconds.

Cooper recovered sufficiently to win the next three races in a row, Sears Point, Detroit and Des Moines, a Corvette Challenge record for consecutive victories. Cooper was obviously a force to be reckoned with this season. Other drivers such as Tommy Riggins, Peter Lockhart and Boris Said were also doing well by mid-season.

The last four races of the year were won by Said, Hendricks, Lockhart, and Lagasse, although Bill Cooper's magnificent mid-season charge, and other high finishes, were enough to give him the 1989 championship. The top ten for 1989 were:

1. Bill Cooper
2. Peter Lockhart
3. Scott Lagasse
4. Shawn Hendricks
5. Tommy Kendal
6. Andy Pilgrim
7. Boris Said III
8. Stu Hayner
9. Tommy Riggins
10. Lou Gigliotti

When Car Meets Tire

The second year of the Challenge saw one of the most incredible crashes in motor sports history. At the second race, in Dallas, Stu Hayner took a wild ride when his Challenge Corvette vaulted over a runaway wheel and tire. The errant wheel had come off another Corvette just emerged from the pits, without lug nuts tight on one wheel. The wheel and tire were rolling along in the track when Hayner blasted around the corner and hit it.

Catapulted into the air, Hayner and his 'Vette flew into the chain-link fence. Then the car dropped to the track on its roof. The crowd gasped. Hayner was not amused by it at all.

"For 1989," he said, "I decided not to do the Corvette Challenge at all. I'd already won it."

He had come to the second season late because his promised Trans-Am ride in a factory Camaro didn't materialize. Sponsorship from GM Division EDS (Electronic Data Services) was then offered to Hayner, but Challenge promoter John Powell responded that he could race two cars for the budget EDS was planning to give Hayner alone. EDS went for the two-car deal and had their cars painted with matching logos. However, this didn't make Hayner and driver Scott Lagasse teammates, as far as Hayner was concerned. Still, when Hayner rounded a turn and saw the free-rolling wheel on the Dallas street circuit, he didn't think it posed a threat to him.

"But never did it occur to me that a tire standing twenty-five inches tall could go under a car that was eight inches off the ground," he said. "The physics of it just did not make sense. So when I hit the tire I actually closed my eyes, because I thought it was going to come up the hood and maybe go into the windshield. And the next thing I know, I open my eyes and see lots of blue sky and then concrete and then a fence.

"But because I was accelerating, and going around a left-hand turn, the left front of the car was much higher than typical and because the tire was rolling in the same direction, the car just crawled up the front of it. Then, when it was going under the seat, it caved the floorboard in about four or five inches which rammed me way up against the roll bar.

"Then when the car hit, it made it short from the top and the bottom. I didn't move, even when the car came down, I was so crammed up in that thing. So, if it had been a taller guy, it wouldn't have just been a great crash, it would have been a devastating crash.

"Then I landed on the roof," Hayner said, clearing his throat, "and it seemed like forever, but it was just a couple of minutes till I got out. I had to take my helmet off to move my head. And I let go of the belts, but I was so crammed up in there, I didn't even drop away. So, I'm upside down and I don't know if somebody's going to hit me. I didn't know if I was on the track or on the other side of the fence. They were afraid to look inside. I didn't see anybody's face till I stuck my head out. They looked surprised to see me!"

Dramatic and spectacular crashes were not the hallmark of the Corvette Challenge. Overall, it was a very safe series. That's not to say that there wasn't plenty of contact between race cars both years, or between the cars and the walls of city street circuits too, because there certainly was.

Other Drivers' Views

Robin Dallenbach was one of the drivers toward the back of the pack in the Challenge, even though she was an experienced racer before she came to the series. From age eight, she has competed in sprint cars and quarter midgets, even had a couple of NASCAR rides in 1982, and is steady and reliable on the track. In early 1988, she spoke to Doc Bundy about the Corvette Challenge.

A formidable pro racer whom we last met in the Rick Hendrick Corvette GTP car, Bundy was driving for Ed Miller in the Corvette Challenge and told Dallenbach that Miller might want to run a second car. She called Miller and he agreed to put her in a second Corvette Challenge car—for the rest of the season. She had missed the first race, at Dallas, in 1988.

She would be flown to Detroit to pick up the car, then she would drive it to Sears Point in California for the next race on the calendar. *Corvette Quarterly* later ran a story about Dallenbach and her sister-in-law making this cross-country jaunt.

"The first time I drove the car, it was totally different from anything I had ever raced," Dallenbach explained. "I was always on racing tires. I had never driven on street tires, so that was a big difference. I think it's easier to go from racing on street tires to slicks; it's a lot harder to go the other way. I was used to having a lot more grip in a car and having the horsepower to compensate when you slide.

Bearded Bill Cooper had a remarkable string of victories in the second year of the Corvette Challenge and won the points championship at the end of the year. Not a flashy driver, Cooper concentrated on consistency, and it paid off. Chevrolet

Times have changed since Betty Skelton drove a Corvette at Daytona Beach in 1956. Robin Dallenbach used her sprint car experience in the Corvette Challenge, finishing fifteenth in the points in 1988. She had trouble adapting to racing on street tires, but still finished the year ahead of such able drivers as Bruce Jenner, Tom Kendall, Jeff Andretti and Paul Tracy.

Yes, even the windshield wipers work. This is how we want to remember the Corvette Challenge: a beautiful car, an aggressive driver, and the thrills of close, wheel-to-wheel racing. We may not see its likes again. Chevrolet

"So it was a totally different type of driving. That was really hard for me to get used to. I didn't get into road racing until 1984, that was in the IMSA American Challenge Series. So all my background was with bigger cars, more horsepower and racing tires.

"Driving it on the street from Detroit to San Francisco, it was one of the best cars I'd ever driven. And it helped in racing the car, but it didn't help learning about sharp, tight turns. It handled really well, it had good horsepower; I liked everything about it, really. Comfortable to drive, shifting was good.

"At one of the races, Mosport, I was side by side with Bill Cooper quite a bit. And there were times when Johnny Rutherford and I were close on the track a lot. Johnny and I never qualified real well. My best qualifying was, I think, tenth or twelfth at Portland. There were a lot of cars out there. I ran around Doc Bundy a lot, my teammate, and Mark Wolocatiuk, he was my teammate also, and he did real well—so did Doc."

Dallenbach continued: "Everybody was really friendly and the guys that were in charge of tech inspection were really helpful in a lot of things. If you ever had any questions, they were there to answer them.

"The drivers that were used to those type of cars, with the exception of Juan Fangio, who had never driven Showroom Stock, but did great, it was those drivers who were usually in the front—because they had mastered the technique of driving on street tires. And then everybody else was just crazy in the back.

"The bumping wasn't so bad but sometimes there were some moves that were like, there's just

no way they're gonna make it. The series was very frustrating for me because I never felt that I was doing as well as I should be doing. It was a lot of fun but it would have been more fun if I would have done better. I'll drive anything if I get the opportunity."

John Greenwood was another old Corvette hand who gave the Challenge series a fling. But for Greenwood, the Challenge was not his cup of tea. He liked to be able to set the car up to his own personal specifications and had an unbearable itch to massage the engines in the cars he raced. This was not acceptable to the tech stewards from Corvette engineering. After a few races with disappointing results, Greenwood dropped out of the series.

An unknown at the time, Scott Lagasse, had his first Corvette ride in 1987 in a GTO race car at the 24 Hours of Daytona, with Greg Walker Racing, a Daytona Beach team. He had also driven a Showroom Stock Corvette for RCG Racing out of Midland, Texas. In those four races he was teamed with such luminaries as GTP drivers Doc Bundy, Sarel Van Der Merwe and Trans-Am pro George Folmer. Lagasse started the Corvette Challenge in its first year, 1988, and ran in nine of the ten races.

"From a racer's standpoint," Lagasse said, "it was an opportunity to showcase driver ability. Corvette being the flagship car of Chevrolet, it made the series seem like a sellable item to dealers and their customers. So, I contacted my local Chevrolet dealer and we did a very low-key, small-budget program in 1988 and came back in 1989.

"We kind of got caught with our pants down in '88. There were a lot of serious, experienced Corvette racers in this series. Teams who had been doing the Escort Endurance Championship and obviously they had done more homework than we had.

"We found ourselves running very well in the first five races but scoring hardly any points due to this and that. 1988 was more of a learning year for me. But by the end of 1988, you couldn't have drug me out of the Corvette Challenge in 1989.

"These cars are really amazing in the rain," Lagasse bragged. "You wouldn't believe the lap times we were running in the wet. And that's a combination of a couple of things. The Goodyear Eagle tires worked exceptionally well in the rain, and the Corvette suspension works well. At Mosport, we qualified really well and started on the front row, led the race for about half a lap until Bobby Carradine's foot slipped off the brake pedal or something and he T-boned me into—I think it was turn three. And that put me back to the back of the field.

"That's the way 1988 went for me; I couldn't do anything right," Lagasse joked.

"In 1989, in St. Petersburg, the last race of the year, I got a flat tire on the first lap. It was kinda interesting because all through '89 I had to forget about winning races and try to just run consistent and finish in the top five every race. So, throughout the season it was a points battle and coming into the final race at St. Petes I was third in the points and Shawn Hendricks and I were real close to being tied for it. And I had to finish ahead of him by one position. So, Shawn and I raced aggressively all year long, and on the first turn he kinda pushed me into the wall, bent the rim and flattened the tire.

"Luckily, a caution came out and I was able to come in the pits and change the tire, go back out in last place. We had been fastest in practice and second fastest in qualifying, and we had a good race setup, so I was able to work my way back through the field and got another caution late in the race, which closed the gap up and I had fifth or sixth place at that point. I didn't get a scratch on my car after that first incident, and everybody else was beatin' and bangin', being really aggressive and for me it was the highlight of all the Corvette Challenge races.

"To come from the back of the pack on a street course is somewhat exciting," Lagasse said with a hint of understatement. "Then we went ahead and won that race. After the second year of driving them, you really get to love how the Corvette handles.

"I was very comfortable in the car by the end of 1989 and I was very sorry to see the series go away. I needed to move on and continue my career, but that's a series that I would have enjoyed to do another year or two. I can't ever remember being around a series where the competitors loved it that much. They were really into Corvette Challenge and thought we had a good deal."

End of the Challenge

And so it came to pass that a large number of beautiful and well-driven Corvettes raced against each other, stole the very thunder from the skies and then vanished.

Almost as a frightening playback of the 1957 AMA racing ban, Chevrolet pulled the plug on John Powell's noble experiment at the end of 1989. This time, however, Chevrolet had better reasons. For one thing, there were the realities of corporate budgets. Chevrolet had been sold the Corvette Challenge as a no-cost venture and it wound up costing them a great deal of money.

While both Powell and Chevrolet seemed correct in their optimism that a Corvette Challenge would draw sponsorship as quickly as Picasso drew bullfighters, they turned out to be far from accurate. The beginning of a recession in the latter days of the 1980s saw sponsors pulling in their horns on all advertising and promotion projects.

Unique, memorable, perhaps impossible to duplicate, the Corvette Challenge provided a glorious moment in time. It fittingly capped the decade when the Corvette rose to unquestioned world-class status.

Some Challenge drivers such as Stu Hayner and Scott Lagasse were later recruited to help set a new world speed record in a ZR-1. Others like Juan Fangio III, Mark Dismore, Bobby and Tommy Archer and Boris Said have gone on to solid careers in racing, with perhaps more than one champion among them.

Surprisingly, one voice of dissent about the Corvette Challenge came from where you'd least expect it—Dick Guldstrand. This veteran Corvette racer and tuner was not impressed by the series: "What's so exciting about running Corvette against Corvette? You've got IROC to do that. Who cares; what's it prove? A Corvette can beat a Corvette! Wonderful. They should have run Corvettes against Ferraris and Lamborghinis and Maseratis, and Porsches and Jaguars or whatever."

Well, Dick, you get your wish. In 1991, IMSA inaugurated a Super Car racing series to pit Corvettes against Lotus Esprit Turbos, Ferraris, Lamborghinis and all the other big boys. The Bridgestone Potenza Super Car Series debuted in the summer of 1991.

Chapter 14

The ZR-1 and the Future of Corvette Racing

We had a physics major figure out that if we left the track at the speeds we were averaging, we would fly 360 some yards before landing. You were traveling a football field per second, is what you were doing.

—Stu Hayner, Corvette racer

As the decade of the 1980s was ending, a time which had been phenomenal for Corvettes racing

This ZR-1 Corvette withstood over twenty-four hours of blistering top-speed pounding to set new world's speed records. The run took place at Fort Stockton, a huge Firestone test track located in the West Texas scrublands. Although the turns were long and wide, the high top speed, about 180 mph, brought with it the danger of a catastrophic tire failure and spin. Morrison Motorsports

in production classes such as Showroom Stock, Chevrolet was preparing an even more heady surprise, the ZR-1 Corvette, familiarly known as the King of the Hill. This extra-special Corvette would be produced in limited numbers and would boast an exotic 5.7 liter DOHC engine with four-valves-per-cylinder head, an engine with the capacity for 400 bhp and 400 lb-ft of torque without catalytic converters. Times of 0-60 mph under five seconds would be no problem.

There had been a ZR-1 Corvette in the early 1970s. Intended as a club racer, the ZR-1 badge was for an RPO group of stiff springs and big brakes, a delete of the air conditioner and other comfort items to turn the Corvette into a production racer. The new ZR-1 was nothing like that at all.

It was a fully featured Corvette with a specially developed evolution of the traditional push-rod small-block 350 ci engine. Based on twin-cam, four-valves-per-cylinder head, the magnificent LT5 engine was developed by new GM acquisition, Lotus Engineering of Hethel, England. Except for immensely wide tires and broadened rear bodywork, the ZR-1 would otherwise be like the L98 Corvette.

Projected top speed for the car was in the 180 mph range, perhaps much higher—even as much as 200 mph, with some minor modifications for aerodynamics. One interesting note. There is a key switch on the center console of the ZR-1 which allows the keyholder to switch the engine from full to half power, by means of blocking-off one set of intake runners.

Corvette fans, uncertain about the durability of the $60,000 machine, wondered when some racer would buy a ZR-1 and throw away the power key. They didn't have to wait long.

A remarkable set of circumstances, set into motion by a creative but reclusive West Coast automotive writer and publicity agent, led to a ZR-1 Corvette setting a new world speed record for twenty-four hours. It was a great way to start the 1990s.

Texas Twisters

The big oval outside Fort Stockton, Texas, looked like the landing site for a monstrous UFO. Banks of lights had been set up at each of the four corners, so the drivers could see their way into and out of the bends at 180 mph. Stretching over 6,073 acres of Texas desert, this slightly banked oval is a Firestone Tire test track. It is 7.712 miles long, has 1.5 mile straights and 2.35 mile turns. The turns are so wide and gentle that you can go through them flat out, or close to it. At the end of turn four there is an overpass, a concrete bridge with 2 ft. thick posts supporting it. Tonight, the lonely facility crackles and booms with Chevy thunder.

On the night of March 1, 1990, a ZR-1 Corvette and its cousin, an L98, were being driven around the clock to establish a new world record. In a few more hours the ZR-1 would set a blistering pace of 175.885 mph for twenty-four hours. The ZR-1 with its Lotus Engineering developed LT5 thirty-two-valve DOHC engine was about to prove that it was a durable as well as a fast car.

This particular speed record had been set fifty years ago by cars running on huge circles drawn on the Bonneville salt flats. A car known as the *Mormon Meteor III* currently held the record, driven by flying Mormon, Ab Jenkins, onetime mayor of Salt Lake City. Set in 1940, the twenty-four-hour speed record stood at 161.2 mph. The *Mormon Meteor* was a behemoth of a car that weighed close to 5,000 lb. and was propelled by a 27.5 liter aircraft engine that developed a whopping 850 hp.

This record run had come about to showcase the durability of the ZR-1s and to generate excitement for a group of Corvettes that were being exported to Europe by GM's International Export Sales division. The gutsy attempt for a world record was the result of a union between three separate forces: Morrison Motorsports, CPC engineering's Corvette group, and Pete Mills, an independent West Coast automotive writer and publicist.

Mills had come up with the idea for breaking the existing twenty-four-hour speed record a few years before, to showcase the products of a tire recapper. After a warm initial reaction, the tire company changed its marketing plans and the speed record idea was kaput.

When he heard about the ZR-1, Mills thought that it represented a real contender for the twenty-four-hour speed record as itself, not just the plat-form for a tire maker. Bringing the idea to Stu

R. K. Smith is another experienced Corvette racer who lent his expertise to the ZR-1 speed record run. Even though there were plenty of drivers, every one of them was exhausted by the stress of the speed record when it was over. Chevrolet

Hayner, a successful Corvette racer in the late 1980s, Mills suggested that the world record would provide a quick way for the ZR-1 to establish itself as a well-made and reliable car.

Hayner carried a proposal to Chevrolet's John Heinricy at a race where they both competed in Corvettes. Heinricy liked the idea and helped the proposal get to the right people at GM. When Tommy Morrison was brought into the mix, he got the assignment of prepping the cars and providing his skilled pit crew for the long day and night of the record run.

After several meetings, the idea was approved and a budget was established for the overall attempt. Sponsorship would come from Electronic Data Systems, the former Ross Perot company that is now a General Motors division, Goodyear, and Morrison's longtime sponsor, Mobil 1 lubricants. While Pete Mills was still somewhat involved, Chevrolet had taken over the project and reor-ganized it as its own.

At about this same time, the Chevy Corvette engineering group decided to run a standard Corvette L98 Coupe as well as the ZR-1. It wouldn't hurt if the L98 set some records on its own, and if it

187

didn't, the reason it failed would be instructive anyway. The cars would be prepared in Morrison's shop in Georgia and trucked to Fort Stockton, Texas.

According to Warren Hall in Morrison's race shop, the cars were left mostly stock. Roll cages were added to both cars. In addition, data acquisition electronics were added to the ZR-1. The ZR-1 would be broadcasting a number of its parameters back to a computer terminal in the pits.

This system was to prove its worth when, between the twenty-fourth and the thirtieth hours of the run, a fastener worked itself loose on the fan shroud and allowed the fan to move back a bit. In its new position, the fan wore a hole in the upper radiator hose and the car began to heat up. The technician had programmed the system with a number of upper and lower limit alarms. If any one of these values such as oil pressure or engine temperature got too low or too high, the computer would beep an alarm.

When the overheating alarm was triggered, the driver was contacted immediately by radio. When the driver looked in his rearview mirror he could see the cloud of steam vapor trailing out behind him. He came into the pits and repairs were made in about fifteen minutes. The hose replacement was considered "routine maintenance" and was allowed under the rules of the record run.

Making their competitive debut at the Daytona Continental in 1991, the Corvette ZR-1s proved tough competition for purpose-built race cars. Although they had some mechanical problems, both ZR-1s entered by Morrison Motorsports finished the twenty-four hour race, a tremendous feat for a racing debut. Chevrolet

Provision was also made against a flat tire spoiling the record. Several piles of tires, jacks and other equipment were spaced around the track. It was legal for a driver to stop and make minor repairs—as long as no parts were brought to him and no outside help was given. To save the extra weight of the tire and jack inside the cars, the caches were prepared, although they went unused; no tires were changed out on the course.

Other technical changes to the stock ZR-1 included removing the headlights and placing oil coolers in their place. They would receive cooling air from a high-pressure zone along the car's chin spoiler. Two little plastic tubes were pasted on the front of the car, which generated a loud, ultrasonic whistle to scare animals, mostly coyotes, away from the race cars. You don't want to hit a 50 lb. coyote at 180 mph!

A 45 gal. fuel cell replaced the stock 20 gal. tank, and a suitcase was carried inside the car with a stash of assorted replacement parts. If something failed along the way, the driver could make repairs on the track and legally continue with the record. But parts could not be brought to him.

Morrison at the Wheel

Tommy Morrison's Morrison Motorsports prepared the speed-record ZR-1s and crewed the event in Texas. "Heinricy and I talked about that sort of thing for a long time before getting real serious about it," recalled Morrison. "The thing that started this particular project was when Pete Mills talked to Stu Hayner about the idea of doing this as a world record thing, and they sent a letter to John. John and I were coming back from the Mosport race together in a car and we talked it over and he said, 'What do you think?' And I said, 'Well, let's try to do it.'"

Morrison put together the funding, put together the team "and all that. I was in the car when the record was broken," Morrison said proudly. "We also had an L98 car that we had built up to about 390 horsepower, and the ZR-1 with about the same horsepower. And we ran comparable times. But we could only keep the L98 for six hours because it had to leave there and go to Geneva for the auto show. So we pulled that car out after six hours and then everybody started rotating cycles to drive the ZR-1. I just happened to be in it when the twenty-four-hour record was broken." Sure, Tommy, sure.

Stu Hayner Sees It Come True

Stu Hayner was in on the record run at a very early stage, at the beginning, actually. Pete Mills had come into Hayner's office and mentioned that he visited Jim Busby's shop in Orange County, where Busby's Porsche 962 IMSA endurance racer is kept. Mills told Hayner that he had tried to interest Busby in breaking a fifty-year-old speed record held by a Mormon from Utah.

Hayner immediately visualized a Corvette ZR-1 breaking the record. His mind kept skipping back to that image. By the time he and Mills had completed their business, Hayner was determined to bring the idea to Chevrolet's Corvette Group and see if they could pull it off.

One day, when Hayner and John Henricy were racing together, Hayner sprang the idea on Heinricy and found a surprisingly positive reception. Morrison was brought in and a date was set for the attempt. Then, the idea seemed to chill at GM and the date was pushed back indefinitely.

A month later, the event was on again, but now under Corvette Group's direction, with the cars managed by Tommy Morrison and sponsorship by EDS. Stu Hayner and Pete Mills, the originators of the project, were nearly left out altogether.

"I had to beg to be one of the drivers," Hayner said, "and hustled down to Fort Stockton, Texas.

"We were down there for nearly two weeks. When we got there, the cars were not quite ready to go. We were testing. The telemetry system wasn't completely in. We had a three-day wait before we could start the run, just because we weren't ready for it.

"We were just about ready to go when the rains came. And nobody wanted to go out there on slicks in the rain. So then we had rain delays."

Finally, it was the first of March. Would the month come in like a lion for the Corvette speed record team?

Hayner went on: "Then we started at nine o'clock one morning. We decided that we'd waited enough so we started it, and that L98 kept plugging along. They finally pulled it off and it went to Geneva.

"John Heinricy was in the car at first so a couple of records like the 100 mile, he would have set those. And I believe that I was in the car at the twelve-hour mark, which was a new record. And that was 175.523 mph. Tommy Morrison was in the car for the twenty-four-hour and then I was in the car for the 5,000th mile, which was the end of the thing at twenty-eight hours and forty-six minutes. And 173.791 mph was our overall record, which to me is the cool record, 'cause I was in there.

"We had tuned the cars like a tractor, so you could only open the throttle 75 percent. We really wanted to keep the car somewhere around the 180 mph mark for a lot of reasons, like tires and fuel consumption.

"The track was nearly eight miles around, so the turns were not like turns on racetracks. The tires weren't skidding, you weren't oversteering all the way around or anything. On the track there were three lanes to work with. The very inside lane was flat all the way around. The second lane had

about four degrees of banking. Then the outside lane was a pretty good banking. In the outside lane you could have comfortably gone another 20 or 30 mph faster, which sounds good. Except, on the other side of that third lane, one foot past that outside lane, is desert. We had a physics major figure out that if we left the track at the speeds we were averaging, we would fly 360 some yards before landing. You were travelling a football field per second, is what you were doing.

"So we decided not to use the high banking. We used the middle lane. And at 180 mph that lane is about a thread thickness wide. So it took a lot of concentration, even though the G-forces were not that high. If you were on that inside lane it was a mess, there was a lot of junk down there. And if you got caught on the transition from one lane to the other, it was so drastic, it upset the car, and chances of spinning were very good too. And to make this record stand for the FIA, we had to stay inside our lane."

Jim Mineeker Is Tickled to Death

One of the men who kept the Corvette Challenge on the straight and narrow was Corvette Group engineer Jim Mineeker. One of those guys with gasoline in their blood, as Bill Mitchell used to say, Jim Mineeker got out of the tech center and saw life in the real world. This gave him an edge in developing the next generation of Corvette. He went so far as to win the Corvette Challenge drag race in 1988 at Brainerd.

Mineeker was one of those who believed in the speed-record project from the earliest time. "In the course of development for the LT5/ZR-1 we had spent a considerable amount of time on racetracks, both high-speed tracks like Talladega, to sort out high speed and oil management in the sump," Mineeker said, "and we spent time on the road

With all that power it was hard not to spin the ZR-1's tires at Daytona, said several of the drivers. Here the Z car leads a Trans-Am Camaro. Chevrolet

Is this car the future of Corvette racing? It's too early to tell, really. If the ZR-1 stays in production, it could grow into a formidable racing platform. But no one will say for *sure if Chevrolet's grand experiment will continue.* Chevrolet

courses. We would take an LT5 road car along to the various Corvette Challenge tracks and during practice, we would put an LT5 mule on the race-track. So we had a pretty good idea that the car would run for twenty-four hours and essentially go at top speed for that time.

"I was tickled to death to be part of this, not only as a driver but having lived with the LT5 project struggling through its infancy and then all the way up into production. You always have those naysayers who say, 'Yeah, it's got a good zero-to-60 and a good top speed but is it durable?' And when you got out and do something like we did, the questions stop."

Mineeker didn't just brainstorm on this record run, he pulled on a crash helmet and slid in behind the wheel himself, putting in shifts of an hour and forty-five minutes, the duration of one tank of gas. They had a 44 gal. tank and would run it down to about 4 gal. before pitting. So they had roughly 40 gal. of fuel for each stint.

"The actual circulating speed was pretty close to 180. So with the slow-down time, speed-up time and the actual driver's change the clocked time was 175 and some change for twenty-four hours. I think I had three shifts. We started out with two crews of

four in two cars, and then when we retired the pushrod car to get it over to Geneva for the auto show, we were time constrained on that car. The other four drivers joined us for the duration of the twenty-four hours.

"The car was very stable at 180. Of course it was sensitive to wind shifts. And the track is slightly tipped, so at one end it is cut into a little bluff. So, between turns one and two it was essentially blind through there. You could not look across the track and see the other side. Then there was a dip and a rise between turns two and three and that's where the coyotes typically crossed the track. That part of it was unnerving, especially at night. It was never boring, I can tell you that!"

On April 9, 1990, Burdette H. Martin, Chairman of the FIA/FISA Records Commission, sent a letter to Tommy Morrison. It said:

"On behalf of the Federation International de l'Automobile and with the greatest admiration I am very pleased to confirm the following World Speed and International Endurance Records established by your team in the new ZR-1 Chevrolet Corvette during its successful record attempt at the Fort Stockton Texas Test Center on March 1-2, 1990.

World Records—Class

100 Miles 282.601 kph	Time	00:34:10.103		175.600 mph
500 Miles 282.445 kph	"	02:50:56.211		175.503 mph
1,000 Miles 280.715 kph	"	05:43:58.772		174.428 mph
5,000 Kilometers 282.788 kph	"	17:40:53.748		175.710 mph
5,000 Miles 279.690 kph	"	28:46:12.426		173.791 mph
12 Hours Distance 282.477 kph			2,106.278 Miles	175.523 mph
24 Hours Distance 283.061 kph			4,221.256 Miles	175.885 mph

"And in surpassing World Record marks that have been in place for almost 50 years, we are particularly pleased to recognize the following new achievements established during these record breaking runs by the Tommy Morrison Motorsports ZR-1 Corvette.

World Records—Irrespective of Category or Class

5,000 km 282.788 kph	Time	17:40:53.748		175.710 mph
5,000 Miles 279.690 kph	"	28:46:12.426		173.791 mph
24 Hours Distance 283.061 kph			4,221.256 Miles	175.885 mph

"FIA/FISA President Jean-Marie Balestre joins me in congratulating Chevrolet Motor Division of General Motors Corporation for the excellence of its fine new product, the ZR-1 Corvette, the driver team of: John Heinricy, Scott Lagasse, Stuart Hayner, Jim Mineeker, Scott Allman, Don Knowles, Kim Baker and yourself as well as their entire record breaking support team in this most significant motor sports achievement."

In setting these records, the ZR-1 did not silence all of its critics. But it began to establish a track record which will one day speak for itself, just as every Corvette racer has done before.

Gazing the Corvette Crystal Ball

The future of Corvette racing is a yet unwritten book. Whether Corvettes will ever win at the 24 Hours of Le Mans, will race in the GTP class of IMSA, dominate drag racing and triumph against the world's super cars is uncertain. Even the future of the production car is in flux, with new reasons for saving energy appearing every day, and a troubled economy making hard times for Chevrolet, General Motors, Detroit.

The light on this gloomy horizon showed briefly at the 24 Hours of Daytona in February of 1991. At that race, two slightly modified, but mostly stock ZR-1 coupes prepared by Tommy Morrison and driven by such Corvette stalwarts as John Heinricy, Stu Hayner and Scott Lagasse finished the twenty-four hours and placed well in the overall standings. And they did so against a field of purpose-built race cars. If this first competition outing for the ZR-1 is any indication of future trends, Corvette racers are again headed toward those waving checkered flags.

It seems clear that another golden era of Corvette racing is at hand. The strength of the L98 Corvette and the promise of the ZR-1, a true nineties hot rod, indicate that Corvette racing will be better than ever. Another hopeful sign is the continuing health of the Chevrolet Raceshop, the official source within General Motors for Chevy high-performance parts and advice to the amateur and pro racer. Modern factory speed parts such as Bowtie, special, alloy engine blocks and trick ECM chips help give Corvette racers an edge on the competition.

With interest and enthusiasm for the Corvette at a new high, the horizons look to be flat out, in top gear. For a Corvette, how natural.

Index